FIT TO PRINT

The Canadian Student's Guide to Essay Writing

SIXTH EDITION

JOANNE BUCKLEY
McMaster University

THOMSON ™

NELSON

Australia   Canada   Mexico   Singapore   Spain   United Kingdom   United States

THOMSON

NELSON

Fit to Print: The Canadian Student's Guide to Essay Writing Sixth Edition

by Joanne Buckley

Editorial Director and Publisher:
Evelyn Veitch

Executive Editor:
Anne Williams

Marketing Manager:
Lisa Rahn

Senior Developmental Editor:
Katherine Goodes

Production Editor:
Carrie McGregor

Copy Editor:
Kelli Howey

Proofreader:
Kelli Howey

Indexer:
Jin Tan

Production Coordinator:
Ferial Suleman

Creative Director:
Angela Cluer

Interior Design:
Sonya V. Thursby, Opus House
Incorporated

Interior Design Modifications:
Peter Papayanakis

Cover Design:
Ken Phipps

Cover Image:
Faye Digulla, "Untitled 1/1"
monoprint

Compositor:
Nelson Gonzalez

Printer:
Webcom

National Library of Canada Cataloguing in Publication

Buckley, Joanne, 1953–

Fit to print : the Canadian student's guide to essay writing / Joanne Buckley. — 6th ed.

Includes index.
ISBN 0-17-641631-5

1. Report writing. 2. Exposition (Rhetoric) I. Title.

LB2369.B83 2004   808'.042
C2003-905888-3

Preface

The sixth edition of *Fit to Print*, like its predecessors, is aimed at the problems students encounter when they write essays in a scholarly environment. The book may be used as a textbook in writing courses or as a supplementary guide in the humanities or social sciences at the university, college, or secondary-school level.

The sixth edition continues the tradition of teaching students how to organize and write an essay and how to overcome specific difficulties of grammar and style. It has also, however, added some features to improve its coverage for contemporary students and instructors:

1. It includes a more complete discussion of research methods, both accessing the Internet and using the library.
2. It uses more contemporary Canadian examples than previous editions.
3. It gives students updated advice on how and when to incorporate material from the Internet.
4. It contains new and varied authentic sample essays by students.
5. It contains almost entirely new exercises.
6. It has a very complete Instructor's Manual with additional exercises and answers for use as test materials.
7. It reflects the latest editions of MLA, APA, and University of Chicago in documentation.

Canadian in authorship and in much of its content, *Fit to Print* is a readable guide that is aimed at helping students improve their mastery of the writing process and their grasp of the particulars of style and documentation. It may be used as a self-help guide or as a classroom text. Its examples are frequently drawn from student work and essay assignments across a variety of disciplines.

Acknowledgments

The sixth edition of *Fit to Print* owes its existence to a number of students, reviewers, editors, and friends. I would like first to thank Katherine Goodes, the Developmental Editor, for being so willing to search things out, so helpful, so sensitive to my needs, and so encouraging throughout the process. I would also like to thank those students whose work I used in this edition, and a number of colleagues at McMaster University who provided samples of student work and helpful suggestions. For support and inspiration, I would also like to thank Kim Harrison, Alex Stevens, and Anne Williams. Neither *Fit to Print* nor I would exist without the steadfast support and patience of Mary Buckley.

A Note from the Publisher

Thank you for selecting *Fit to Print: The Canadian Student's Guide to Essay Writing*, Sixth Edition, by Joanne Buckley. The author and publisher have devoted considerable time to the careful development of this book. We appreciate your recognition of this effort and accomplishment.

Contents

Introduction—Defining the Essay

The essay is a literary device for saying almost everything about almost anything.
—ALDOUS HUXLEY

If at First You Don't Succeed . . .

The essay, as any dictionary will tell you, is an attempt. This definition itself ought to be reassuring if you have ever worried about how you would be able to write an essay. You can't fail as long as what you write is a sincere attempt to come to terms with a particular subject. The finished essay succeeds insofar as it is an honest attempt to elucidate some aspect of your topic.

An essay need not fail as long as your ideas are treated fairly, honestly, and in a spirit of thorough and intensive investigation—and you have communicated these ideas to the reader! If the essay seems an especially burdensome assignment, it may be because most of us are not accustomed to independent thought. Try to think of the essay as an opportunity to stretch your intellectual muscles and to think your own thoughts.

To write an essay is to engage in a creative process, to bring an idea to life. The essay itself, however, is a finished product, not a record of the process by which you wrote it.

Whether you are writing an expository essay (meant to explain something) or a persuasive essay (meant to argue something), the essay's chief purpose is to present a thesis that focuses your ideas and conveys them to the reader in a way that shows their worth and their validity. Depending on the occasion, an essay may be formal or informal; however, academic writing usually demands formality. Depending on the nature of the assignment, the essay may be a product of reasoning or of a combination of reasoning and research.

This text deals both with the essentials of essay writing and with the variations expected in different kinds of assignments. Skim its contents first to acquaint yourself with the most important steps of essay writing. If you are unfamiliar with the basic requirements of the essay, pay special attention to Parts One, Two, and Three. If you are unsure of the specific guidelines for a particular kind of essay, check the pertinent section in Part Four. Then, as you write your next essay, use this book as a step-by-step guide. It will provide helpful suggestions on how to organize your thinking, and how to present your material in the most effective manner.

Remember that the essay is an attempt to think through your ideas in a structured way. Each attempt will teach you more about how the process works for you.

Try, Try Again

As you plan and write the essay, you will be trying various ideas on for size. The process of writing an essay involves finding some part of a large topic that fits your attitude toward and interest in the subject. Compromise is essential. The essay must fit both you and the topic: it will show you and the reader what you know and what you have yet to learn. For best results, choose a topic in which you have some personal stake. Make sure that you can treat the topic satisfactorily within the required word limit and within the time constraints of the assignment.

Overcoming Your Fears

Writing is hard work, even for those who choose to write for a living, as a glance at some of the epigraphs that begin each chapter of this book may well illustrate. You may find it difficult to get your thoughts down on paper, or even to feel that you have any important thoughts to record. Here is some advice meant to make starting to write easier.

1. Divide the writing process into smaller steps; don't try to do everything at once.

   Look again at the table of contents in this book. It should suggest to you that your first task is finding some central focus; your next task, building an outline; your third task, writing a preliminary draft; and your final task, revising the whole. Don't skip any of these steps.

2. Don't ignore your real questions about a topic because you feel they betray your ignorance.

   The essay is meant to be an exploration of something; if you knew everything about the subject before you began, you wouldn't need to write. In large part, the writing process is meant to help you and your reader discover something.

3. Pay attention to your real interests in and your real objections to the subject matter.

   Let the focus of your conversations and your wondering become the focus of your essay.

4. Don't approach the assignment in a perfunctory manner.

   Ask yourself why the assignment is a good one and what connections it makes with the course, or with other courses, or with other things you have read.

5. Don't expect too much from an essay.

   An essay is not meant to provide a definitive answer; instead, it explores what you think, and why you think it, in as clear a way as possible.

6. Gather information and ideas, and write them down as you go along.

   Remember that you need to keep good track of your findings, particularly of ideas that are not your own. Things you encounter on the Internet, or in your reading, need special acknowledgment. Keep track of authors, titles, page numbers, and URLs, so that your steps may be retraced as your ideas gel.

7. Ask questions of your instructor and seek his or her help with the delineation of your topic.

   Reading, both on- and off-line, can also help accomplish this task. Preliminary reading is an essential step to getting a feel for your topic and your take on it.

8. Try not to think of your instructor as an enemy, seeking to trip you up.

   Think of your reader as someone engaged in the topic and deeply interested in your point of view.

9. Explain your ideas to a friend.

   The transition to paper should involve little more than careful documentation and editing.

10. Learn from your mistakes.

    Diagnose what went wrong with previous assignments and resolve not to make the same mistakes again.

Part One

DEVELOPING THE ESSAY

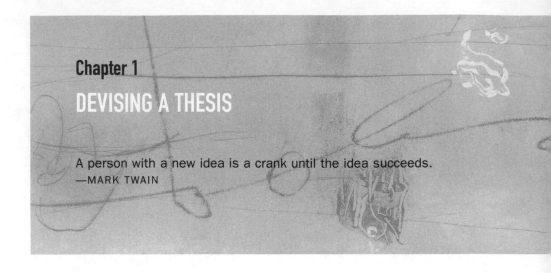

Chapter 1
DEVISING A THESIS

A person with a new idea is a crank until the idea succeeds.
—MARK TWAIN

Usually when you begin to write an essay, you will have in mind a broad area of concentration or a fundamental topic that you mean to explore. To write a successful essay, you must find the focal point of your discussion—the centre of your thought, from which the points you make may radiate outward. This focal point is the thesis statement.

Topics are only the starting point for your thinking. They tell you only the general area of investigation. Whether you are given a topic by the instructor or you find your own, the topic must be narrowed down to serve as the focus of your paper. Like the bull's eye in the middle of a dartboard, the thesis statement is the centre that holds your argument together. An essay succeeds because the point to be made is directly on target, and the significance of the point is firmly established.

Discovering a Topic

If your instructor has not suggested areas for exploration, you will have to create your own, usually subject to his or her approval. This process need not be drudgery; it gives you the opportunity to explore your own interest in the subject. The following are some suggestions for finding a general topic or area of interest:

1. Skim the index and table of contents of any book mentioned in class as a useful source.
2. Skim through class notes and texts for ideas that catch your imagination.
3. Ask questions about the meaning and value of the subject.
4. Look at class assignments and essay questions, and ask yourself what their point is. Why are these questions particularly fitting to the subject area you are dealing with?

5. Listen to yourself. What issues and matters of concern come up in your conversations outside of class?
6. Allow yourself the chance to express your real puzzlement about something you have read. If you don't understand something crucial in your area of study, make finding out more about it one of the goals of your investigation.
7. Always write down ideas as you go along.

Shopping for a Thesis Statement

Often, you will be given a general topic and be instructed to narrow it down. Remember, though, a topic is only a general idea in need of development. Suppose you were asked in a political science course to write an essay of 2500 to 3000 words about American–Canadian border relations. Obviously, this is a broad subject that could yield several promising thesis statements. By itself, however, it is just a phrase and makes no meaningful statement. Keep this example in mind as you read through the following tips on developing a specific thesis statement.

Consider the Writing Situation

When you develop a topic, keep these determining factors in mind:

1. your interests, strengths, and weaknesses
2. the reader's expectations
3. the restrictions of the assignment

Use Whatever You Have at Your Disposal

1. supplemental bibliographies you may have been given
2. advice from the instructor
3. material from the course itself
4. your native wit
5. library materials—books, journals, and audio-visual materials
6. the Internet

Ask Questions about the General Topic

Your first question with regard to our sample topic might be "What about it?" Your sources, both in class and out, may have revealed to you that American–Canadian border relations have changed drastically since the tragedy of September 11, 2001.

Your next question might be "Why?" suggesting a cause-and-effect development, or even "How?" suggesting an argument based on classification (the breakdown of ideas into categories) or on process (the orderly presentation of steps). Refer also to Chapter 5 for some suggested approaches to topic development.

Consider Your Topic in Conjunction with Something Else

Try joining your topic to these conjunctions: "and," "or," "but," "so." These linking words should give you some idea of what might be productively attached to your topic to yield interesting results.

"And," for example, might help you think of things that can be compared (or contrasted) with your subject: variations in attitudes toward the defence of the American–Canadian border at different periods in our history, for instance.

"Or" might lead you to consider a controversy about the causes of the change in American–Canadian border relations: national perceptions or ongoing trade hostility, for example.

"But" might allow you to refute the position of a particular authority on the subject, or to prove that the change in American–Canadian border relations was a political change based on government defence attitudes rather than fear of terrorism.

Consider Key Words That Form Part of the Topic

Ask yourself about the nuances of the question or topic for discussion: is there ambiguity or potential for development in the wording of the question? When setting questions, instructors usually have only a sketchy idea in mind; try to see in the topic as much as or more than they have.

In our sample general topic, one phrase to which this tactic might apply is "drastic change." To develop your topic, you might investigate what particular areas have most drastically changed, to find a clue for your response. You might also want to explore exactly what is meant by "border relations" and how they are defined and characterized in the popular press.

Consult Your Own Taste

Your taste in topics should be consulted before you settle on anything. About the only serious mistake you can make is to choose a topic simply because it looks easier than the others. A challenge is often the best choice because it allows you to ponder the topic rather than assuming, probably incorrectly, that the main point is clear or the answer obvious.

Try On the Topic Before You Decide

Always play with the topic before you work on it. Play with ideas by scratching them down haphazardly on a sheet of paper without regard (for now) to problems of order or clarity. This kind of unstructured thinking will open up the possibilities of the question or the topic for you in a way that no amount of tidy compartmentalizing can.

Brainstorm by Writing Ideas Down

1. Try clustering ideas together according to their associations for you.
2. Try drawing diagrams, connecting various ideas.
3. Check the meanings of words in the topic, and perhaps even their etymologies, for clues to the direction you should take.

A Working Thesis versus a Polished Thesis Statement

If you follow the guidelines above, you should be able to arrive at a narrow focus for your paper. But even a thesis statement should be subject to revision. Because it is normally part of the introduction to a paper, writers often mistakenly assume that it should be written first. In fact, your real thesis statement may emerge only after you have made several false starts.

Since you have to start somewhere, begin with a working thesis. It will allow you to consider your material from a tentative point of view. If you find that the evidence begins to contradict it, or you no longer consider it the centre of your discussion, redefine your statement to suit the new circumstances.

The thesis statement that appears in your finished introduction will be the best description of what you are trying to prove and of how you propose to do it. For example, your thesis statement on the subject of American–Canadian border relations might look like this:

> Changes in border relations between America and Canada can be understood in political changes between the two countries and an increasing mistrust, quite apart from any fear of terrorism on the part of the Americans.

Example

Look Before You Leap

Once you have formulated a contention, that is, some idea of what your approach to the topic is going to be, you must formulate a thesis statement, along with some sense of the essay's ultimate direction. You may want to visit the library to take note of what relevant books and journal articles are available on your specific subject, and of whether they support or contradict your working thesis.

To write a good thesis statement, you need to remember that a strong thesis is a contention that forms the basis of your argument. It is what you are trying to show the reader. A good thesis statement takes into account the purpose of the writing and its audience, but it does more than that. For instance, your purpose might be to define for a beginner the perfect golf swing. Although this idea shows promise, it is not a thesis statement. To transform it, you need to make a claim. Look at this statement:

> A perfect golf swing demands a proper grip, delicate balance, and excellent timing.

Example

It is a strong thesis statement because it makes a claim that the rest of the essay, presumably, will go on to support.

Suppose, now, that your topic is "learning a foreign language." Your purpose is to tell your reader what you consider the best way to learn a language. You must not, however, leave the topic too vague. Instead, you might compose a thesis statement like the following:

Example   The best way to learn a foreign language is through active practice and immersion among native speakers.

This thesis is stronger than, say, one that argues that learning a foreign language is difficult, because this one is contentious: some might, after all, disagree and claim that study and reading are more important than practice and immersion. It is your job to make your case convincingly.

What to Look for in a Thesis Statement

Personal Conviction

No writing of any power is ever possible without commitment to the subject. No motivation is ever as pressing as the need to say something on a subject that matters urgently to you. Your first task is to find an approach to the topic capable of moving you to care and to work and to write. If you can find such an approach, the process of writing—the reading, the thinking, even the reworking of your thoughts—will be carried along by the desire to know and not only by the need to complete the assignment.

Pertinence

An essay should not be a trivial pursuit. It should matter to you and to its reader. As you shape your thesis statement, keep the *value* of your subject in mind. When selecting a point of view, allow yourself to think about its broader implications, even if there is no place to include all of these in the essay itself. You don't have to tell readers how relevant your topic is, but you should believe it, and you should be able to show that you do. Ensuring that your perspective is new and making your point of view matter to your reader are fundamental requirements.

Proportion

The thesis statement indicates what size the essay will be in its finished form. A well-measured thesis statement is snug, not loose, in its fit. If it does not fit properly, the arguments that follow may sag. To ensure a good fit between thesis statement and essay, ask questions. Ask yourself if there is room in a 1500-word essay to discuss all the implications of unemployment in Canada. If not, then trim the thesis statement to fit: for example, unemployment among students seeking part-time jobs in Canadian cities.

Precision

As in a legal contract, the essay is the delivery of promises made in its thesis statement. And, as with all such contracts, the issues to be dealt with must be clarified at the outset. Make sure before you develop your thesis statement that you have made clear to your readers both what your essay will do *and* what it will *not* do. Feel free to announce (without apologies) in or near the thesis statement what the limits of your treatment of the subject are.

Point

Not only should your thesis statement have a point to make, but it must also point in a particular direction. A useful addition to the thesis statement itself is the "route map." The route map informs readers of the highlights of the journey they are about to make. For instance, in a sociology essay comparing the changing attitudes toward women in advertisements from the 1940s to the 1990s, as reflected in two issues of the same magazine, you can briefly outline the steps in your discussion:

> Three major changes can be noted in the presentation of female figures: women   **Example**
> are shown less often in domestic situations; women are more often featured as
> authority figures; and women are more often shown in active, rather than pas-
> sive, roles.

Such a statement contains the direction of the entire essay in miniature and points toward the arguments to follow.

How Can You Tell a Good Thesis Statement from a Bad One?

A good thesis statement is credible, relevant to the course you are taking, narrow enough to be treated in the space you have available, and specifically focused on the point you are making.

Here are some bad thesis statements. Can you tell why they don't do the job they were intended to do?

> Prime Minister Brian Mulroney was one of Canada's most controversial prime   **Example**
> ministers.

The problem with this attempt at a thesis statement is that it doesn't go far enough. It leaves us wondering what exactly the word "controversial" means. You could improve this statement by continuing with a precise route map. You could, for example, write this:

Example   Prime Minister Brian Mulroney was one of Canada's most controversial prime ministers because he forged new trade links with America that have a continuing effect on the economy today.

Now consider this unsuccessful thesis statement:

Example   Myths of creation reveal a great deal about the philosophy of a people.

The chief difficulty with this statement is that it leaves the reader asking "So what?" And the thesis in this case could be the subject of an entire book. Better to say something like the following:

Example   Myths of creation, like the story of Prometheus's theft of fire, sometimes illustrate the dangerous consequences of humankind's attempts to create something that imitates the gods.

This second example narrows down the topic from the outset, leaving the reader in no doubt about the ultimate direction of the paper.
  What is the problem with this next example?

Example   Why does Canada need to provide more protection for some endangered species?

What makes this thesis statement inadequate is that it is not, in fact, a statement at all. Resist the temptation simply to ask a question at the beginning of your paper. Essays usually demand a clear statement of what the results of your thinking and findings are.
  Finally, look at the following thesis statement:

Example   Technology is a threat to human life.

This thesis statement fails to get its point across because it is too general. First, the reader needs to know what kind of technology is so threatening. Is it airplanes or X-ray machines or computers? Next, it is probably too strongly stated to be entirely credible. Try this revision instead:

Example   Computer technology is dangerous to initiative because it encourages too much dependence on something external to the human mind: trust in computers is gradually replacing trust in common sense.

This thesis statement is doubtless still controversial, but at least now it has identified which technology and what kind of danger are meant.

Now That You Have a Thesis Statement . . .

Use your thesis statement as the springboard for the outline. Keep it in mind as you develop your thought. With your thesis statement on paper, you are now ready to set the tone for the readers you have in mind.

How Much Time Should Preparing an Essay Take?

The answer is, of course, that it depends. For a typical student paper in college or university you ought to spend about three weeks, at least if the essay is intended to include research materials. Your tentative schedule should allow about one week for library and Internet research, one week to write up your results in essay form, and one more week to let your essay get cold and to give you time to revise it adequately. Approach your revision both in terms of small details, like checking notes and rewriting to ensure effective word choice, and in terms of larger elements, like the solidity of the argument and the reliability and completeness of your facts. You probably won't devote the entire three weeks to the paper, but that length of time should allow you the leisure to procrastinate a bit and the opportunity to double-check details. It will give you a chance to recover if things go wrong, too.

CHAPTER 1 EXERCISES

1. Develop a focus for the following topics, using some of the techniques listed above. Each is meant to be the subject of a 1500-word essay in the discipline suggested.

   a. the *Youth Criminal Justice Act* in Canada and its implications (sociology)
   b. gay marriage and the church (religious studies)
   c. Olympic scandals (physical education)
   d. international management styles (business administration)
   e. women's suffrage in Canada (history)
   f. the theme of racial differences in Shakespeare (English)
   g. access and accommodation of special education students (education)
   h. artificial intelligence and its moral implications (philosophy)
   i. Canada's peacekeeping role in the Middle East (political science)
   j. the effect of immigration on Canadian cities (sociology)

2. Examine some of your past essays to see if the thesis statements you have written have narrowed the topic down sufficiently. Try rewriting them to give them more focus.

3. Develop a thesis statement for each of the following topics:

   a. attitudes toward reality TV
   b. styles of dress among students
   c. the role of examinations in higher education
   d. taking responsibility for one's actions
   e. approaches to learning
   f. reconciling with an enemy

    g. your attitude toward your physical body

    h. what constitutes happiness

    i. finding your vocation

    j. choosing a place to live

4. Evaluate these thesis statements:

    a. There are pros and cons that must be considered when one decides whether to apply for a student loan.

    b. Shakespeare's romances explore the development of the self.

    c. Arts funding in Canada would benefit from more corporate sponsorship.

Chapter 2
SETTING TONE

All the fun's in how you say a thing.
—ROBERT FROST

Tone is one of the most elusive features of a writing style, whether your own or someone else's. The tone of your essay writing, if it is to avoid clashing with the reader's expectations, should be neither too loud nor too soft. Harsh tones may antagonize your readers. Conversely, gentle tones may make your arguments seem too weak or too bland.

Tone in writing may be compared to tone of voice. It is the personality of an essay. What follows will show both which tones to avoid and which to emulate. When you read your paper aloud to check for errors at the revision stage, you will listen for potential problems. But even before you write, it is important to think about the impact of your ideas on the readers.

The tone you choose must fit the purposes of your essay. If the assignment is a formal research paper, the tone must be appropriately formal as well. If, on the other hand, you are writing an informal, more personal paper, your tone may be correspondingly more casual. The expectations of your readers define the tone for you.

In large part, setting tone is a process of audience analysis. In order to communicate with your audience effectively, your writing must show that it takes the reader's reactions seriously. Some of the preparation you go through to write an essay necessarily involves anticipating how your audience is likely to react to your subject. When you have thought about the potential problems, you are ready to set the tone of your paper.

Tones to Avoid

Avoid Whispering

A tone that is too "soft" suggests that the writer is unsure of the words and the thoughts behind them. Words that are too tentative, too hesitant, are one sign of a whispering tone. Phrases like "it seems to be" or "perhaps" or "it could be that" are indications of the problem. Another signal is the overuse of qualifying phrases such as "however" and "to some extent." Although some qualifications are a good idea, too many may cause the reader to doubt your confidence in your own position.

Example   ✗ It seems that the World Health Organization may have perhaps been too quick in putting Toronto on its travel advisory list during the SARS incident.

Avoid Chatting

A chatty essay is most often the result of incomplete planning and outlining. If your paragraphs or your sentences seem to trail off or to lead to unexpected conclusions, if your ideas seem linked by random association, if your language seems too colloquial or offhand, and if you treat the reader as a chum rather than as an interested observer, you may be accused of chattiness. The cure for chattiness is care, revision, and a polite, though distanced, regard for the reader.

Example   ✗ What was the main cause of the War of 1812? Well, let's look at the question as carefully as we can to see if we can scout out an answer.

Avoid Emotiveness

An emotive tone is struck when a writer attempts to describe his or her feelings in a high-flown, exaggerated way. Often, what results sounds falsely sentimental or hackneyed. Such a tone is often found in introductions and conclusions, particularly when a writer tries to wax poetic about his or her opinions. Although opinions are warranted in an essay, it is nevertheless not necessary to praise Shakespeare as a great playwright at the end of a paper analyzing the structure of *Macbeth,* or to tell the reader of an essay on nuclear disarmament that the issue is a matter of life and death for the human race. Show your feelings by supporting your opinions; don't just declare them.

Example   ✗ Michel Marc Bouchard is a brilliant Canadian playwright whose works, such as *The Coronation Voyage* and *Written on Water,* have been very successfully produced in major theatres in Canada.

Avoid Declaiming

Treat your reader as an equal. Though you may well be playing the role of expert, your role is to reason with your reader and to assume his or her rationality. Any style that repeats points too often, or goes on too long, or explains more than the reader needs is declaiming. This tactic, in combination with a pretentious vocabulary, is disastrous. When you revise, check to see that your writing is transparent, that it does not need to be deciphered to be understood. Avoid words that intimidate the reader because of their length or their obscurity. Choose instead the word that will most clearly express your meaning. Check also to see that the essay is within the required word limit.

In a formal essay, it is also wise to limit the use of rhetorical questions, or to avoid them altogether. Your job is to tell the reader something, not to ask questions.

   ✗ Isn't it true that teachers like you go on strike without regard for the consequences for their students?   **Example**

Avoid Shouting

Make sure that your essay does not inadvertently antagonize its readers. Even though it is your job to defend your viewpoint, you must not assume that your readers are opponents. This problem with tone is especially prevalent in essays that attempt to refute someone else's position. In these cases, the force should be in the logic of your argument, rather than in the tone of your writing.

   ✗ Only an idiot would argue that capital punishment is a humane solution for the problem of life-threatening crimes.   **Example**

Use Personal Pronouns with Discretion

Avoid directly addressing your reader in formal essays. "You" and "your" may alienate the readers if your assumptions about their knowledge or their attitudes are incorrect. It may even sound cheeky or overbearing. If you can, keep the readers on your side; if you know they disagree, keep them at a formal distance.

   ✗ You should have learned from this essay how losing weight will improve your overall health.   **Example**

A research or formal expository essay also may demand that you avoid the use of "I" in writing. If you are forbidden the use of "I" by an instructor, respect that condition.

Do, however, try to avoid awkward impersonal constructions and self-conscious references. Never refer to yourself as "the writer" or "the author."

On the other hand, if "I" is acceptable, *use* it. Your relationship to your reader in a formal essay is meant to be a professional one, but that does not mean that personality has no place, simply that you must know its place and respect the polite distance imposed between you and the reader.

Examples   ✗ It is the opinion of this writer that . . . (too stuffy)
    ✗ In my opinion . . . (too weakly subjective)

    ✓ This paper contends that . . .
    ✓ I will show that . . .

Tones to Emulate

Modulate Your Writing Style

A modulated voice is controlled. Despite the moods of the writer, it shows restraint, politeness, and judgment. Your tones in private conversation may be more varied; in the essay, however (except in the freer personal essay), your tone should be cool, professional, unruffled, and firm.

Imitate the Best

Read newspaper editorials and newsmagazines, as well as your fellow students' essays. Textbooks and critical material may also serve as examples, though you must choose with discretion. And listen: the tone of classroom lectures is often a good indication of what is expected in a paper.

CHAPTER 2 EXERCISES

1. Find an essay in a learned journal and analyze its tone. Find an essay on a related subject and do the same with an article in a popular magazine or newspaper. Describe the tone of both pieces. How do the works differ in terms of audience and purpose? Compare them in terms of vocabulary, use of personal pronouns, use of specialized language, complexity of sentence structure, and assumptions about the reader's familiarity with and interest in the subject under discussion. How is the tone, whether formal or informal, created in each case?

2. Write four paragraphs, each with roughly the same story written for different ears. The story is how you returned home late after a party. Write the first paragraph to your best friend, in whom you confide everything. The second is to your brother, who does not like the people who gave the party. The third is to your mother, who has always discouraged you from going out on weeknights, and the fourth is to your roommate, who was awakened when you returned in the middle of the night.

3. On the Internet, find an interview with a well-known writer or public figure whose written work you know or are currently studying. Compare and contrast the tone of the interview with your impressions of the written essay. How does the tone of the interview differ from the written work? How is it similar? A good source for information and interviews with Canadian writers is located at Athabasca University <www.athabascau.ca/writers/>.

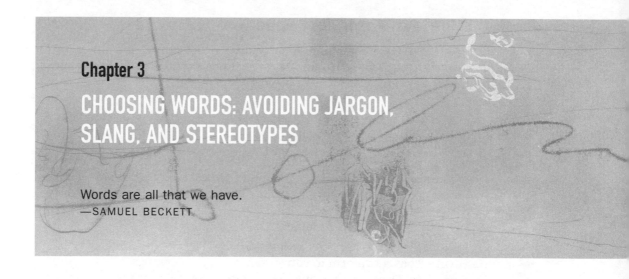

Chapter 3
CHOOSING WORDS: AVOIDING JARGON, SLANG, AND STEREOTYPES

Words are all that we have.
—SAMUEL BECKETT

Word choice is perhaps the most accurate index of the status of a writer. The words you choose depend in part on the role you mean to play in relation to the reader.

Not only is word choice important to tone, but it is also crucial to clarity. The words you use should be weighed carefully: you need to be fully conscious of all the nuances of meaning that they may conjure up. We often use words in a number of quite different ways; if we substitute one for another too blithely, we may find ourselves rather embarrassed. Take, for example, the simple adjective "dirty." If you were to look it up in a thesaurus, you would find a list of words, including, perhaps, "soiled," "unclean," "polluted," "filthy," "foul," "lewd," and "obscene." In this example, it is obviously not adequate to substitute "lewd" for "dirty" in the context of someone's dirty hands. Exact meaning is absolutely demanded if word choice is to be clear.

Good writing demands more than clarity, however. It demands attention to the delicate relationship it has with a reader. It must strive not to say more than it intends, or to create unpleasant, unsuitable, or ludicrous associations in the reader's mind. When you choose your words, stay aware not only of their denotations, but also of their connotations. It is now, for example, important to use language that is deliberately inclusive. While standard grammar used to sanction the use of "his" or of generic words like "men" to mean "humans," readers are these days more likely to take issue with such an exclusive approach to the sexes. Here is another area that demands close attention if you are to form a good relationship with your reader.

Diction: Fit, Form, and Function

Choose language that satisfies the criteria of fit, form, and function for the assignment in question. What follows are some pointers on how to choose (and to revise) the language of your essays.

Observe the Dress Code

Paying attention to the conventions of a dress code does not mean that you must wear a uniform inhibiting all expression of personality. It means, simply, that you must conform to certain standards—happily, in this case, quite flexible standards.

Keep these guidelines in mind:

1. Fit—Does your writing suit its purpose and audience?
2. Form—Does it conform to convention?
3. Function—Does your writing make your message clear?

If the idea of conforming for the sake of conforming disturbs you, remember what the consequences of not conforming may be: perhaps being misunderstood, ignored, or considered offensive. To avoid any of these perils in your use of language, and in your word choice particularly, keep these hints in mind.

Write to Impress—Not to Intimidate

When you write an essay, you should address your reader as an equal; the information you impart and the viewpoint you defend are offered as reasonable choices for readers as clear-thinking as you are.

To impress a reader, you need to show what you know and to express a willingness to share it. If your words do not allow you to share your results, because they are too technical or too vague or carelessly chosen, you will have alienated your readers. Remember that, in the formal essay, the emphasis is less upon you and the reader personally than it is upon the subject at hand: your relationship is entirely professional. But in the informal essay, your personality and that of your reader play more pronounced roles: you expect that the reader will enjoy your company.

Make Yourself Comfortable in the Language of Your Subject

Determining your status, and thus the proper diction for an essay, is sometimes a great challenge. After all, you may not feel much like the equal of the professor giving a course in which you feel shaky or ill prepared. Obviously, the more conversant you become with the terminology of a discipline, the easier it will be to feel like an equal and to write a stimulating learned discussion.

Just as important, however, is the confidence with which you can play the role of an equal. Think of your paper not as just another assignment, written by a student to an instructor, but as an opportunity to speak the language of the discipline to someone who understands it.

Choose Your Words Stylishly

The "rules" that govern diction cannot be listed here, simply because word choice depends upon context. A formal essay demands formal language, just as a formal occasion demands evening dress. Likewise, informal writing allows you more freedom in self-expression and a more casual approach.

Avoid Overdressed Language

1. DO NOT USE TOO MANY TECHNICAL OR SPECIALIZED TERMS OR ACRONYMS. Too many terms may actually prevent your reader from seeing your underlying meaning. Technical subjects clearly demand some technical terminology, but while it is partly your task to demonstrate your ability to use terms with skill and ease, you must not use them to confuse your reader or to avoid the issues. Acronyms like DAT (for "digital audio tape") may be meaningful to you, but if you intend to use such shortened forms throughout your essay you should identify them at the outset in order to avoid confusion. The best form is to use the term in its entirety first:

> Digital audio tape (DAT) is available to consumers who wish to make high-quality   **Example**
> recordings in their own homes.

2. AVOID NEOLOGISMS USED OUT OF CONTEXT. Words, like everything else, have a history. A word like "lifestyle," of modern derivation, is inappropriate when used to describe the feudal way of life, for example.

3. AVOID THE CURRENT TENDENCY TO MAKE VERBS OUT OF NOUNS. "Impact" is a noun and not a verb; something may therefore "have an impact on" something, but may not "impact on" something. A similar problem occurs with words ending in "ize" and "ization." Many are now acceptable, but some are questionable recent coinages, often unnecessary and vague. "Prioritize," for example, should be replaced with "establish priorities."

4. AVOID PRETENTIOUS WORDS AND CONSTRUCTIONS. Often these pretentious constructions appear as groups of nouns, attached in such a way that the reader cannot visualize the object described. The tendency to use such abstract and depersonalized language comes partly from our desire to appear sophisticated, but the effect is rather like wearing designer labels on the outside of our clothes. Such a high-sounding style may intimidate or amuse, but it does not really communicate.

Example   ✗ Mimi found it difficult to orientate herself in the library.

Replace "orientate" with "orient." When in doubt, check usage in a dictionary or a guide to usage.

Example   ✗ Irregardless of her negative attitude, Gloria got the job.

Replace "irregardless" with "regardless." "Irregardless" is nonstandard usage.

5. AVOID "FLASHY" WORDS. Sometimes a student will fervently consult a thesaurus, seeking some clever ways of varying vocabulary. Although this is a commendable practice, never forget that no two words mean exactly the same thing or have precisely the same impact. When you find a synonym, check it in the dictionary to make sure that it means what you think it does. Make sure your words know their place.

A longer word is not necessarily a stronger word. A word selected simply "for show" may be as out of place as a diamond tiara worn with a soccer uniform. Context is the first consideration in these matters. Don't use a word just because it sounds elevated.

Example   ✗ At any time of year, upon entering this voluminous structure, one cannot help but notice the low roar of conversation as the voices of the library's patrons reverberate from one concrete wall to the other.

How can a library be "voluminous"? Replace this word with something more suitable—like "huge" or "imposing."

Avoid Sloppy Language

1. AVOID SLANG. There are, admittedly, times when slang fits the mood. You may, for instance, wish to draw attention to the common language for a particular term, or report some dialogue. Beware of enclosing slang in quotation marks ("swell"); it may seem forced and unnatural. Unless you are sure that slang will add colour and character to your writing, avoid it. Careless slang is sloppy and perhaps more revealing than you wish.

Try to be conscious of your use of slang. It is easy to pick up words and phrases that seem to be in vogue and to use them unthinkingly. A word or phrase that comes too easily will not help you do any original thinking; the reader may just glide over the usage without reflection as well. Worse still, the reader may not know the particular usage you have in mind.

Examples   ✗ I avoid reading psychology books because I think the subject is flaky.
            ✗ The idea of euthanasia weirds him out.
            ✗ I was really clueless on that last exam.

2. AVOID COLLOQUIAL CONSTRUCTIONS. Colloquial constructions may include slang, but they also include language that is chatty, takes too much for granted, or is not completely clear. A carefully selected colloquial word or phrase may add unexpected life to a formal paper, but the overuse of language generally confined to speech may lead the reader to dismiss the value and importance of what you are saying.

Because you have no chance to reinforce your words with body language (a raised eyebrow, a smile, a frown), your reader will need the most precise, specific language you can possibly find. You need all the power and clarity of the words at your command.

> ✗ Voters were initially enthused with Jean Chrétien's plans to increase employment among Canadians.   **Example**

Replace "enthused with" with "enthusiastic about."

3. AVOID SAYING THE OBVIOUS, ESPECIALLY IN A HACKNEYED WAY. What you have to say may not be entirely new, but your approach to the subject should be fresh, and your way of expressing yourself should give the reader a new angle of perception.

Avoid language deadened by overuse, whether it be jargon or cliché. Use language that enlightens, that sparks thought, that provokes discussion, that wakes up your reader. Saying the same old thing in the same old way may be the easy way out, but it will not have the same impact that a thoughtful or inventive use of words may have.

The cliché does, however, have its place. For instance, in the paragraph above, the phrase "the easy way out" is a cliché. In the midst of some fairly abstract prose, its presence can startle just because it is a different kind of language than what precedes it. Use clichés sparingly, and don't use them thoughtlessly. Otherwise they may have all the impact of a joke too often repeated.

> ✗ Those who are employed in the service industry often feel they are working for peanuts.   **Example**

Replace "working for peanuts" with fresher, more thoughtful phrasing, perhaps "not paid enough to eat properly."

4. CONSULT A DICTIONARY TO FIND THE PROPER USAGE OF A WORD. When you look up a word in the dictionary, you will find information vital to its usage. Usually, one of the first things you will see in a listing is an abbreviation that denotes what part of speech the word is. For example, if you look up the word "impact," you will find it listed as a noun. If you are in doubt about what any of the abbreviations used in your dictionary mean, check them in the list of abbreviations, usually provided at the beginning of the dictionary. Also pay special attention to samples of idiomatic usage that may be given; such examples may offer you more help in how to use a word more accurately than an abstract knowledge of its meaning alone. Dictionaries give current information about

how to use a word in standard English: they are reliable sources in determining whether a word's usage is archaic, dialect, colloquial, or slang.

5. BE ESPECIALLY CAREFUL TO AVOID BIAS IN YOUR LANGUAGE. Unintended bias occurs when people are not scrupulously careful about their language. To avoid bias, you should be sure to use inclusive language. For example, in a letter you should use the salutation "Dear Sir or Madam" rather than "Dear Sir" if you are unsure of the recipient's identity, thus avoiding accusations of sexism. You should be cautious about assuming things; make sure that you respect the terms that individuals or groups use to identify themselves rather than assigning labels to them. This tactic usually ensures that you will be using a specific term rather than a generalized or even a stereotypical one. For instance, the word "Korean" is more specific than "Asian" and may be more accurate. Be wary of "pseudo-generic" words such as "mankind" or "chairman" that seem to be inclusive but are not. "Humankind" and "chair" are preferred in these cases. Make sure that the language you choose treats everyone equally. An expression like "the man and his wife" does not accord equal treatment: substitute either "the man and the woman" or "the husband and wife." Why, after all, should one of the individuals be identified only in relation to the other? Finally, it is always a good idea to use a term that puts people first. Do not say "the disabled," but "people with disabilities," or, if the characteristic is irrelevant, don't mention it at all.

6. AVOID CONTRACTIONS IN FORMAL ESSAYS. Contractions, such as "don't," "can't," or "shouldn't" generally are not acceptable in formal writing. While they are acceptable in spoken language and in the reporting of dialogue, make a special effort not to use them when you are writing an essay meant for the classroom.

CHAPTER 3 EXERCISES

1. Make a list of common expressions we use to describe drinking too much. The list might include such phrases as "getting loaded." Try to analyze the origins and the functions of these expressions. Do the same thing with words and expressions used to describe sleeping.

2. List slang expressions that are dated, such as "groovy" or "the cat's pyjamas." Can you list some contemporary expressions that are similar?

3. Look for clichés or stock phrases in newspapers or magazines. Many words seem automatically and unthinkingly to go together, such as "illegal alien." Make a list of phrases you find and explain why they are ineffective.

4. Read over essays you have written, and note any slang you find. Though slang can be colourful, its context is significant. Rephrase the sentences, substituting fresh language.

5. A. Identify problems in the following sentences and suggest alternative wording. (Turn to p. 218 to check your answers.)

    1. Diana Krall and Avril Lavigne are well-known Canadian songbirds.
    2. The perpetrator of the crime was an illegal alien.

3. A victim of polio, Lou used a scooter.
4. The handicapped need your help.
5. The girl who works on the switchboard must be well-spoken.
6. Call the firemen if you smell smoke.
7. Sarah Binks is a celebrated fictional Canadian poetess.
8. Man cannot live by bread alone.
9. Whenever he went to the variety store, he felt that he was gypped.
10. Lin Song was an Oriental student.

B. Identify problems in the following sentences and suggest alternative wording.

1. Indians often choose to live on the reservation.
2. A victim of West Nile virus, Bette is paralyzed and confined to a wheelchair.
3. There were many men in the office, along with the girls at the reception desk.
4. The aged and the infirm use this transportation system.
5. A man and his wife came in this morning to rent an apartment.
6. AIDS victims take special medications.
7. The disabled can apply for supplemental income.
8. Dodi was committed to a school for wayward girls.
9. Men accompanied the ladies to the celebration.
10. May I speak to the master of the house?

Part Two

DESIGNING THE ESSAY

Chapter 4
DESIGNING AN OUTLINE

The discipline of the writer is to learn to be still and listen to what the subject has to tell him.
—RACHEL CARSON

Once you have decided upon your topic, determined your thesis statement, and considered your audience and purpose, you need an outline.

Never attempt to write an essay without some kind of outline—whether it be a formal, detailed itinerary or a hastily jotted map showing your destination, your direction, and the stops you wish to make along the way.

When preparing an outline, remember that it is only a sketch of your paper. The final design of the essay may be quite different from what you originally intended. A sketch does not need to be perfect. The outline is meant to help you write the paper, not to restrict your line of thought. Keep the outline flexible so that you can tinker with it as you go along. It is simply a tentative blueprint, a description of the contents of your paper, rather than a prescription of its requirements.

Make a Table of Contents

Think of the outline as your own flexible table of contents. It is, after all, your note to yourself, your reminder of what details you wish to include and what arguments you want to make. Like a table of contents, the outline labels what the reader may expect to find contained in the work itself.

Take a look at the table of contents of this book to see what information can be gleaned from it. Not only does it tell you what is included in the book, but it also tells you what the major and minor divisions of the work are. For instance, you will find the chapter entitled "Devising a Thesis" under the part heading "Developing the Essay."

In other words, the table of contents gives the reader a sense of the book's dimensions. You see, for example, that the book you are holding in your hand has seven major parts, each of which is divided into a number of chapters. Thus, it gives you a sense not only of the work's overall shape, but also of the size of each component, and, at the same time, of the orderly arrangement of its position within the work. What follows is not a set of rules for composing outlines, but a series of suggestions about what they may contain.

To make your outline as useful and as organized as a table of contents, keep the following steps in mind:

Sort Through Your Ideas

1. MAKE SURE YOU HAVE ESTABLISHED YOUR PIVOTAL POINTS: THE THESIS STATEMENT AND PURPOSE. Use your thesis statement (subject to revision) and your selected purpose as the launching points for your outline. From them will emanate all the ideas, arguments, facts, and figures you have gathered.

2. GATHER YOUR NOTES. With your tentative thesis statement on paper in front of you, gather your tentative remarks, your research, and your questions about the topic. One good way to take notes is to list separate ideas on index cards (remembering to include sources, if any). This way, you can shuffle or discard material easily.

Keeping your purpose in mind, organize the material you have selected, discarding any information not strictly related to it. If you are discussing kinds of stage props, for instance, don't include material on their development in the history of the theatre.

3. CLASSIFY YOUR MATERIAL. Decide how many steps your argument contains. Then classify your notes accordingly. If, for example, you mean to consider three reasons that border relations have deteriorated between Americans and Canadians, decide in which of the three discussions to include a statistic about people detained at the border.

4. ORDER YOUR MATERIAL IN A LOGICAL WAY. This process demands that you decide at what point a particular argument should be mentioned. Here you must decide what your opening point, your follow-up, and your last word should be. Keep in mind the tried-and-true notion that a strong point is best placed at the beginning or end of an essay. Keep in mind, too, that some of your organizational decisions are dependent upon the pattern of argument you selected at the outset. If you know, for instance, that your reader will need to understand your definition of national security to get the most out of your essay, put it where it will be most accessible. Or, if you are explaining a process, make sure the reader is able to follow it step by step.

5. RANK YOUR POINTS ACCORDING TO THEIR IMPORTANCE. Sorting your ideas according to rank means deciding whether an item has a major role or merely a minor one to play. The ranking itself will give you an excellent idea of what you have to say and of how developed your thought is. Where you have much to add or to explain, the idea is vital and may serve as a significant part of your evidence;

where your idea is almost all you have to say on the subject, you may relegate the point to a minor status.

In order to rank your ideas, assign them numbers or letters, beginning perhaps with capital Roman numerals for major sections, moving to capital letters for important supporting sections, through to Arabic numbers for less important support material, to lowercase letters for the minor details. The points you are making are primary in rank; the support you gather for them is secondary.

Example I. Border relations between Canada and the United States have deteriorated for a number of reasons.

    A. Americans became extremely cautious after the terrorist attacks of September 11, 2001. (REASON #1)

        1. America felt that Canada was too lenient in its immigration policies.

            a. People were allowed to enter Canada from a number of destinations from which America would not accept immigrants.

            b. Canadian policies toward refugees and toward deportation are notably less strict than American ones.

        2. America felt that Canada was too lenient in its policing of the world's longest undefended border.

            a. People were simply "waved through" without investigation, even after September 11.

            b. Airports in Canada tended to be loose on security measures, according to American standards after September 11.

    B. Canada believed that America was blaming it and other countries for the events of September 11, without sufficient evidence to back up its claims. (REASON #2)

        1. Canadians did not approve of the war against Iraq, launched by America partly as a response to perceived terrorist threat.

            a. The Canadian government did not support the war in Iraq.

            b. Surveys show that the Canadian people largely did not support it either.

The form of notation does not matter particularly, but it should permit you to see *at a glance* the relative scope of the point you are making. A carefully ranked outline will show you the ideas within ideas.

6. INVENT A TITLE. Although you still have not arrived at a finished product, the argument you make in your essay should be clear enough to you that a title should pose no problem. Just bear in mind that a title should give the reader specific information about the subject you are writing about. Don't entitle your paper "Margaret Atwood"; instead, call it "Atwood's *Oryx and Crake* as a Departure from Formulaic Science Fiction." Do not underline your title; reserve underlining for the titles of published works. A title should be catchy and not too lengthy, but don't sacrifice clarity for flourish.

Tailor the Outline

As you outline, you may well notice some rags and tatters among your papers, bits of research material that seemed valuable at the time you took the notes, though they now seem unrelated to the development of your thought. If you cannot use these scraps in the final fabric of your argument, do not hesitate to toss them out. Remember that one of the main functions of the outline is to show you how well the material you have gathered actually fits the viewpoint you have chosen. Each point of the outline ought to represent an area that you can fill with developed thoughts, facts, and evidence. If you find that all you have to say on a particular point can be fleshed out in one sentence, then you must find a way to incorporate that small point into another place in your argument, or perhaps you may have to eliminate it altogether. What isn't useful or appropriate for your thesis statement should be left behind.

The outline below shows a short persuasive essay developed by examples, definition, classification, and even comparison/contrast. Basically, the essay consists of three or more arguments to defend the thesis, plus supporting evidence. These patterns of argument will be discussed in the next chapter.

Note that each section has a small thesis statement (or topic sentence) of its own. These are best written as sentences in the outline to ensure clarity. Note also that the subdivisions allow you to see at a glance what items have the most support (and conversely, what might be in need of greater support or development).

The example below provides one of the commonest structures for the essay—the funnel. In this structure, the essay develops from a general point that is narrowed down in the thesis statement. Not every essay, however, will move from the general to the specific. Some may follow a pattern dictated by the internal structure of the particular evidence that you uncover in your research. Also, while this essay uses a familiar three-part structure, an essay is easily expanded or contracted depending on the breadth and depth of information you have to include.

TOPIC: Headaches   **Example**

PATTERN OF ARGUMENT: Classification

I. INTRODUCTION: Everyone suffers a headache at one time or another, though the pain can vary in degree. Some headaches respond to Aspirin; others are excruciating, perhaps chronic or debilitating.
THESIS STATEMENT: In order to treat a headache properly, one must be able to diagnose it correctly.
PREVIEW: There are four types of headache: the tension headache, the cluster headache, the sinus headache, and the migraine.

II. BODY
   A. A tension headache
      a. Cause: muscle contraction
      b. Symptoms: dull, steady ache; tightness around the scalp or neck
      c. Triggers: stress, anxiety, repressed emotion
      d. Treatment: Aspirin

   B. A cluster headache
      a. Cause: unknown
      b. Symptoms: burning, piercing pain, often behind one eye; occurs periodically for days, weeks, or months; less than an hour in duration
      c. Triggers: smoking, alcohol consumption, histamines, or nitroglycerine
      d. Treatment: medication, such as ergotamines, inhaled or held under the tongue
   C. A sinus headache
      a. Cause: any disturbances blocking the passage of fluid from the sinuses
      b. Symptoms: gnawing pain, rise in temperature
      c. Triggers: same as cause
      d. Treatment: nasal decongestants and antibiotics
   D. A migraine
      a. Cause: not known
      b. Symptoms: nausea, dizziness, cold hands, tremor, sensitivity to light and sound; sometimes a day or longer in duration
      c. Triggers: irregular eating and sleeping; ingestion of cheese, chocolate, red wine, or caffeine
      d. Treatment: no cure, but some medications prevent or abort headaches; lifestyle changes are recommended
III. CONCLUSION: Relief from headaches is possible for most people if they learn to seek the safest and most effective treatment available.

CHAPTER 4 EXERCISES

1. Develop outlines, complete with thesis statements, for the following topics:
   a. the school registration process
   b. your favourite local band
   c. the importance of family dinners
   d. making ends meet
   e. turning a hobby into a job
   f. getting along with superiors
   g. censorship on the Internet
   h. political correctness

2. Read a classmate's essay and sketch an outline of its structure. Is each section clearly delineated? Is adequate support given for each point that they raise? Is the movement of the paper logical and easy to follow? What advice would you give on how to make the essay's structure clearer?

3. Read a chapter in a textbook related to your field of study. Make an outline of it, complete with thesis statement, arguments, and support.

4. Find an online set of instructions, such as a help file. Analyze how the information is put together in order to make the process clear to the reader. Are there strategies for making an online set of instructions clearer? Can you see differences between an online help file and a set of instructions written exclusively on paper?

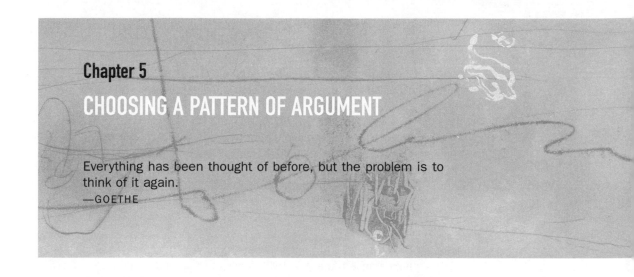

Chapter 5

CHOOSING A PATTERN OF ARGUMENT

Everything has been thought of before, but the problem is to think of it again.
—GOETHE

After you have established your thesis statement and made your outline, you need to choose the pattern or patterns of argument that will do it justice. Arguments make an attempt to persuade the reader of something; the pattern of argument gives structure to your thoughts.

Arguments present evidence and reasons that an idea is valid or that a course of action is the best one to take. Arguments can be quite complex: not only do they present reasons for accepting a particular line of reasoning, but they also attempt to counter possible opposing arguments, anticipate objections that might be raised, and analyze the assumptions on which any reasoning is based. To be persuasive, an argument must win a reader over, by engaging emotions and by presenting reasons and support for them that are trustworthy and reliable.

Audience analysis is a major factor in writing a persuasive argument. You need to use authorities, statistics, examples, and reasons that will strike your readers as convincing and commanding respect. Argument is thus the process by which you lay out the good reasons for making your case: the reasons that any right-minded reader would also accept as compelling.

Look at the following outline. An argument is stated and a number of kinds of support are used to defend its position and win over its readers:

THESIS: Dieting is not a good way to maintain one's health.   **Example**
Reason 1: Most diets are unbalanced to begin with, encouraging dieters to
          skimp on starch, or to avoid entire food groups, like carbohydrates,
          unwisely.

Your support for Reason 1 might include examples of low carbohydrate diets (like that espoused by Dr. Atkins) or fat-free diets (like that advocated by Susan Powter).

Reason 2: Diets are too often considered the key to avoid being overweight when, in fact, a sedentary lifestyle may be the real culprit.

For Reason 2, you might cite the words of an authority, such as a physician who has worked extensively with overweight people and who has had success in developing exercise programs for them.

Reason 3: Most diets fail because dieters are not willing or able to change their eating habits permanently.

In support of Reason 3, you might cite the statistic that fully 85 percent of all diets fail since the dieters in question regain most of their excess weight within a year.

Reason 4: Diets can lead to problems because they encourage obsession with appearance rather than with feeling strong and healthy.

Your last claim, Reason 4, might be supported by the reason that dieting is based too often on a cultural obsession with appearance that has nothing to do with health and, in fact, may be detrimental to it.

This argument does not prove conclusively that diets do not work to maintain health, but it does muster a number of powerful reasons that they do not. Arguments in general do not prove anything beyond a shadow of a doubt; they do, however, marshal forth facts and reasons that together work to persuade a reader. Your job, when constructing a good argument, is to assemble pertinent facts and reasons with an eye to making your audience see things your way. To be persuasive, the facts you choose and how you assemble them should form a pattern or patterns of argument.

Usually an essay will demand several patterns in support of its thesis, as the sample outline in the preceding chapter demonstrates. In order to support your thesis with a similar variety of arguments, you must look for methods by which to direct your thought. The following tactics may serve as structural guidelines or blueprints for your thought:

Definition/Description
Example
Classification
Process
Comparison/Contrast
Cause and Effect
Narration

These patterns cannot be entirely separated from one another. Usually, a writer will use several patterns to develop one essay. Refer, for example, to the outline in the preceding chapter. It uses many different kinds of argument, including definition, classification, comparison/contrast, and example.

A paragraph that defines "dreams," for example, may contrast a simple dictionary definition with a more elaborate definition offered by a psychologist. Examples of dreams may be given to show something about their essential nature, perhaps demonstrating the creativity of the unconscious mind.

The patterns listed below should offer you some inspiration when you get stuck in the process of outlining your thoughts. Refer to this section when you need help in amplifying an argument.

Definition/Description

Definition suggests the use of a dictionary to define a term explicitly. This tactic ensures that there is a general consensus between writer and readers as to the term's meaning in the context of the essay.

Although dictionary definitions are important, don't rely too heavily on them. Belabouring a definition already familiar to your readers may alienate them: it may sound condescending. Furthermore, a critical reader will be concerned more with what you *make* of a definition than with its content per se. If you do cite a dictionary definition, make sure that you use it to make a point.

What comprises a useful definition? First, it must supply the reader with characteristics that describe something. Occasionally, it may describe by way of comparison/contrast, by showing what the thing is not. And, it may give some enlightening history of the term, showing how it came to have the meaning it has. It may then show what something does, in order to describe more concretely what it is. Lastly, it may give an example, meant to epitomize the nature of the thing described.

> What, exactly, is a dream? Webster's says nothing more than that it is a "hallucination in sleep."[1] This rather bland attempt at definition masks the essential problem. The truth is that we do not really know what dreams are, though there has always been a great deal of speculation about their nature. Some modern psychologists, such as Carl Jung, maintain that dreams are unconscious subjective re-creations of reality: "the dream is the theater where the dreamer is at once scene, actor, prompter, stage manager, author, audience, and critic."[2] But, even among modern psychologists, there is still considerable disagreement about the source of dreams.

Example

This definition introduces the subject and provides two possible definitions of what dreams are.

Example

Because readers usually find it easier to understand what they can picture, examples are often the best means of amplifying an argument. Whether you use an extended example, meant to illustrate your general point in a series of specific ways, or whether you use a variety of small examples to achieve the same end, examples lend support to your argument.

Example   One of the most famous recorded dreams is Kekulé's account of his discovery of the nature of benzene. In 1865, Kekulé, a chemist, fell asleep and dreamt of a snake with its tail in its mouth.[3] His intuition about the structure of benzene—that its molecules were not open structures but rings—was one of the cornerstones of modern scientific thinking. This episode illustrates that some dreams have a creative component capable of communicating, in a flash, something that the conscious mind has been seeking in vain. Some dreams apparently can bring about a breakthrough in understanding.

This example supports the idea that dreams are sometimes creative.

Classification

In order to explain something more precisely, a writer often has recourse to methods of classification, by which he or she can make necessary distinctions within a subject area. Classifying different parts of a subject involves making decisions about what belongs where. A large subject may be divided into smaller or more manageable sections to make important distinctions clear. In order for classification to work convincingly, the reader must be assured that the categories are tidy, include everything essential, and do not substantially overlap.

Example   Although dreams have been a subject of much study throughout history, there is still no consensus about what dreams mean. Some philosophers, like Bertrand Russell, contend that dreams cannot be differentiated from reality, that, in fact, we do not know which is real, the waking state or the dreaming state.[4] Others maintain, even in certain modern cultures, that dreams have divinatory qualities that tell us something about what might happen. Modern psychologists argue that dreams are proof of unconscious activity in the mind, and their studies of dreams seek to understand the springs of behaviour.

This classification lists some of the different interpretations of what dreams mean.

Process

It is often necessary in the course of an essay to explain how to do something or how something works. When describing a process, think of yourself as a teacher. It is part of your job to supply your readers with all the information they require to understand, without confusion, a given process. At the same time, you must be careful to assess their level of understanding accurately, if you are to avoid writing that is boring or condescending. It is also part of your job to present the material in a logical, step-by-step manner, so that the reader is spared needless cross-referencing and rereading. Check your description of the process to see if its steps can be easily followed.

Example   The Freudian view of the process of dreaming, recorded in *The Interpretation of Dreams* in 1899, suggests that dreams are stimulated by bodily reactions, experiences during daylight hours, and infantile memories. When people dream, according to Freud, they give way to primitive impulses, to repressed wishes, often displaced or represented in symbolic terms. When they awaken, dreamers revise their dreams by rationalizing and elaborating upon their reports of them. To understand these subconscious processes, Freud suggested that the content of dreams be analyzed through free association that would allow the dreamer to become aware of the hidden meanings and symbols of the dream.[5]

This paragraph outlines the steps in Freud's interpretation of the process of dreaming.

Comparison/Contrast

Comparisons are an essential part of expository writing. No pattern of argument is more common on examination questions, for instance, than comparison/contrast.

A comparison includes both similarities and differences. When you contrast, however, you focus exclusively on the differences between things.

When comparing, keep the overall structure in mind. You may present first one thing and then the other, or you may present the two things in combination. Alternating between the two is best if the material to be covered is complex or lengthy.

Example

From earliest times, there has been sharp disagreement about the sources of dreams. One school of thought sees dreams as a natural phenomenon; the other sees them as something supernatural. Even the basic division between Freud and Jung on the nature of dreams can be seen this way. Freud holds that dreams are explainable in terms of what he calls "day residue" and of external stimuli;[6] that is, they are borrowed from the images of daily life accompanied by bodily disturbances. Together these elements produce a dream that reveals much about the dreamer's repressed desires and feelings. Jung's account of the source of dreams is more spiritual and less a part of natural human functions. He argues that a "dream is the small hidden door in the deepest and most intimate sanctum of the soul,"[7] and his studies of individuals' dreams attempt to relate the dreamer to the larger patterns of human consciousness throughout history.

This paragraph illustrates the main differences between Jung and Freud on the subject of dreams.

Look at the table below. Point-by-point comparisons usually succeed better, especially if the topic is complex, because you do the comparison more overtly in that argument structure. You make three points about apples and oranges, and then you organize your argument around your points, rather than just doing one side of the comparison (the apples) and following with the other side (the oranges). After all, the point of a comparison/contrast essay is for you to compare and contrast. Don't make the reader do it.

BLOCK COMPARISON (for simple short topics only)	POINT-BY-POINT COMPARISON (usually the better choice since the reader doesn't have to do all the work alone)
APPLES	*POINT 1*
Point 1	Apples
Point 2	Oranges
Point 3	*POINT 2*
ORANGES	Apples
Point 1	Oranges
Point 2	*POINT 3*
Point 3	Apples
	Oranges

Cause and Effect

This pattern traces the relationship between the cause of an event or a condition and its results. When seeking to develop an argument by tracing causes and their effects, keep in mind two potential dangers. First, beware of trusting the idea of causality too much. Simply because one thing follows another chronologically does not mean that the second event was caused by the first.

Second, do not limit effects to one cause alone. Usually more than one determinant brings about an event or a trend. Don't wear blinders in your zeal to establish connections.

Example   Recent studies show that there is a physiological correlation between sleep patterns and the frequency of dreams. In the 1950s, researchers found a link between bursts of rapid eye movement (sometimes called REM sleep), increased electrical activity in the brain, and frequency of reported dreams. If a dreamer is awakened during a period of REM sleep, there is a much greater chance that he or she will report and remember a dream. These studies show that dreams usually, though not always, occur in conjunction with certain patterns of activity in the dreamer's brain.[8]

This paragraph points out a relationship between sleep patterns and dreams. It also illustrates one of the problems in establishing an argument; note that while the author of the paragraph does mention a correlation between two things, there is no claim of a definite cause-and-effect relation between them. Often, there can be no positive declaration of cause and effect. Be cautious in your claims.

Narration

Telling a story, like telling a good joke, is hard to do. You narrate, or tell a story, in a piece of expository writing in order to bring your argument to life.

To be effective, the narrative you use in an essay should contain carefully selected, telling details—enough to be vivid, not so many that it is boring. The narrative must be well timed: it should draw your reader into the writing or graphically illustrate a point you are making. It should hold the reader's attention: do not expand the story endlessly with "and then . . . and then . . . and then."

Use narration sparingly in essay writing. Most commonly, you will find it used to relate case studies, brief anecdotes, and extended examples.

5

The Bible contains many stories of dreams used as prophecies. Perhaps the most famous is the story of the dreams of the Pharoah of Egypt. He dreamed of seven fat cattle, followed by seven lean cattle, which devoured the first. Then he dreamed of seven good stalks of corn, which were destroyed by seven lean stalks of corn. These dreams Joseph interpreted as prophecies about the fate of Egypt. First, it would experience seven years of plenty, then seven years of famine. In response to Joseph's interpretation, the Pharoah stored enough food from the seven good years to protect the country from starvation during the famine that followed.[9] Such treatment of dreams as prophecy are part of many religions and illustrate the captivating power of the dream on the human imagination.

Example

This paragraph retells a familiar biblical story to make a point about the imaginative appeal of dreams.

The superscript numerals used throughout the sample paragraphs indicate places where a writer would have to acknowledge sources. In this case, traditional note numbers have been used. For more information on the subject of citation of sources, see Chapters 13 and 14.

Tips on Choosing the Right Pattern

Your choice of pattern may depend to some extent on your subject. In English, for example, one of the most common patterns is *comparison/contrast*. In political science and sociology, you may find yourself most often choosing *definition* or *classification*. History makes most use of the *cause-and-effect* pattern. The most common pattern in all writing is *example*. Choose your pattern wisely; keep its relevance to the overall thesis statement always in mind.

CHAPTER 5 EXERCISES

1. Develop the following thesis statements by using at least two appropriate patterns of argument:
   a. Genetically altered foods, or so-called "frankenfoods," should be monitored carefully.
   b. Tuition for colleges and universities needs to be drastically reduced to allow greater access for lower socioeconomic groups.
   c. Reaction to terrorist activity has led to a greater incidence of racism.
   d. The Internet has led to a severe diminution in users' level of physical activity.
   e. Arts education needs to be more integrated in school curricula.

2. Develop a thesis statement for one of the following topics:

   a. Canada's relationship to American popular culture
   b. The advantages or disadvantages of chain stores

   For the topic chosen, develop a short introductory paragraph ending with the thesis statement. Go through the patterns of argument listed, and decide which methods would be most appropriate for developing your thesis statement. Then, outline the essay.

3. Analyze the patterns of argument in a paper written by a classmate. What are the most common patterns? What patterns could be used more effectively?

4. Analyze the patterns of argument you find in a chapter in this textbook. List any techniques you find that you could emulate in your own work.

5. Write a set of instructions for how to make or to fix something. The instructions should guide the reader clearly through the process involved to create the final product. Use the basic structure of a recipe as a guideline for your set of instructions, remembering to tell the reader what materials are needed and what methods are to be followed in a logical, step-by-step order.

6. Listen carefully to a speech delivered by a politician or a media celebrity, or study the text of a speech (sometimes these are available online). How do the techniques of an argument delivered orally differ from those used in essays?

7. Write two definitions of a word you commonly use. Design the first definition so it explains the word to a group of your peers; next, rewrite the definition so it is suitable for a grade-one class. What techniques did you use to accomplish the second task?

8. Write an essay that compares two places you have lived. Obviously, you need to first decide what the point of the comparison is. For example, you might compare Edmonton and Winnipeg in order to show that one is more pleasant than the other, or to show that one of the places is more interesting than the other. Make sure that the comparison is not simply perfunctory; you are comparing the two places to make some point to the reader.

Part Three
DRAFTING THE ESSAY

Chapter 6

SHAPING THE ESSAY

The wastepaper basket is the writer's best friend.
—ISAAC BASHEVIS SINGER

As you develop your outline from its bare structure to its fully dressed form, remember that the shape of the essay is in your hands. Though there are guidelines you can follow, the essay is not a form to be filled in. You create the form itself, by selecting what is included and what is left out.

The First Draft

To make the first draft of your essay easier to write, keep the following advice in mind:

Write While You Think, Not After

To move from outline to essay, you need to develop your thoughts. This development does not involve long delays and cautious planning. Writing is not the expression of thought; it is thought itself. To avoid getting tangled up in a web of confusion, or worse, procrastination, write as you think, rather than after you have thought. Putting pen to paper, even in an unpolished way, will help you overcome the terror of the blank page and will enable you to examine your thoughts more objectively later on.

That many students now use a computer to write their papers from start to finish is a great boon, or can be. The initial fear of the blank page is less daunting when you use a computer, if only because everything can be so easily changed. The computer screen indeed seems to demand less commitment from a writer than paper and pen. Use that quality to good effect. The ease with which revisions can be made should mean that you experiment more often and write more drafts in your efforts to achieve clarity.

Think of the advantages a computer screen can provide as you write your first draft. First, you can add, delete, move, or change text with surprisingly little effort. Next, you can save multiple versions of your draft, in different stages of your thinking; that means your good ideas won't get away. You can leave formatting decisions like spacing, margins, font, and titles for afterwards. And, best of all, you are not at all restricted to beginning at the beginning and continuing on till the end. You can start wherever you feel comfortable, assured that sooner or later you will fill in the gaps essential to creating a brilliant introduction or a strong opening argument.

Worry as You Write

This may sound like odd advice in a book meant to help you compose an essay, but the worrying stage, uncomfortable though it may be, is usually productive. Worrying is thinking. Keep the essay in the back of your mind as you do other things; carry a small notebook and make a record of passing ideas.

Plan to Rewrite

Don't demand perfection of your prose the first time out. Writing demands rewriting, not only to correct, but to beautify as well. The need for revision does not mean that your first draft is a failure. Writers revise not only to correct errors, but also to find the smoothest, the most succinct, the most elegant way to say something. Writing without revision is like getting dressed without looking in a mirror.

Revision involves a conscious decision to take several passes at the essay. Word processors make this an easy thing. Do not make the mistake of thinking that the first draft will suffice, even though the first draft that spews from your printer may look quite respectable, unlike the pen and paper version. Take the opportunity that the computer provides to revise your paper, with an eye to making it the best it can be. Revision is a snap when even large chunks of text can be easily moved, changed, added, or deleted. Don't let the computer's convenience make you a lazy reviser.

Allow Yourself Freedom to Experiment

Say something. The essay is your chance to say what you want to say (within the limits of decorum!) the way you want to say it. All that is demanded in an essay assignment is that you think independently (perhaps with a little help from source material) and write in your own words (perhaps with the occasional quoted expert). Don't allow the fear of criticism to paralyze you at the outset. In your first draft especially, write to suit yourself.

Allow Yourself Space to Write and to Make Mistakes

Although the preferred method of composing these days is sitting directly in front of the screen, you don't have to do things that way. Some of the strategies incorporated into the computer are the same things many of us have done regularly on paper. You can, if you like, cut and paste on paper, if you have glue and scissors handy, and if the physical layout of the paper helps you think more clearly. Either way, give yourself the chance to see the complete sequence of ideas.

At the very least, make an effort to take frequent breaks from the computer screen. It is easier to look at a draft with fresh eyes; for that reason, don't hesitate to print out a small section, read it over, make some changes on paper, and then revise later on the screen. Such things will keep your mind more awake to subtle nuances of phrasing and make you more able to question minute points.

Double or triple space. Leave wide margins. Leave one side of the page blank. Use pencil if you like. Or use coloured markers so you can see immediately what is being added or deleted.

Develop Your Own Methods of Quick Notation

As you write, include references immediately after their occurrence in the text. Generally, use the author's last name and a page number in parentheses just after the quotation or the reference in your paper. If you use the documentation style suggested by the MLA or APA (see Chapter 14), this notation may be all you need. If not, your notes can be amended later.

If You Are Using a Computer

If you compose your essay on a computer, take advantage of any of its special features that will enable you to write more quickly and efficiently. Here are some guidelines:

1. Experiment. Use the speed of the computer to allow yourself a look at various possibilities in wording and in structure.
2. Write more critically than when you write on paper. Take advantage of the freedom from drudgery offered by the word processor to move paragraphs and to revise wording.
3. Learn to proofread from the screen. Better still, double-check your proofreading. Check the screen first and then make a hard copy and check it.
4. Don't expect the machine to do everything for you. Even though the mechanical aspects of the essay should be simpler on a computer, don't fool yourself that careful writing or rigorous revision can be eliminated.
5. Use the time you save by writing on a computer to think your topic through more carefully, to do more intensive research, and to ferret out every small error. Remember, of course, that if you have an Internet connection and access to the World Wide Web then you may do some part of your research

there. While you do need to develop some skills to discriminate among reputable and disreputable Web sites, your research can often benefit from a careful search of this quick, broad, and current source of information. Bear in mind, however, that the Internet is an unregulated body of material, so don't believe everything you read there.

6. Don't approach your paper as if it must be done in a linear fashion. Take advantage of the computer's ability to work on any section of your essay that you feel ready to tackle. If the introduction is giving you problems, skip over it for a while. Move on instead to some part of the paper over which you have more control. The writing process is recursive, rather than linear; if technology permits, you can make your composition mirror the creative process.

7. Simplify your thinking about the revision process. When you come to revise your paper, there are only four operations available to you: you can add, delete, move, or change materials. The computer makes all these aspects of revision much easier than they are with pen and paper.

8. Since it is unusual for a writer to produce his or her best work in one single draft, you would be wise to save several drafts of your paper, shifting back and forth between them as you decide how best to express your ideas.

9. Take advantage of features that are often part of word-processing software packages, such as the spell checker and the thesaurus. These functions are intended to help you overcome your own inadequacies as a writer and to speed up the entire process. Don't rely too heavily on them, though, since they can miss many small errors.

10. Let the speed that a computer gives afford you the time to revise more carefully and rethink more deeply.

Assembling Evidence

Remember the Purpose of Your Research

Your research is intended to help you find support for the claims you make in your paper. Because an essay presents an argument, you want to confine your search to those things that will help you defend yourself: your evidence will explain why you think what you think and why your reader should be inclined to do so as well. Because the research is not meant to give you information on everything about the subject in question, and because what you are writing is an essay, not a report, you must keep this purpose firmly in mind.

The purpose of your research is especially important when you use the Internet to help you gather information. Most instructors believe that the Internet is a good current supplement to library information, but not sufficient as a source of information in itself. When you use the Web as a source, it is vital to consider what you will be using the information for, because that will help determine which of the many sources you will cite. The Internet is a body of information, both expert and amateur, both objective and subjective, with authors of all ages and with all kinds of reasons for being there. It is up to you to determine which sources belong in your paper.

Determine What Counts as Evidence

In any kind of essay, there are really only four kinds of support that you could gather from your research materials: examples, statistics, authorities, and reasons. Seldom would you use all four kinds of evidence in any one short paper. When you assemble your research material, working outline in hand, you want to be able to isolate relevant parts of others' work to strengthen your own. Keep your priorities straight. What is important here is that you select research material relevant to your particular focus on the subject. Examples and reasons are more likely than the others to be drawn from your experience and from your own thinking, though this is not always the case; they are the most common and closest to home, and may be either real or hypothetical. Often examples are the best way to make an abstract point concrete. Reasons, by contrast, represent your thoughts and questions about key terms and your critical evaluations of the arguments of others. Statistics and the citing of authorities are both useful methods of garnering support for your position. In both of these cases, however, you must be careful how you use the material in question and don't make the mistake of assuming that it speaks for itself; otherwise, your meaning will be obscured, and you will lose control over the paper itself. When you cite someone else's words, you must show the reader what you intend him or her to see in the passage; the meaning is not self-evident. Similarly, the meaning of a statistic must be related to your overall position in the paper; it is your responsibility to draw conclusions about what these findings mean for your claims.

The Internet makes the question of what sources to include an even more complex one since everyone, from scholars to children, is part of that vast conversation. With care, you can find the best sources for your purposes, and use them properly. What makes it challenging is that everything is there, in a fluid, unregulated state. Before, reference librarians and teachers imposed some order on the information you were likely to turn up. Now, you have access to more materials, and it falls to you to figure out how to use them wisely. It is best to think of the Internet not as a source of information, but as a means by which you can examine an issue from a variety of different points of view in order to arrive at your own take on the question in front of you.

Make Outlines of Relevant Arguments in the Research

Strengthening your own case is often easier if you have made brief outlines or paraphrases of the arguments you encountered as you went along. It is often a wise idea to summarize your findings from a particular chapter or journal article in your own words, so that you can make the transition from notes to essay more smoothly. A summary of a journal article might consist of one page that outlined its thesis, its main points, an assessment of its support, and some general comments of your own in response to it. This method will record your engagement with your research materials better than any mere transcription of quoted materials might do.

Take the Opposition into Account

The best approach to take with materials that argue against your position is to approach them head on, assuming, of course, that you have decided your position is reasonable and defensible. Once you make up your mind to argue on a particular side of a question, your best line of defence is to read opposing views carefully and use materials from them to show flaws in their thinking and your own counterarguments. If you take this advice, your argument will be more complete and more encompassing in its perspective.

Bear in mind that the Internet, if your instructor sees it as a possible avenue of research, will provide something close to field research. In other words, your online searches will probably uncover a multitude of differing opinions and perspectives. In general, you should search for sources that bear the marks of authority, usually because of the reputation of their authors. You should also beware of inordinate bias and of problems with accuracy in materials found online.

Avoid "Tunnel Vision"

The success of your essay depends not only on your ability to make your case, but also on the maturity of your critical approach—your fairness, objectivity, and sensitivity to flaws in methodology (yours and others'). Don't let emotions prevent you from assessing the evidence. You may, for example, feel strongly that Canada should provide aid to developing countries, yet when writing an essay on the subject of development aid you will have to assess the claims that such aid leads to economic dependency. Objectivity is essential. When in doubt about sources, particularly those on the Internet, ask a teacher or a reference librarian what you should be reading and how you can make sure that you have arrived at a balanced approach to your subject.

Interpret Your Findings

You cannot expect the citation of a statistic or the inclusion of a quotation to make your point. You must *interpret* the meaning of such evidence. A survey that indicates that 75 percent of the student population approves of aid to developing countries does not speak for itself. In order to interpret such findings, you need to know how many people were actually surveyed, whether or not the survey involved a fair random sampling, and whether the questions that made up the survey were clear and unbiased in their wording. Only when you have taken these factors into account can you use the figure to claim, for example, that the student population is, to a large extent, willing to support developing countries.

Avoid "Blind Spots"

An essay demands that you take a position with regard to the evidence you uncover. That position must, however, be based on an objective and unbiased reading of the facts. To ensure that you do not willfully (or otherwise) misread your evidence, try to formulate both the case for and the case against your position. Include in your essay not only a defence of your thesis, but also arguments that have led you to reject contrary interpretations. For example, if you are arguing that aid to developing countries is a humanitarian obligation, you must consider the charge that the resulting private foreign investment is exploitative. You may find that you must concede some points. Such qualification makes your argument all the more objective in its evaluation of the data.

Realize that the shape of your essay is in your hands. Do not make the mistake of thinking that you can "cover" all the material that you find. Your job is to make editorial decisions as you go along, searching out and reading materials. Aim at currency, but don't forget the value of credibility and accuracy. The ease of research these days sometimes lulls writers into accepting as true all the "facts" that they can so easily discover. Be discerning in your use of sources.

Aim at a Better, Not an Ultimate, Theory

When you use evidence to defend your thesis, be realistic in your goals. Your research and your thought together have led you to understand the data in a certain way. Your task is to show that your reading of the material exhibits common sense and attention to recent data. Your theory about the meaning of the evidence should help to explain something. You may find, for instance, that economic dependency only partly explains the continuing problems in developing countries and that internal, national factors play a part as well. Your theory won't be perfect—just the most reliable interpretation of the facts you have found.

The Conventional Shape of the Essay

In order to control your material, you must strive to achieve unity within your essay. An essay's unity is the wholeness of the vision, the focus that holds the disparate parts together. Without such wholeness, your essay will seem incomplete or rambling.

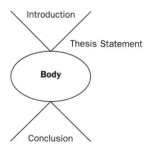

To do justice to your assembled arguments and support, the shape of your essay should meet certain of its readers' expectations. To make a good first impression on the reader, your essay should include these basic elements:

1. an *introduction*, moving from general topic to specific thesis, perhaps including a preview of its content
2. a *body*, developing in turn each of the main points used to support your thesis statement
3. a *conclusion*, reinforcing and/or summarizing what has been the focus of the essay and suggesting further implications

Observing these conventional forms will ensure that your essay is clear, pointed, and emphatic from beginning to end.

A good essay possesses a sharp, comprehensive introduction and conclusion, with an expansive body that develops and supports the thesis.

Maintaining Unity in the Essay

An essay is a unit: a discussion centred on one basic point. Remember that your essay should focus on your thesis statement. An essay meant to grapple with the causes of the War of 1812 should not discuss its aftermath, just as an essay treating the issue of free will in *Paradise Lost* should find no place for a discussion of epic conventions.

To keep your essay unified:

1. Keep your purpose and basic pattern of argument firmly in mind.
2. Avoid digressions, however interesting, if they cannot be connected to the thesis statement.
3. Avoid padding for the sake of word length. Instead, develop your ideas by referring to Chapter 5, on patterns of argument, and relating them to your proposed thesis statement.
4. Redesign your thesis statement (within the limits of the assignment, of course) if you find your initial focus unappealing or too limited in scope.

Above all, remember the principle of unity: **Everything in an essay should relate directly to the main focus of the paper.**

CHAPTER 6 EXERCISES

1. Develop a line of argument in an outline for each of the following topics:
   a. Mortgages should be tax-deductible in Canada.
   b. Courses that teach life skills should be mandatory.
   c. Schools should operate year-round.
   d. Young people are discriminated against because of their age.
   e. Marijuana should be legalized.
   f. Separate schools should not be publicly funded.
2. Read over an essay for a classmate, and note every time the writer digressed from the main focus of the essay and every time you find "padding."

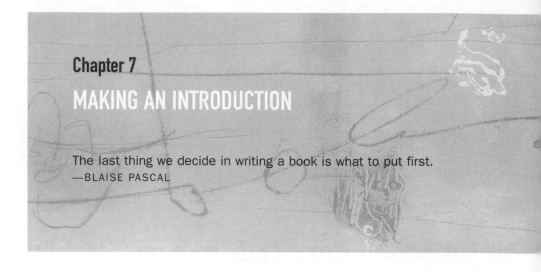

Chapter 7

MAKING AN INTRODUCTION

The last thing we decide in writing a book is what to put first.
—BLAISE PASCAL

Think of your essay, for a moment, as if it were a person. Since an essay will establish some kind of relationship with its readers, the analogy is not altogether far-fetched. Here is some advice on how to proceed after you say "hello."

Strike Up a Conversation

Obviously, writing a formal essay is more complicated than starting a conversation. But the analogy should provide you with a place to start. How should you begin a conversation? One way is to startle your listener by presenting an exciting piece of information, as a preview of coming attractions. Or, as a recommendation of the value of the work you have done, you can report the words of a well-known, respected authority in relation to your topic. Another method is to pick a fight, by stating the claims, or defining the terms, of the accepted position and then challenging them. Remember that your first task is to convince your audience to pay heed to what you are saying. What all of these tactics have in common is their ability to provoke a response.

Human judgment being the superficial, lazy thing it sometimes is (and professors are by no means exempt), an essay must overcome certain prejudices about its nature. In order to present itself proudly to an instructor, an essay must show immediate signs that it will not be boring, vague, pretentious, or long-winded.

Write with Control

Perhaps the most common pitfall among essay writers in establishing the basis of their arguments is long-windedness. Remember that an introduction should be no longer than about one-fifth of the entire essay's length (the best introductions are short and comprehensive—don't go on). If you find that your introduction demands more space than that, you have not narrowed your topic down to a manageable size, or you should be writing a book instead! Never promise in the introduction more than you can deliver in the paper. The first few lines are the best place to limit the scope of your discussion and state the qualifications of your theories. Maintain control of your material, and have some consideration (if not some pity) for your poor beleaguered reader.

Avoid writing introductions that are too broad in scope. You can't do everything in 1500 words, nor should you try. Here are some examples of the kind of thing to avoid:

7

> ✗ The advent of the electronic book, as heralded by Stephen King's decision to publish his most recent work online rather than via a traditional publisher in book form, indicates that the book, as we know it, is dying. Printed books are becoming a thing of the past, and more and more people are turning to the Internet as the most convenient source of information available.

Example

In this opening paragraph, the author sets out to establish that all books have become redundant now that the Internet is here. This approach does not, however, take into account that only 40 percent of homes currently have access to the Internet, nor does it consider how much the Internet relies on the form of the book for its own formatting of information. No one essay could take on this entire subject. It would be better to concede that the electronic book is making inroads in our reading habits, rather than to overstate the case.

> ✗ Censorship of any kind is reprehensible. American schools that ban Mark Twain's *Huckleberry Finn* because of its allegedly "racist" language, and Canadian schools that ban Margaret Laurence's *The Diviners* are both acting against our right to read whatever we want.

Example

This introduction oversimplifies the case that might be made. While it is true that the censorship of some books in schools seems ludicrous, it is difficult out of hand to argue that all censorship is inappropriate. Much will depend on age groups that are reading or accessing materials. Much, too, will depend on the accuracy and the purpose of the materials being circulated. Would hate literature, for example, be acceptable in a world without censorship?

Write with Conviction

To avoid accusations of boredom, make sure that the introduction shows *how* what you have written matters—to you and to anyone concerned with the subject. Convincing readers that a topic is important is not simply a matter of telling them so; you have to show them, by the tone of your writing, that you are deeply engaged with the topic. Write with conviction, with the feeling that what you are saying will make a difference. Don't negate its value by suggesting that the essay's position is only your opinion. Approach the essay as if it were one side of a lively conversation. Because there is some distance between writer and reader this interchange is not as immediate as that of conversation, but remember that there is a reader "at the other end of the line." Imagine your reader's responses as you introduce your material, just as you imagine your friend's face as she answers the telephone.

Be Conversant with Your Subject

Your introduction is meant to foster an existing knowledge and interest on the part of the reader. Don't tell the reader what he or she already knows. In the case of a literary essay, for example, there is no need to provide a plot summary. Any reader of such an essay should have that material well in hand. In other disciplines, this advice means avoiding the mere recital of material discussed in class, or the careful delineation of a definition that is neither contentious nor germane to what will follow. Write to communicate.

To avoid sounding pretentious, you must use your own voice and your sense of what is appropriate to the occasion. In the introduction, you must lead the reader into your way of thinking. The introduction must make both you and your reader comfortable. To get comfortable with a topic that, three weeks ago, may have been completely unfamiliar to you is part of the task of essay writing. Only when you can *talk* knowledgeably about the subject of your paper are you ready to write about it.

Communicate with Your Reader

If carefully designed, your introduction should tell the reader some essential things about you and your work: that you sincerely wish to communicate; that you are conversant with your subject and have convictions about it; that you are confident, in control, and considerate of your reader. All these words beginning with "con" or "com" suggest the necessity of forming a relationship *with* someone or something. An introduction with these attributes demands attention and commands respect.

Ice-Breaking: Tactics for Opening the Essay

If you are at a loss for words when writing your introduction, try one of the strategies in the following list. Suppose, for example, that your essay topic is "health hazards in the environment caused by humans."

1. Take the straight and narrow path.
State your thesis bluntly and without preamble. Follow it with a brief statement of the steps in your argument.

Example   It is our fundamental human right to live in a healthy environment. For this to happen, we must protect the environment from health hazards caused by humans.

2. Try shock treatment.
Give your reader a striking, perhaps shocking, example, statistic, or statement to get him or her interested in reading further.

One-year-old Diane Fowler woke up in the middle of the night in the midst of a convulsion. Her temperature was dangerously high. She was rushed to the Hospital for Sick Children in Toronto, where she was diagnosed as suffering from lead poisoning. Soon after, five more members of Diane's family were diagnosed as having lead poisoning. Within two years, a large group of citizens, all living near a Toronto-based lead plant, were found to have elevated levels of lead in their blood.

Example

3. Engage your reader.

Remind the reader that the subject under discussion matters to him or her by showing its general importance, before you settle down to your specific line of argument.

While some people think that environmental health hazards affect only those who work in risky occupations or who live in certain neighbourhoods, it is clear that the problem is more widespread than that. Everyone's life is endangered. Lead, for example, is in the water we drink, the air we breathe, and the food we eat. For Canadians, the likelihood of exposure to serious environmental hazard is now 100 percent, and even low-level exposure to substances like lead can cause serious health problems.

Example

A good introduction captures the reader's attention, provides necessary background, and gives some indication of where the rest of the essay is headed.
Here is an example of how this might look:

When Canadian novelist Yann Martel won the Man Booker Prize in October 2002, he thanked his readers for "having met his imagination halfway" ("Joyful"). Indeed, reading a magic-realist fable like *Life of Pi* involves something akin to a leap of faith for readers, in several ways: first, the story tests the credulity of readers by asking them to embrace a surreal parable; second, the story helps readers have faith in the god of their choice; and third, the story reminds readers that reality is a story we choose, and it is our responsibility, along with the writer, to pick the better story between the two options provided for us.

Example

This introductory paragraph pins down the subject matter of the essay in its first line, and in the second demonstrates how the essay will explore that magic realism in a three-part structure that illustrates the relationship between writer and reader.

CHAPTER 7 EXERCISES

1. Write introductory paragraphs, complete with thesis statements, on the following topics:
   a. a goal you would like to accomplish
   b. a movie that made a lasting impression on you

    c. a constant preoccupation

    d. the influence of other people's advice on your life

    e. your relation to your relatives

2. Analyze the opening paragraph or so of one of your classmates' essays. What introductory techniques are used there? Try making suggestions to rewrite the opening to make it stronger.

3. Locate an introductory paragraph in this textbook. Analyze how an introductory passage has used particular techniques to introduce its subject.

4. Read the following student paragraphs, all of which served as introductions to essays. Analyze the techniques by which they arouse the reader's interest.

    a. Some say that television cannot teach me anything about real life, and that is the reason why I am currently engaged in a staring competition with my set. So far the tube has won best three out of five, but as Dr. Schuller says, "If it's going to be, it's up to me." That TV has to blink sometime. So, while I wait for sweet victory against the naysayers of educational TV, I will set my mind to learning and become a couch potato.

    b. A person whose soul has already been separated from his or her body is still able to experience feelings such as regret, fear, and isolation. This is the belief of over 33% of the world's population—the Muslims. Therefore, Muslims are very gentle with their dead, and the washing and shrouding of the body are done very methodically, leaving no room for error. Because Islam lays significant importance on the existence of the afterlife, its followers are often flabbergasted by the degree of vanity in the burial practices of the West. Since the Islamic code emphasizes simplicity, burial practices are straightforward, with no unnecessary expenses.

    c. Canadians are holding their heads high in admiration of the Liberal leadership's decision not to follow the Americans into a non–UN sanctioned war against Iraq. Although Canadians remained hopeful, the notion that Jean Chrétien would actually say no to our powerful friend to the south seemed doubtful. For once, a Canadian leader listened to the voice of the people and didn't cower in front of Americans. Euphoric, Canadians seem to have chosen to applaud this decision without even considering its true motivations. Has the Canadian government taken the high road of diplomacy, or are there some underlying factors that may have influenced this choice? The Canadian military proudly participated in the Kosovo campaign, shoulder to shoulder with the Americans. Since the Kosovo campaign was executed without a UN resolution as well, what is different about the war in Iraq?

    d. Leslie Marmon Silko has found a way to transfer oral Native American stories onto the page. She does this by keeping in her stories many of the conventions of Native American storytelling, especially the unconventional and non-Western form of her work. In her works "Yellow Woman," "Cottonwood *Part One: Story of Sun House*," and "Cottonwood *Part Two: Buffalo Story*," Silko maintains the idea that stories are tools for the community. Though she is often not considered among mainstream writers of literature, her use of the oral tradition in her work has led to her popularity as an author who is widely respected by critics and by her own community.

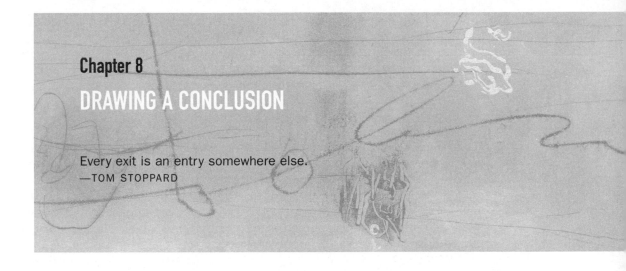

Chapter 8
DRAWING A CONCLUSION

Every exit is an entry somewhere else.
—TOM STOPPARD

Your concluding paragraph is not only your last word on the subject but also an opportunity for you to reinforce your argument. Listed below are four techniques by which you may reinforce your argument in order to end your paper strongly and convincingly. The essay that builds toward a powerful conclusion will not fade out but will reverberate in the reader's mind.

Retrace Your Line of Thought

Retracing does not mean repeating. Since both you and the reader know where you have been, all you need to provide in your conclusion is a reminder of the steps of the journey. You need only mention key words that have gathered meaning as the argument has proceeded in order for the astute reader (the one for whom you have been writing all along) to "catch your drift." Echo for effect, rather than for reiteration.

To remind the reader of the inherent structure of your essay, make certain to restate the thesis statement in a conclusive manner, and in different words from those that you used in the opening. Doing so will enable you to check to see if the essay has really lived up to your expectations of it. Keep in mind that the essay is meant to be a lively, though formal, conversation. A subtle reminder of the point you have made will aid the readers; a word-for-word repetition will annoy them.

Refocus Your Argument

Just as a film director may end a scene by changing the camera focus to wide angle or softening it, so too can the essay take a broader and less stringent view of its subject in its closing.

Widen the focus as you conclude by showing the importance of your topic beyond the immediate concerns of your paper. Beware, however, of writing an overblown conclusion such as "Milton is the world's greatest poet." Instead, include a suggestion for change or perhaps a solution to the problem you have so carefully outlined in the core of the essay.

Encourage Response

While the body of your essay requires you to provide answers and to be clear and definite in your thinking and wording, there is *some* room in the conclusion for you to mention tentative ideas, to pose questions, or to offer challenges to the reader. You shouldn't open the floodgates too widely, but it is a good tactic to provoke a response in your reader, provided it is relevant to the topic in question. Beware, though, of starting something you cannot finish, or of introducing a topic that sounds suspiciously like what your essay should have been about.

Make Your Words Resound

By the time you reach your conclusion, you should feel that no important argument for your thesis statement has been neglected. This attitude of confidence will allow you to end your paper with a bang rather than a whimper (to invoke, or rather invert, the words of T.S. Eliot). Make sure that the tone conveys a sense of finality, a sense that you have done all that can be expected within the precise bounds of your thesis statement. The conclusion should not, of course, make grand claims that your essay cannot substantiate.

Note that the concluding paragraph of an essay reverses the structure of the opening paragraph, where the writer typically moves from the general to the specific. In the conclusion, the paragraph most often moves from the specific points the essay has been making to some generality, often taking a broader view of the subject and opening other questions up for the reader to ponder.

Drawing to a Close: Tactics for Ending the Essay

When you come to the end of your essay, consider one of the following ways of formulating a conclusion. Suppose, for instance, that your paper is about the dangers of pollution:

1. Decide that enough is enough.

If you find you have nothing pressing to add, say nothing. Make sure, however, that your argument ends on a strong note. Don't stop writing just because you are tired, though.

Example   There is nothing that we do, nothing that we eat or breathe, that does not contribute to the state of our planet, and therefore to environmentalism.

2. Take the wider view.

Examine some of the broader implications of your thesis and the questions it may have raised.

> As you read through this paper, you probably thought of some things you can do to make your contribution to the preservation of the environment. Although some of these solutions may involve giving up a few of your comforts, you have probably realized that we can no longer blame the other fellow and do nothing ourselves. The poverty, pollution, and poisoning were caused by all of us and can be eliminated only with everyone's cooperation.

Example

8

3. Reinforce your claim.

Remind the reader gently of your line of thought and reiterate your thesis in a slightly different form.

> We are all affected by pollution, but just as we are part of the problem, so we can be part of the solution. Remember these guidelines: reduce, reuse, recycle, and rebel. Reduce the use of electricity and fuel. Reuse things, rather than automatically disposing of them. Recycle refillable containers made of glass, paper, and metal. And rebel by encouraging the government to back tougher legislation to protect our environment.

Example

CHAPTER 8 EXERCISES

1. Read and discuss the following conclusions:

   a. I am gravely concerned for the future of quality childcare in our community. The Liberal government has refused to listen, has refused to help. The result is gross imbalance, injustice, insensitivity, indeed cruelty so that some may have more than they can ever use and others go without even enough to eat. The fate of quality childcare is in the hands of the people. To help remedy this imbalance, we must exercise the power to change. Contacting government representatives is one way to exercise this power. A national policy on regulated childcare that provides access and affordability to all, where all are welcome, is a solution. All children have the right to be treated with the respect they deserve: we are their loudest voice. Our numbers need to be seen, and our voices need to be heard. This is my voice: let it be heard, let it be listened to, let it be read, but most importantly, let it be understood with compassion, respect, and dignity.

   b. In *Frankenstein* the conceptualization of nature with regard to landscape, society, human experience, and behaviour seems, on first analysis, Romantic. That is, for the most part, the novel evokes a pantheistic natural world that elevates emotion and individualism as sources of virtue. However, I would like to posit that the novel contains arguments for restraint and qualification of this concept along lines compatible with Enlightenment thinking. In Mary Shelley's concept of nature, some accommodation of both rationality and natural law is seen as essential to avoid catastrophe. Enlightenment notions of nature remain important reference points, creating a fundamental tension in Shelley's work.

c. Given the circumstances surrounding Canada's refusal to participate in a unilateral campaign against Iraq, the government would like the public to believe that the sole reason for its decision was the lack of UN support. Perhaps the government expects the public to forget Canada's involvement in Kosovo, prior to UN approval. The reality is that although the public embraced the choice not to go to war, they were deceived by the government's motivations. Canada has demonstrated that it would go to war without UN support, so what was different this time? In this case, the leader of the government was obsessed with his personal legacy, the Liberals were starving for public approval, and the military machine was suffering from Liberal cuts. In this case, it had nothing to do with foreign policy and everything to do with self-preservation on the part of the government. In this case, it was not about setting an example for the international community, but about saving face.

2. Read the following outlines, and then write a concluding paragraph suitable for each.

a. Thesis statement: Physical exercise has many health benefits.
It helps with weight control.
It increases the strength of your bones and muscles.
It raises your endorphin levels and thus improves your mood.

b. Thesis statement: Credit cards are dangerous to the financial well-being of many consumers.
Consumers are encouraged to buy more than they can afford.
Consumers run up enormous debts at huge interest rates.
Credit card companies increase credit levels to facilitate even greater levels of debt.

c. Thesis statement: Stricter rules are needed to keep impaired drivers off the road.
Many accidents are caused by elderly drivers.
People with bad driving records are currently treated too leniently in the courts and thus tend to be repeat offenders.
The rate of mortality due to traffic accidents has increased every year in Canada for the past ten years.

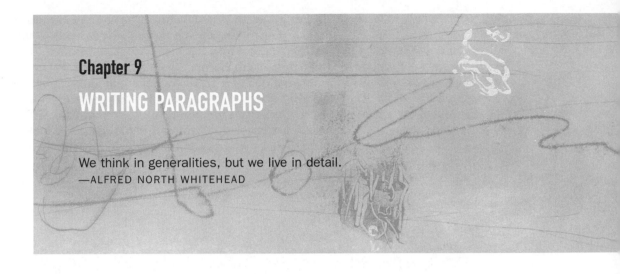

Chapter 9

WRITING PARAGRAPHS

We think in generalities, but we live in detail.
—ALFRED NORTH WHITEHEAD

Though an essay may not be, strictly speaking, a work of art, it does offer infinite opportunities for the artistic development of your material. What follows are some suggestions on how to develop your paragraphs and how to check to see that paragraphing in the final paper is unified and coherent.

A paragraph must be about one thing. This principle of unity should be so clear that you could compose a heading for each paragraph if the assignment demanded it (and some may).

Logical connections within each paragraph must also be clear. Leaps in logic or unstated assumptions are flaws in your argument that will affect the coherence of the final paper and lose your reader's good will.

Each paragraph is a small step in your total argument, meant to lead the reader onward through your thought process. Hence, each small part must contribute to the whole pattern. Remember that each small section of your argument, each paragraph, is in fact a miniature model of the essay structure itself.

Each paragraph, like the larger essay, should contain the following elements:

1. a topic sentence that reveals the controlling idea, or thesis
2. support related to the topic sentence
3. unity of focus
4. a smooth transition to the next paragraph

The Topic Sentence

A typical paragraph in an essay begins with a topic sentence, a general "umbrella" statement that explains what the rest of the paragraph is about. Anything that does not relate to this controlling idea should be left out. Sometimes, writers feel that it is unprofessional to make the topic sentence too obvious, but, despite their fears, a clear topic sentence is an asset. Because the essay is, by its nature, rather repetitive in structure, you may be simply repeating, in different words, a point that you previewed in your thesis statement. For instance, your thesis statement may be that triage is an essential, if difficult, part of a good health-care system because it enables medical teams to decide which patients must be attended to first. In your first paragraph, you have defined the term "triage." In the second paragraph, you might begin by stating that one of the criteria for setting priorities for care is the patient's chance of survival. Your next paragraph might begin with a topic sentence that mentions the next criterion: the patient's ability to wait. Each of these criteria would be developed in turn.

A topic sentence need not necessarily begin your paragraphs, but for less experienced writers, and in essay writing generally, it usually does.

The Support

Your support may take several forms:

1. examples
2. statistics
3. connected reasons/definitions
4. authorities

Approach the undeveloped arguments in your outline with these four categories in mind. The sources of support will depend on the nature of the assignment: a formal research essay may require all four; a less formal paper will rely chiefly on reasons and examples for its strength.

Developing Support for Your Paragraphs

Remember, as you weave your outline into paragraphs, that each discrete unit must ultimately contribute something to the illustration of the essay's thesis statement. The paragraphs argue in its defence or show its validity.

Some of the following methods are formal adaptations of techniques of argument you may have used before. The list is by no means complete; try to think of other equally effective battle plans.

Present the Facts of the Case

These facts may include statistics to prove your point. Don't take for granted that your readers know what you know about the subject.

Example   Frozen dinners, according to their manufacturers, are steadily increasing in popularity, perhaps because of the widespread use of microwave ovens and because of the pace of modern society. Indeed, according to one producer of these goods, more than 80% of households buy these products on a regular basis. One wonders, however, how anyone can bear to eat them.

Show and Tell

To keep the line of thought going, remember that it is always best to argue by example, rather than by precept. Don't just tell your readers about something. Show them, wherever possible, how your idea works by giving an example.

Lumped in one plastic partition of the frozen dinner is a white, viscous mound with a substance faintly resembling butter sliding greasily down its pasty sides. Its likeness on the box wrapper indicates the presence of potatoes in that location, but the taste is reminiscent of the last stamp you licked. The texture is perennially similar across all brands of frozen dinners—that of wet plaster. Incredibly, manufacturers of frozen dinners even get their potatoes to taste like wet plaster, an unfortunate consistency, if you will excuse the pun.

Example

9

Establish Connections

Find something in the point you are making that relates to your own experience or to that of your readers. If the essay is formal rather than informal in tone, adapt this advice to show your readers why the subject is important to them.

Hope springs eternal as the harried consumer tries different brands of frozen dinners. The diabolically clever chemists must do freelance work for all the major manufacturers, because Brand A's "Chicken Marengo" tastes disconcertingly like Brand X's "He-Man Beef Platter." You may wonder how they do it. A better question may be "Why do we let them?" The answer is probably that fast food, despite its drawbacks, is ubiquitous and unavoidable in a society in which no one has time to cook.

Example

Define Your Terms and Use Details

If the terminology is clear, don't bother telling your readers what they already know. If, on the other hand, you think that a closer look at a word or phrase that is part of your topic will help your case, draw their attention to it.

Although frozen dinners claim to be made of frozen food, the claim is debatable. Take, for example, what passes for dessert in one of these trays. Gustatory delight is expected because of a tantalizing picture on the box and an imaginative description—spiced apple supreme, for instance. Alas, the unsuspecting fruit has met a fate similar to that of the potatoes. Magnificent, tart, crunchy apples have been reduced to apple-facsimile chunks, improved by the thoughtful addition of a charming artificial flavour mixed in with a gelatinous goo. When the fruit is eaten, the fleshy texture is so odd that, except for the absence of pain, the consumer cannot be sure he has not bitten his tongue and is happily chewing on it.

Example

Call in an Expert or Cite a Source

Convince your reader by turning to an expert for support. Don't expect readers to take your word for something if the words of a specialist in the area are available to buttress your own. If the person to whom you refer is a respected authority, your argument will be enriched by his or her utterance.

Example   The sad truth is that diners everywhere exist on frozen food because no one has time anymore for home cooking. While we all still have to eat, none of us is eager to prepare dinner—for ourselves or for others. Because time is precious, and frozen food is ubiquitous, we do not rebel against the horrors of monosodium glutamate, salt, and artificial colouring. As Shirley Conran says, "Life is too short to stuff a mushroom."

Note that the source of this quotation would have to be acknowledged, using some consistent form of documentation—a subject covered in detail in Chapter 14.

Unity

A paragraph, like the essay itself, should have demonstrated the development of your thought by the time your reader finishes it. Each paragraph should lead the reader along in a logical and coherent manner. If your outline has been well planned, the progress of your thinking should be orderly and your conclusion clear. Your paragraphs should each form a discrete unit, and each paragraph should be clearly connected to what precedes and to what follows.

Example   It is interesting that beets are rarely offered in these frozen dinner simulations. Possibly that is because beets stubbornly insist on having a beet-like tang no matter how they are diced, sauced, or otherwise adulterated. Such a renegade authentic flavour might take the targeted "average consumer" by surprise. He or she might then realize that the other items on the slab are pale imitations of the real thing. Since that realization could have dire consequences for the manufacturer's cash flow, only cooperative vegetables grace the microwaveable plastic tray.

In this example, the author discusses the quality of vegetables normally used in frozen dinners by pointing out one variety that never appears. The paragraph then goes on to offer a theory for the beet's conspicuous absence, one that connects this paragraph to the overall notion of the lack of flavour found in frozen dinners.

Pinning the Pieces Together—Transitions

Despite the basic structural independence of the paragraph, the reader must be able to appreciate how it fits into the whole essay. To make the connections clear to the reader, an essayist must use appropriate transitions and linking devices.

Transitions are signals of a turn in thought. They often pose a problem for the novice essay writer simply because our methods of changing or developing the subject in conversation are much less formal and much more spontaneous than in written, rhetorical form.

Ask yourself what your favourite techniques of transition in speech are. Then try to categorize the situations that prompt you to use them. You may find that your list of transitions includes such statements as "And you know what else?" to add to or elaborate on a point; "You see," to explain in greater detail; "Sure, but," to disagree with another's argument, at the same time conceding to some degree; "What if . . . ?" to put forward a hypothesis; "Anyhow," to dismiss the view of your interlocutor; or "As I said before," to reinforce an earlier point.

Many of these transitions cannot be easily transferred to the printed page. They are too casual to suit the public occasion of the essay. In their stead, the writer must become familiar with and use more formal transitions to enhance the power of his or her rhetoric.

Transitions have many uses. Here are some examples of various transitions:

TO ADD
and
also
in addition
furthermore
as well

TO CHANGE DIRECTION
but
however
conversely
although
whereas

TO ILLUSTRATE
for example
for instance
in other words
that is

TO SUMMARIZE
to conclude
in short
finally

TO QUALIFY
often
generally
specifically
usually

TO CONCEDE A POINT
although
though
whereas

TO ENUMERATE
first, second
first, next, last

TO ESTABLISH CAUSE
because
for

TO STATE A REASON
because
since
for

TO DRAW A CONCLUSION
thus
finally
hence
therefore
as a result
consequently

TO POINT AT A PREVIOUS REFERENCE
this
that
who/whom
which
few
many

Good transitions are like carefully sewn seams. Although not readily notice-able, they are the means by which the garment is held together. Shoddy work-manship in your transitions may cause your essay to fall apart—an embarrassing state for something that is appearing in print and is being presented to someone you wish to impress.

Checking the Overall Pattern of Your Paragraphs

There are two basic tests for the aesthetic appeal of the paragraph. One of these is to read the first sentence of each paragraph to check whether the line of thought is clearly maintained throughout the entire work. That is, do the sen-tences themselves act as subheadings to guide the reader through your design? (*Note*: This test assumes that most paragraphs begin with a topic sentence. Sometimes, however, the topic sentence may appear at the end.) Another test of effective paragraphing involves looking at the length of the paragraphs them-selves on the printed page. Is each of them a manageable length? Note that the length of paragraphs is typically governed by some basic guidelines. You need to make sure that all the essential elements are included; that is, there must be a topic sentence, some support for it, and some elaboration of that support. That generally means that a paragraph in a self-respecting scholarly essay is usually at least three lines long, though rarely you may see a one-sentence paragraph used for its startling effect, most often in less scholarly material.

The layout counts too. As a rule, it is wise to include at least one paragraph break per printed page, and no more than about three. To have no breaks is to invite boredom on the part of the reader; to have more than three breaks is to suggest your thoughts lack integration. Paragraph length, in other words, is often fairly arbitrary: witness how newspapers often use one-sentence paragraphs simply because they look better in column form. Break your paragraphs with an eye to avoiding a "choppy" page or one that presents a daunting block of type.

CHAPTER 9 EXERCISES

1. Develop a paragraph using your own definition of a term. Compare it with the defi-nition you find in the dictionary. Try one of these words:

   innocence
   turbulence
   zeal
   rapture

2. Develop a paragraph using a statistic or a quoted authority as support. Look through newspapers or weekly magazines for topics, or try these:

marriage
children
crime
obesity
weather
a medical breakthrough

3. Write a paragraph establishing a connection or making a comparison. Develop your own comparison, or work with one of these:

DVD vs. the big screen
love vs. infatuation
herbal medication vs. drugs
habit vs. addiction

4. Develop two paragraphs, one using an example from your own experience and one paraphrasing a case study or a news report. Find your case study in a magazine or a textbook, and make up another on the same subject. Try one of these subjects:

someone who has an illness
someone who being treated unjustly
someone who triumphs against the odds

5. Write two paragraphs, one using a series of small examples to make a point and one using an extended example to support the same point. Pick any one of these:

how to win someone over
how to memorize facts
how to be assertive
how to make a speech successfully
how to develop muscles
how to overcome a setback

6. Use the following quotations in paragraphs that you devise:

a. "In the confrontation between the stream and the rock, the stream always wins—not through strength, but through persistence."—*Anonymous*
b. "It's not how smart you are, but how you are smart."—*Howard Gardner*
c. "If you aren't the lead dog, the view never changes."—*Unknown*

Chapter 10

PARAPHRASING SOURCES AND INTEGRATING QUOTATIONS

It is the little writer rather than the great writer who seems never to quote, and the reason is that he is never really doing anything else.
—HAVELOCK ELLIS

Not all essays will demand that you use sources other than your own imagination and general knowledge of the world. Many essays, however, will include, as part of the requirements, a knowledge of background sources, all of which must be acknowledged to avoid charges of plagiarism. Plagiarism is a serious charge. If a student deliberately plagiarizes someone else's work and passes it off as his or her own, there are often strict consequences, which may include expulsion from the class, the program of study, or even the institution in question. You must acknowledge where you found facts, ideas, and exact wording to avoid the charge that you are plagiarizing. Whether intentional or not, plagiarism seriously affects the credibility of your work and undermines your abilities as a researcher. If the reader might at any point ask, "How do you know that?", the essay is likely remiss in acknowledging sources. It is the writer's duty to give credit where credit is due and to assist readers to find and check the sources used. Not to do so is to violate the reader's trust and also to defeat the purpose of the research essay in the first place.

Source material, while often a significant part of the essay, does not speak for itself. Remember that the function of paraphrased and quoted matter is to provide support for your arguments. You are responsible for the use you make of the source material. Not only must you be accurate in your representation of it, but you also must be prepared to use it thoughtfully to support your viewpoint.

When you find an idea or a quotation in another source, you are obliged to inform your reader of its origins, even if it is an idea that you already had yourself. Except for the classroom, which is usually considered common domain, the sources of your ideas must be listed in your papers. If you are in doubt about whether or not to include a source for some particular information, put yourself in the reader's place. Would he or she ask, "How do you know this is true?" If so, you need to mention the source.

Quotations and paraphrase are used as support in rather different ways. Quotations are most often used in an essay dealing with literature or a book review, where the main trustworthy source of information is the text of a work itself.

Paraphrase, on the other hand, is used when the exact words are not as important, but the facts they present are; hence, paraphrase is the most common method of using source material in the social sciences. If you find that you must refer to a theory or to an explanation of the meaning of some data, the best plan is to paraphrase. Remember, as you take notes, to paraphrase rather than to quote, taking special care with statistics and their implications.

When you paraphrase some part of a book or article for inclusion as support in your essay, try to get at its meaning. Try to rephrase the thought as if you were teaching the material to someone. Make notes with this principle in mind, taking care to "boil down" the facts and reduce them to their simplest terms, without distorting them. Focus on the thesis statement, topic sentences, and key words, and don't let yourself get bogged down in details. Think the words through rather than just copying them.

Both quotations and paraphrase are used to support your arguments. When you select material from sources, consider the use you intend to make of it. None of the sources will speak for itself; you must demonstrate how a source relates to the case you are building. For this reason, you should usually introduce source material and comment on its function in your paper, rather than assuming the reader will make the necessary connections.

Borrow Only What You Need

Borrow words, phrases, and sentences only if they add something essential that you do not already possess. Among these essentials are **credibility, power,** and **eloquence.**

The quotations that follow are taken from Michael Hornyansky's brilliant essay "Is Your English Destroying Your Image?" in *In the Name of Language!* Ed. Joseph Gold (Toronto: Macmillan, 1975).

Credibility

Quote to improve credibility by citing a respected and recognized authority. Or use the quotation as a target for attack, to illustrate that the source itself is doubtful and the object of your critical scrutiny.

The CBC's newsreaders, once modestly reliable (meaning they could be counted on to apologize for errors), have lost their supervisor of broadcast language and now commit cheerfully such barbarisms as "It sounds like he's going to reform."

Example

Power

Quote to demonstrate the power you have at your fingertips, but only to the extent that you will use the quotation. A carefully integrated quotation will show the reader that you have made yourself at home with the sources you have used. Your work will then illustrate your power to cut through trivial details to find the point that demands attention.

Example   Not all change is progress. Some of it has to be resisted, and when possible reversed. If the last ditch needs defending, I'll take my place alongside Samuel Johnson:

> If the changes we fear be thus irresistible, what remains but to acquiesce with silence, as in the other insurmountable distresses of humanity? It remains that we retard what we cannot repel, that we palliate what we cannot cure. (Preface to the *Dictionary*, 1755)

Eloquence

Quote rather than paraphrase when no rewording could ever hope to recapture the obvious eloquence of the original writer. Bear in mind that these instances are rare.

Example   As Samuel Johnson observes, "languages are the pedigree of nations."

Begging, Borrowing, and Stealing

In order to avoid accusations of theft, a writer, when quoting, must acknowledge a debt to a source. Don't interpret this to mean that you must quote whenever you borrow. When you paraphrase or when you make reference to an idea, you will also admit your indebtedness. Quote only when it is rhetorically the best tactic: that is, when it adds credibility, power, or eloquence.

Technically, you have not stolen an idea as long as you document its original occurrence. Failure to acknowledge a source is illegitimate borrowing, or plagiarism.

Legitimate borrowing takes place when a writer makes sparing use of some source material by fitting it carefully in the body of his or her essay, without altering it or distorting it in a way that would upset the author.

Avoid borrowing quotations in such a way that the original meaning is changed or even contradicted. The classic example of this shifty tactic is the movie review cited in an advertisement. It may read, for example, "stunning . . . amazing . . . not to be believed," when what the reviewer really said was, "A work stunning in its ignorance, amazing in its clumsy handling of the script, and not to be believed when its advertising describes it as the movie of the year."

The Fit, Function, and Form of Quotations

The quoted material must fit. It must relate directly to the point under discussion, and it must say something significant. Although quoting often seems like a form of pedantic name-dropping, that is not its rightful purpose.

The function of the quotation is usually to illustrate a point that you have already made in your own words. Bringing in an authority on the subject does not, after all, prove anything; it simply shows your awareness of the position of the experts, whether they are on your side or against you.

The form of the quotation is often the most difficult part of essay writing for the novice. Wherever possible, weave borrowed material unobtrusively into the body of your paper, rather than simply tacking it on.

10

Tacking Quotations On

While it may be a relief to stop writing and turn over the responsibility for illustrating your thesis to an authority, proceed with caution. Stopping in the midst of a sentence to introduce someone else (usually with a grand and unnecessary flourish) will diminish your own authority as writer.

When you quote, you must remain on the scene, controlling the situation, rather than giving the floor to someone else. Remember, at all times, that the essay is *your* work. When you quote, do not withdraw completely as if another speaker has been hired to do the job for you.

If you have been in the habit of employing long quotations from your source material, try this experiment with one of your past essays. Read the material through quickly. Do you find yourself skimming over the quoted material, or worse, skipping it altogether? Imagine what effect this kind of reading will have on an essay that depends heavily on outside authorities to make its case.

Weaving Quotations In

Wherever possible, make quoted material part of your own sentence structure. This tactic is more difficult but worth the extra effort. First, it will ensure that your reader cannot so easily skip those sections of the paper. Second, it will probably force you to cut quoted material down to the bare essentials, to look at it more closely, and to think of its direct relation to your own thought.

> When a mechanic reports that "she's runnin' real good," it takes a pretty stuffy professor to reply that "it is running rather well." **Example**

To make this technique work to its fullest advantage, there are some rules to keep in mind.

1. Use an ellipsis (. . .) to indicate words that have been left out. But never use ellipses in a way that misrepresents the original. Ellipses are permissible only

when you are making cosmetic changes (such as omitting a connective structure that would not make sense out of context). Keep in mind that you do *not* need ellipses at the start of a quotation, even if you did not include the beginning of a sentence in what you quoted, and remember that four dots are used when the omitted words come between two sentences. In other cases, only three dots are necessary.

Example   Hornyansky comments that "in our democratic, colloquial society you are more likely to be censured for using no slang. . . . But of course there are risks in using it too. . . . argot that suits one milieu may draw sneers in another."

The original reads as follows:

I would repeat that in our democratic, colloquial society you are more likely to be censured for using no slang at all. But of course there are risks in using it too. Some sober groups may find your flip ways unacceptable; argot that suits one milieu may draw sneers in another.

2. Use square brackets (even if you have to add them in black pen) to indicate words that you have added. Usually, you will need these only to indicate small cosmetic changes (such as changing a pronoun to a noun or changing a verb tense to make it consistent with the rest of the verbs in your sentence). Occasionally, you may need square brackets to add a word or two to clarify the context of the quotation.

Example   Hornyansky addresses "third- and fourth-generation Canadians who . . . [speak] English (sort of, you know?)."

The original reads as follows:

For I teach third- and fourth-generation Canadians who have spoken English (sort of, you know?) since the crib, yet who have no more sense of English idiom than a recent arrival from the Old Country.

3. When you use a complete sentence to introduce a quotation, follow it with a colon. Otherwise, use a comma or whatever punctuation you would use if the quotation marks were not there.

Example   On the subject of pretentiousness in grammar, Hornyansky remarks, "A question like 'Whom do you mean?' really deserves the answer it gets from Pogo: 'Youm, that's whom.' "

4. Make the terminal punctuation of the quoted material serve your purposes, rather than those of the original. In other words, if the quotation appears at the end of your sentence, close it with a period, even if a comma or other punctuation was used originally.

The original reads as follows:

For he knows that grammar varies inversely as virility; and that if you continue on down to the stadium, you'll find that nobody there plays well.

Your paper will read this way:

Hornyansky believes "grammar varies inversely as virility."

5. Quote exactly. Do *not* distort a quotation, accidentally or deliberately. The first offence is carelessness, the second fraud. If you detect an error of spelling or grammar in the original, you may tell your reader that it is not your mistake by following it immediately with the word [*sic*] (italicize or underline, and set in square brackets as shown). This notation will tell the reader that the fault is not yours.

Hornyansky cites the Hon. John Turner's advertisement "in a British newspaper that his four children require a 'kind and loving nannie [*sic*].' " **Example**

6. Use single quotation marks for a quotation within a quotation, as in the preceding example.

7. Indent passages of prose that are longer than four lines and passages of poetry longer than two lines. When you indent, quotation marks are no longer necessary.

Hornyansky insists on the importance of developing one's own writing style: **Example**

> A man at the mercy of his own style is as comic, and as much to be pitied, as a man at the mercy of drink. Your style ought to express what you are, and you are not the same person on all occasions, in every company. If you seem to be, you are a bore.

8. When you have gone to the trouble to quote a source, use it. Explain it, remark on its significance, analyze it, do something to show what it contributes to the whole paper. Don't assume its importance is self-evident.

9. Use quotations sparingly. The essay is meant primarily to present your views on a given subject.

10. Make sure you use quotations to make a point. Do so by "unpacking" them for the reader; that is, taking them apart in such a way as to make the progression of your thought and your reason for quoting them in the first place clear to your reader. Suppose that you decided to quote the entire paragraph below (taken, once again, from Michael Hornyansky's essay). The onus is on you to explain what exactly you want the reader to take from it.

Example   Are we lapsing into barbarism? Will we soon be unable to communicate except by coos and grunts and formulas? I don't really think so—though there are portents, dammit: such as my wife's hitchhiker, a braw school-leaver of nineteen, personable and polite. When she asked him to find out what was causing the noisy rattle he checked, diagnosed, and reported, "The uh thing . . . is, like . . . Uhhh . . ." Aghast, she conferred: did he mean the back door on the wagon was not properly shut? He heaved a great smiling sigh of relief. "Yuh," he said, having got through. No, what I fear is that well before that, we shall have lost touch with the past. That is the other purpose and glory of language, which the usage-mongers and the progress-peddlers and the flux-worshippers forget. The gift of my tongue does not merely enable me to "interrelate" with my contemporaries: it makes me a citizen of the entire human commonwealth, of an empire across time. I will not exchange that for a wilderness of global villages.

You need to elaborate on this passage in order to make clear what point you wish to make. You might say, for example, something like this:

Hornyansky believes that language is important because it enables humans to understand the past and to read and comprehend the thinking of the past. Without an education in the niceties of one's native language, humans are in danger of losing their ability not only to communicate with one another in the here-and-now, but also to read and appreciate the lessons of history.

Being able to make the point you want in your own words makes the value of the quotation and your meaningful use of it clear to your reader.

CHAPTER 10 EXERCISES

1. Use the following quotations in paragraphs that you devise. In each case, quote only a few words, not a complete sentence. Make sure to weave the quotation neatly into your sentence structure:

   a. "Children don't read to find their identity, to free themselves from guilt, to quench the thirst for rebellion or to get rid of alienation. They have no use for psychology. . . . They still believe in God, the family, angels, devils, witches, goblins, logic, clarity, punctuation, and other such obsolete stuff. . . . When a book is boring, they yawn openly. They don't expect their writer to redeem humanity, but leave to adults such childish illusions."—*Isaac Bashevis Singer*

   b. "Politics is the skilled use of blunt objects."—*Lester Pearson*

   c. "A little sincerity is a dangerous thing, and a great deal of it is absolutely fatal."—*Oscar Wilde*

   d. "Human beings have an inalienable right to invent themselves; when that right is pre-empted it is called brain-washing."—*Germaine Greer*

2. Explain in your own words the meaning of the following quotations:

   a. "Canada will be a strong country when Canadians of all provinces feel at home in all."—*Pierre Trudeau*

b. "Writing is like getting married. One should never commit oneself until one is amazed at one's luck."—*Iris Murdoch*

c. "There is no finer investment for any community than putting milk into babies." —*Winston Churchill*

d. "Happiness is always a by-product. It is probably a matter of temperament, and for anything I know it may be glandular. But it is not something that can be demanded from life, and if you are not happy you had better stop worrying about it and see what treasures you can pluck from your own brand of unhappiness." —*Robertson Davies*

3. Find quotations that you can use as part of paragraphs on each of the following topics:

a. creativity

b. Canada

c. death

d. sex

10

Part Four

WRITING THE ESSAY

Chapter 11

FINDING YOUR VOICE: MODES OF ESSAY WRITING

The essayist . . . can pull on any sort of shirt, be any sort of person, according to his mood or his subject matter.
—E. B. WHITE

Role playing is a vital part of the skill of essay writing. You must write the essay confident of your role as an expert. In this chapter, we will modify the general principles of essay writing according to the various purposes of different types of essays, and describe a role you might adopt as the author of one of these types. In addition, the chapter emphasizes the kind of reader or audience that each of the different essay types has. All of the types described share the general characteristics that we have already discussed:

1. a narrow thesis statement
2. a clear outline
3. carefully delineated patterns of argument
4. a unified structure—introduction, body, and conclusion
5. a coherent approach to the integration of support materials
6. an attention to sentence structure, emphasis, and tone

Remember that many of the steps involved in writing the different types of essays described in this chapter overlap. But whether an essay is meant as an informal discussion or as a formal research paper, the steps outlined above are essential. No less important are the steps in revision described in Chapter 19. This chapter will show you how to prepare yourself for certain specialized types of essay writing. Consult it for advice geared to the particular task at hand.

The Expository Essay

You shouldn't pay very much attention to anything writers say. They don't know why they do what they do. They're like good tennis players or good painters, who are just full of nonsense, pompous and embarrassing, or merely mistaken, when they open their mouths.
—JOHN BARTH

The expository essay is the most common essay assignment. It is based on the premise that you learn best about something by trying to teach it to someone else. In other words, the expository essay asks you to play the role of teacher, by presenting your chosen material according to your sense of its meaning and structure.

The expository essay exposes: it shows your approach to a particular subject. As in all essay writing, you must develop a general topic into a specific thesis statement, you must prepare an outline, and you must determine the patterns of argument appropriate to your discussion. The expository essay is different only because its object is primarily to *teach*, rather than to persuade, to present research material, to review, or to express personal conviction.

Four stages are involved in writing the expository essay:

1. finding your focus
2. planning your structure
3. adjusting your level of language
4. testing your results

These stages, while much the same as those outlined in the sections on developing, designing, and drafting the basic essay, are all affected by your role as teacher, and hence they need special consideration.

11

The Role of the Expository Essay

Before you begin, try to see your task in terms of its audience and its purpose.

AUDIENCE: a curious, but uninformed, reader you address in a professional but approachable way

PURPOSE: to present some important idea in a way that clarifies it, shows your attitude toward it, and answers questions the reader might have

With these criteria in mind, you can now adjust the stages in writing to suit the occasion.

Finding your focus

1. Find a subject that you know something about and are genuinely interested in, if possible.
2. Establish your objectives. Like a teacher, you should know what you want your reader to learn from your work.
3. Limit your subject to what can be thoroughly explained within the word length of the assignment. What you propose to show or explain is, in this case, your thesis statement.

SUBJECT: Forest-fire management   **Example**

OBJECTIVE: To show how it is done

LIMITATION: The step-by-step process of forest-fire management: prevention and control

Planning your structure

1. Break down the parts of your subject clearly in an outline.
2. Choose the pattern(s) of argument that will allow you to explain most clearly.
3. Connect the steps in your thought logically and clearly.

Example

PATTERN OF ARGUMENT: Process: how forest fires are managed

BREAKDOWN OF IDEAS: Rough outline

THESIS: The Ministry of Natural Resources every year sets in motion a regular plan by which to combat forest fires that threaten to destroy Canada's natural resources.

BODY: The Ministry does several things to control forest fires:

1. It establishes central locations where firefighting begins.
2. It predicts what areas are most endangered and maps these areas in detail.
3. It monitors weather conditions and keeps records of soil moisture and amounts of precipitation.
4. It monitors weather predictions.
5. It uses aerial patrols and lightning towers to keep watch.
6. It mobilizes fire crews when fire or smoke is reported.
7. It dispatches water bombers and erects fire camps in crisis situations.
8. It supplies all types of firefighting equipment.

CONCLUSION: Firefighting in Canada's forest regions is a careful process, dedicated to ensuring the protection of precious natural resources.

Adjusting your level of language

1. Keep your reader's level of knowledge in mind.
2. Define all terms likely to be unfamiliar to the reader.
3. Make language concrete, concise, and clear.

LEVEL OF KNOWLEDGE: Provide enough background in the introduction so that the reader will know why forest-fire management is important.

Example

In 1996 alone, despite preventive measures, a total of 1356 forest fires ravaged 371 358 ha of prime timber.

USE OF TERMS: Explain terms like "water bombers" and any other terms unlikely to be familiar to a reader.

Example

A water bomber is a large and cumbersome government-owned plane that can douse a fire with 5400 L of water.

CONCRETE, CONCISE, CLEAR LANGUAGE: Tell what a firefighter does, rather than what fire management is in the abstract. Include plenty of detail.

Maps that show area landscapes precisely enable officers to see what sort of timber may be threatened by forest fires and what buildings, such as summer cottages and outpost camps, are in immediate or anticipated danger.

Example

Testing your results

1. Check your work to see that it is as clear as possible. Put yourself in your reader's place: would you learn from the essay?
2. Have someone else read your work to see that it is readily understandable.
3. Proofread carefully to see that your writing does justice to your thoughts.

The Persuasive Essay

No man would set a word down on paper if he had the courage to live out what he believed in.

—HENRY MILLER

11

The persuasive essay aims at convincing the reader of the truth and validity of your position. Its subject matter is controversial, its thesis one view of the issue. Your task is to win your reader over with your credibility, your wealth of support, and your good reasoning.

Unlike the expository essay, which simply aims to *show* the reader something, the persuasive essay, by taking one side of a controversial issue, aims to *convince* the reader.

Prepare the persuasive essay according to the following stages:

1. Study the issues.
2. Pick a side—your thesis statement.
3. Make a case for the defence—your support.
4. Consider opposing viewpoints, and qualify or refute accordingly.
5. Test your argument for fairness and effectiveness.
6. Direct your argument, first in outline, then in final form.

A persuasive essay may or may not demand that you engage in extensive research to support your case. It does, however, demand that you keep your writing role in mind.

The Role of the Persuasive Essay

Tailor your essay to fit its special demands.

AUDIENCE: readers who have not made their minds up about a controversial matter and who are willing to make a fair and impartial judgment

PURPOSE: to convince them that your informed opinion on a particular subject is the best one

With these points in mind, consider the stages of the persuasive essay. Suppose you are writing a paper on the accessibility of health care. Research is not a major requirement; what is required is your independent, well-formulated view-point regarding this controversial subject.

Studying the issues

Before you take sides, you must examine all the angles of the question. Make a list of pros and cons about any issue that must be decided or possible answers to any question that must be settled.

Example

ISSUE: Should the government continue to influence the distribution of physicians across the country in order to improve health-care access?

PROS
— health care should be accessible to everyone
— rural areas are underserviced; most specialists are located in cities
— rural areas often lack hospital services

CONS
— doctors, particularly specialists, must be near hospitals
— the financial constraints of building and maintaining hospitals in rural areas are overwhelming
— the cost of health care itself impedes access to it

Picking a side

1. Choose the side for which you can muster the most support. If possible, choose a thesis that you genuinely believe in.
2. Define your position by making a claim or by arguing against another's claim.

Example

SIDE CHOSEN: The distribution of physicians has no real bearing on health-care access.

POSITION DEFINED: The current distribution of physicians does not affect health-care access. The high cost of health care is the main constraint to adequate access.
1. Physicians, particularly specialists, must be near medical facilities to run their practices effectively.
2. Physicians, therefore, should not be penalized for their decision to practise in cities, as they have been in Quebec, Ontario, and British Columbia.
3. The number of physicians should not be increased, as it has been in the rest of Canada, since that "solution" only increases the cost of an expensive health-care system.
4. More hospitals cannot be built and maintained in rural areas without increasing expenditures even more.
5. The current situation, where general practitioners tend to work in towns and rural areas and specialists choose cities, is the only workable way of balancing cost and access.

Making a case for the defence

1. Gather support for your arguments. In some instances, this support will come from books or journals, though it may also come from your own clear understanding of the issue.
2. Use your own reasons, and if research is required, use statistics and expert opinion as further support. Remember to acknowledge sources.

Accessibility is a fundamental principle of Canadian health insurance. The 1966 *Medical Care Act* "requires insured services to be delivered in a manner that does not impede or preclude, either directly or indirectly . . . reasonable access."[1] In keeping with this principle, both federal and provincial governments have tried to change the geographic distribution of doctors in an effort to correct a perceived inequitable distribution of physicians. They hoped thereby to improve access to health services in rural areas.

Example

(Expert Opinion)

In the 1960s and early 1970s, the federal government attributed the low physician-to-population ratio in rural areas to an overall shortage of doctors in the country. They believed that if there were more doctors, rural areas would no longer be underserviced.[2] So, the Canadian government responded to the problem by increasing the capacity of domestic medical schools and opening immigration to physicians. Between 1968 and 1974, the number of physicians in Canada grew by 8151, or 36 percent;[3] however, the distribution of physicians between rural and urban areas remained disproportionate, and the gap even worsened in Ontario.[4] In fact, the growth in the number of physicians increased health-care costs, but it did not improve the accessibility of health services.

Example

(Statistics)

Actually, the increase in the number of physicians to which governmental controls has led is responsible for increasing health-care costs; to build more hospitals would increase these costs even more. Given that funds are limited, if every small town were provided with a fully equipped hospital, then the more expensive equipment and treatments—like CAT scans and cancer treatments—would not be available anywhere in Canada. It might also become necessary to impose restrictions on accessibility similar to the rationing of health care in Britain, where—as a means of containing health costs—kidney dialysis is not available to National Health Service patients over 55 years of age.[5]

Example

(Reasons)

Considering opposing viewpoints

1. Anticipate objections to your arguments as you go along.
2. Treat the opposition fairly.

11

Example   ANTICIPATED ARGUMENT: In spite of these arguments, the number of physicians in rural areas is still smaller than it should be to ensure access to health-care services.

FAIR TREATMENT: a counterargument that analyzes the problem closely

Although rural areas tend to have fewer physicians per capita than cities, the difference in available medical services is not necessarily proportional to the difference in the respective physician-to-population ratios. Family and general practitioners gravitate toward smaller towns, while specialists tend to settle in cities.[6] The significance of this fact lies in the kinds of medical care these doctors provide. GPs perform a considerably wider range of services than do specialists. To some degree, then, one GP acts as a substitute for the many different specialists available in the city, so access to health care may not be as unequal as the present geographic distribution of physicians implies.

Testing your argument for fairness and effectiveness

1. Check for fallacies, or flaws, in your argument.
2. Weigh your words carefully, avoiding biased or vague, unconsidered words.

When writing (or reading) any persuasive essay, you may fall prey to a number of logical errors in your thinking. Remember that certain arguments are not in the spirit of fair play. Learn to recognize the following faulty arguments or fallacies and avoid them in your own writing:

1. ACCEPTING GLIB GENERALIZATIONS. An argument that uses catch phrases like "Canadian identity" or "freedom of the individual" in an unthinking way may just be appealing to what the words conjure up, rather than to any thoughtful meaning assigned to them by the writer. Make sure such general appeals can be pinned down to specifics. If the mayor of your city argues that he or she will work to increase "civic pride," ask what specifics such a general statement entails.

2. ARGUING *AD HOMINEM*. This kind of argument distracts readers from the issue being discussed and, instead, uses personal attacks against an opponent. For example, someone might argue that health-insurance fees should not go up because doctors are interested only in making money. Here the personal charge being made may have nothing to do with the issue.

3. ESTABLISHING FAULTY CAUSE AND EFFECT. This kind of faulty reasoning assumes that there is a connection between two events simply because one followed the other. For instance, if a political party claims that it is responsible for a drop in interest rates that occurred during its period in office, we need to ask if such a drop might have occurred regardless. After all, there may be many other ways of explaining changes in interest rates.

4. MAKING A FAULTY ANALOGY. Often we make analogies, or comparisons, in order to show significant similarities between things. We must, however, always take care to make sure that such comparisons are fair. Commercials are often the chief offenders in this regard. Is a day without orange juice really like a day without sunshine? Check to make sure that your own comparisons are appropriate.

5. ASSUMING AN "EITHER/OR" SITUATION. One of our commonest assumptions is that there are always two sides to any issue. In fact, there may be many more than two sides. See to it that you do not phrase your arguments in such a way that they falsify the problem. It is probably not true that if you don't believe in free enterprise, then you are a communist. Be aware of other possibilities between extremes. This fallacy is also known as the false dilemma.

6. JUMPING ON A BANDWAGON. When you deal with a controversial topic, make sure that you examine the issues carefully before arriving at your own point of view. The argument that something is right because it is "modern" or "current" or "up to date," or because everyone is in favour of it, will not stand up.

7. BEGGING THE QUESTION. You beg the question when you assume the truth of what you are trying to prove. For example, if you argue that books should not be taxed, it is not enough to say that no one could possibly support a tax on books because it will lead to increasing illiteracy. The onus is on you to prove that illiteracy will increase; you cannot simply assume so.

You may want to argue against this stated position:

Health-care access would be more equitable if physicians were more concerned   **Example**
with taking care of patients than with making money.

Checking for flaws: Look at the underlying biases of the statement.

This statement assumes that doctors practise in cities in order to make more money than they would in rural areas, but no proof is advanced for the claim. Here, in other words, the argument begs the question.

WEIGHING YOUR WORDS: It is important to find evidence to justify any claim that you intend to make. The argument above rests on an unexamined assumption.

8. THE SLIPPERY SLOPE. This fallacy occurs whenever someone assumes that one event will follow inevitably after another, without any argument in defence of that position. Like the expression "Give them an inch and they'll take a mile," it's assumed that one thing leads to another as a matter of course. This fallacy is also called the domino theory.

11

Directing your argument

1. Remind your readers of the points you are making by reinforcing those points as you go along.
2. Engage your readers as comrades-in-arms, not as antagonists. Assume that they are reasonable and open-minded about the issue. Do not assume that they are antagonistic.

Look at these techniques in the following paragraph that concludes the paper on access to health care:

Since every small town does not have a hospital and physicians are not located in proportion to demand, barriers to access to health services unquestionably exist; however, the cost of breaking down these barriers is higher than the cost of their presence. Ultimately, then, it is the cost of health care itself that impedes equal access. With limited government funds, equality of accessibility to health services is little more than an idealist's dream. So far, measures to make such services more accessible have invariably increased costs by more than they have improved access. Policies aimed at changing the distribution of physicians and hospitals are not the solution. Clearly, the federal and provincial governments need to change their approach to the issue of health-care access.

REINFORCEMENT: Summary of the line of argument

CHAPTER 11 EXERCISES

1. Identify the fallacies in the following examples:
   a. Of course Father Whiteford opposes abortion. He's a priest and believes that the Pope is infallible.
   b. Teens should not participate in chat rooms because abduction of minors is on the rise.
   c. I fixed the picture on the TV by hitting it on its side. The picture improved immediately.
   d. Women do not belong in boardrooms; they are indecisive and emotional.
   e. Lying on your résumé shouldn't matter if you don't get caught. It is the company's responsibility to check the applications it receives.
   f. If you allow students to hand assignments in late, they won't ever hand anything in on time.
   g. Since she has been carrying that good luck charm, she has won two lottery prizes.
   h. What does Martha Stewart know about homemaking? She was trained as a stockbroker.
   i. We must oppose the war for the good of the nation.
   j. Anyone who seriously believes that plastic surgery is acceptable is making a big mistake.

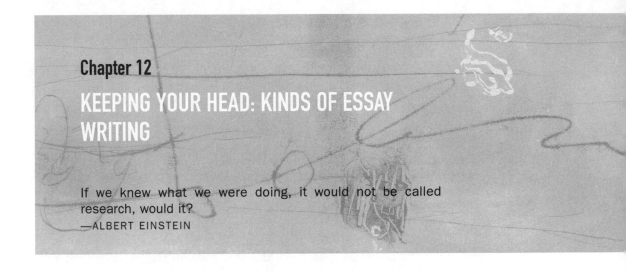

Chapter 12

KEEPING YOUR HEAD: KINDS OF ESSAY WRITING

If we knew what we were doing, it would not be called research, would it?
—ALBERT EINSTEIN

Before your student days are over, you will be required to write varying forms of essays. Knowing the role of each form of essay and what is expected of you will help you "keep your head." This chapter describes the essays you are likely to encounter and gives guidelines that will help you write to fit each form.

The Essay Examination

Eighty percent of success is showing up.
—WOODY ALLEN

Essay examinations are frequently a source of panic because they strip the writer down to the bare essentials. Without hours of preparation to cover your flaws, whether in knowledge or fluency, you may feel exposed—unless your work is genuinely in good shape. An essay examination, because of its time limitations, is brief but not without style.

The advice that follows will help you write a better examination, if you approach it in stages:

1. Getting in shape
2. Coping with exam shyness
3. Making the material fit
4. Taking the plunge
5. Standing out in a crowd

The Role of the Essay Examination

Remember your reader and your aim:

AUDIENCE: an expert (not an antagonist) who wishes to test your knowledge and facility in his or her discipline

PURPOSE: to show what you have learned and how you can apply it

Getting in shape

An examination is only the product. What determines its outcome is your preparation, not only in the nervous hours immediately before it, but in the days and weeks preceding it as well.

To make your performance on the exam less fraught and more predictable, prepare for it gradually. If you have faced your fears throughout the year, the final countdown should not be anxiety-ridden. At least your conscience will be clear if you have attended class, read the textbooks, and completed the course work.

Coping with exam shyness

ANALYZE THE SHAPE YOU'RE IN. Be brave. Take a good hard look at yourself. Judge your past performance in the course. Consider the amount of work you have done. If you're already in good shape, this step will increase your confidence. If not, read on.

LIMBER UP. Even a well-prepared student will need to warm up for the examination by conducting a review. Review course work by setting up a reasonable work schedule and then following it (with some flexibility, of course).

Review does not mean reread. Review should be refreshing, just as a warm-up exercise is meant to get you ready for more and not to drain you of energy. Review is just part of the routine. Look through your notes and your texts, as well as your past essays and tests. This process will be easier if you have highlighted important points beforehand (and if you have done all the required work in the first place).

LOCATE PROBLEM AREAS. To overcome shyness about the exam, you must confront your fears. Ask yourself, unflinchingly, What are you afraid of? If you find that you are worried about some specific problems in your understanding of the course, pay particular attention to these. The benefits will be twofold: you will conquer some of your fear, and you will learn something.

Making the material fit

In order to learn anything, you must make it a part of yourself. You must carry it away with you and get carried away with it (while still keeping your feet on the ground).

To gain full possession of the course material, you will use *memory*, *fluency*, *application*, and *imagination*. Here's how.

MEMORY. There is no learning without memory, though memory is just the first step in turning course material into something of your own. To sharpen your skills of recall, try reading aloud, so that both sight and hearing can register the information.

Concentrate on facts and significant details. Help your memory along by making associations or by visualizing material. These tactics will trigger memory when you're stuck for words.

If memorizing is not your strong point, don't despair. Although an essay exam demands that you have some facts at your fingertips, how the facts are presented, how they are used, and what you create out of them are equally important.

FLUENCY. To make yourself an expert in a discipline, learn how to speak its language as you master its content. Make the terms a part of your language by learning to define them, by including them in speech, and by using them in writing. When imagining how you would answer a question, talk to yourself. Jot down notes. The more conversant you are with specialized language in your subject area, the more gracefully you will write under pressure.

APPLICATION. Make sure you can use what you know. To apply your knowledge, you need to supply a context. Don't just repeat the facts: question the material. As you review, note questions that the textbook may have raised. Keep in mind any questions raised in class or topics distributed for review that strike you as pertinent. These may prove useful when exam time comes.

IMAGINATION. All work and no play would make a dull examination and certainly a grim study period. Approach the test and your preparation for it with a sense of play, if at all possible. Wonder about its potential. Don't confine your imagination to the tried and true; experiment with some ideas of your own. Develop a theory or two, as if you were preparing for a formal essay. You may well get a chance to try them out on the examination. The difference between an A and a B is often a desire to develop your own ideas and to create something new out of the material.

Taking the plunge

Writing an examination successfully depends on two factors: what you know *and* what you can say about it in a limited time. To make the best use of your time, follow this basic pattern: *read, sketch, write, skim.*

READ THE QUESTIONS CAREFULLY. Before you get your feet wet, so to speak, read over the entire exam. Take careful note of the instructions. If you are given a choice of questions, devote a few minutes to their selection. Allot an appropriate amount of time for each question and *adhere to that schedule*. It is wise to begin with the questions you know best.

Look for questions to challenge you. Remember that an essay question does not necessarily have a correct answer. An essay simply tries, as its name suggests, to come to terms with a provocative, perhaps troubling, question.

Become familiar with these common examination terms:

Explain. If you are asked to *explain,* be thorough in your approach and ready to clarify in detail, as though you were teaching the reader. Both structure and substance are needed, so be prepared to show both breadth and depth in your treatment of the question.

Example   The federal Progressive Conservative Party has been called the "normal opposition party." Explain. What must the federal Progressive Conservative Party do to become the "normal government party"?

Begin by using facts to explain the label "normal opposition party." These facts should be available to you from the course material. Then, making sure to refer to appropriate sources, discuss various theories of what is needed to ensure Conservative success at the polls.

Discuss. If asked to *discuss,* use the latitude of the question to focus on some part of the problem that captures your attention and allows you to present a lively, informative, and thoughtful consideration of the problem. Treat the question as if you were writing a less than formal essay—as indeed you are.

Example   Discuss the ways in which family ties and loyalties dramatically expand the inner conflicts and crises of conscience in *Huckleberry Finn* and *King Lear*.

Begin by focusing on the conventional bond between parents and children. Show how the bonds are broken in both works. Then you could go on to show how a new sense of family is created for both Lear and Huck in the levelling process that occurs in both works. Remember to include many examples to support your points.

Outline. If asked to *outline,* put your emphasis on the bare bones of the argument—the facts—rather than the flesh. An outline will require you to place more stress on the shape and the sequence of your subject, rather than the substance.

Example   Outline how and why geographical factors are so strongly evident in classical mythology.

Your outline should be broadly based, isolating a number of examples of geographical factors in a variety of myths, rather than in one or two. Follow these examples with a discussion suggesting some of the reasons for this phenomenon. Aim at broad coverage rather than deep analysis.

Compare and Contrast. If asked to *compare and contrast,* or simply to *compare,* remember that the object is to show the relationship between two things. Focus the essay on the connections and differences you find by setting two things side by side in your sketch.

Example   Compare and contrast the women's movement of the late nineteenth and early twentieth centuries with the women's movement that began in the late 1960s.

Begin by making an outline to discover the main similarities and differences. Say, for example, that the main similarities include the desire to change attitudes toward working women and the desire to gain more influence in the workplace. The differences might include the earlier movement's focus on political rights and the later movement's focus on issues relating to sexual harassment on the job. You could compare and contrast not only the goals of the movements, but also the relative success of each of them. Then you need a summary of your findings in order to compare these two movements more generally.

SKETCH. Sketch out your answers to the questions chosen. First, let yourself go. Jot things down helter-skelter as they occur to you. Then, try to gather material into categories for discussion. Avoid getting embroiled in outlines too complex or too demanding for the time allowed.

Sketch your answers in the briefest possible form. As you do so, use key words in the question to guide your responses. Above all, obey the terms of the question as you work in the things you want to say.

WRITE. Sketching your material enabled you to get warmed up. Therefore, the writing process itself should be more graceful and more organized. To ensure an organized presentation, fall back on established essay-writing habits. Begin at the beginning. Make sure your answer has an introduction, a body, and a conclusion. While these sections will be hastier and less polished, do not abandon structure entirely.

The main thing to keep in mind is the connections you are making between the question and the knowledge you brought with you into the exam. Refer to your sketch and to the original question as you write, but also allow yourself the freedom of an unexpected idea or a unique turn of phrase, as long as it doesn't interfere with the basic flow of your answer.

Let the words flow, but keep the writing legible. Write on every other line as a courtesy to your reader.

SKIM. Force yourself to read your answers quickly and to make small changes. To neglect this stage is to force your instructor to become the proofreader—a proofreader who might become annoyed at your carelessness. A small mistake is forgivable; reckless abandon is not.

Standing out in a crowd

Now that you know how to pass an essay examination, you may well wonder how to surpass expectations. Though you are writing the examination along with perhaps hundreds of other students, there are ways of making your exam style unique without defying the conventions of test writing.

What does a bleary-eyed instructor, marking 200 essay questions, look for in an answer?

DEFINITION. An essay examination is your chance to show your understanding of how some terminology in the subject area works. Unlike a multiple-choice exam, this kind of test will allow you to use the language of the discipline precisely and fluently.

DIRECTION. Your answers should be pointed directly at the questions. Don't make the mistake of trying to say everything; you can't assume that the instructor will give you credit if he or she can find the right answer somewhere in your paper. You also can't assume that your instructor will want to look for your answer. Make your answer easy to find.

DETAIL. While even an exceptional student cannot remember all of the fine points in a complex body of work, it is certainly possible to learn a smattering of appropriate details on a variety of subjects. Such details may be inserted, where applicable, as you are writing the exam. Details have the effect of a close-up. They allow you to focus on something precise, and they reveal your careful reading of your subject matter.

DEPTH. To demonstrate depth of knowledge, an examination must show that the writer has thought about the implications of the subject and of the specific question. Dive in. Don't avoid entirely the deeper complexities of a question in favour of its superficial requirements. Where possible, do more than you need to do. Answer questions seriously; you are writing as a curious and concerned expert. Address your subject, not as an illustration of how well you have learned it, but rather as a serious attempt to advance the subject matter itself.

DISCOVERY. A brilliant exam will show what a student has learned above and beyond what the instructor has taught. If you have some insight or even some questions about the material that have not been raised in class, this is your opportunity to voice them. Never recite the answer to a question based on your memory of a lecture unless you have, sadly, nothing of your own to add to the material. An exam should occasionally allow you to take intelligent, calculated risks.

The Précis or Summary

When you catch an adjective, kill it.
—MARK TWAIN

A précis is a concise summary of a longer passage. Sometimes a précis will be an assignment in its own right; on other occasions, it will be something that you prepare as part of writing a larger essay of your own. The ability to summarize one's own or others' work is important: often, you will be asked to provide short summaries of your written material, whether in abstract form, as is the case with dissertations, or in executive summary form, in the case of reports. Sometimes, too, a précis will provide you with a short memo about what you considered the key features in a work central to your research. The task of writing a précis will help you learn to focus on the line of argument in a passage and will oblige you to reconsider it in your own words; this kind of engagement with source material, or even with your own writing, can be invaluable in honing your critical abilities. In addition, précis writing can help make your writing more concise.

The Role of the Précis

Before you start, conceive of your task in relation to its audience and its purpose.

AUDIENCE: someone who wants you to give a quick overview of a detailed piece of writing without sacrificing central content

PURPOSE: often to reduce a passage to one-third or even one-quarter of its original length, occasionally even shorter, in a way that keeps the original focus and does not obfuscate ideas

Assuming that your task is to reduce a passage to one-third of its original length, you can now follow these guidelines:

Reading the original passage

1. Read the passage to ferret out its main focus.
2. Try to reconstruct the organization of the passage as you read through it.
3. Jot down the main idea of the passage, and mark ideas that are central to it, or peripheral to it, as you go along.
4. Reduce the passage to an outline that constitutes its line of argument.

Condensing sentence structure

Many constructions in English are redundant and can be substantially reduced without adversely affecting content. Here are some suggestions about how to reduce the sentence structure you find in a longer passage:

1. LEAVE OUT APPOSITIVES, WORDS OR PHRASES THAT RENAME OTHER WORDS.

    ✗ Socks, his cat, caught her third mouse this week.   **Example**
    ✓ Socks caught her third mouse this week.

2. LEAVE OUT WORDS THAT ARE INCLUDED ONLY FOR EMPHASIS.

    ✗ Bill was very disappointed.   **Example**
    ✓ Bill was devastated.

3. CHANGE FIGURATIVE LANGUAGE, SUCH AS SIMILES AND METAPHORS, OR OMIT THEM.

    ✗ Tilly worked like a dog on the project.   **Example**
    ✓ Tilly laboured on the project.

4. LEAVE OUT INTRODUCTORY CONSTRUCTIONS LIKE "IT IS . . . WHO" OR "IT IS . . . WHICH."

Example   ✗ It is Cathy who works in the library.
✓ Cathy works in the library.

5. FIND ONE WORD THAT WILL DO THE WORK OF SEVERAL.

Examples   ✗ Cole is a man who had once taught school.
✓ Cole is an ex-teacher.

✗ Dil left the room without a sound.
✓ Dil left the room silently.

6. FIND WORDS THAT ALLOW YOU TO GENERALIZE RATHER THAN PARTICULARIZE.

Example   ✗ Nelly bought hamburgers, french fries, and soft drinks.
✓ Nelly bought fast food.

7. TURN RHETORICAL QUESTIONS INTO STATEMENTS.

Example   ✗ What kind of person would be interested in yet another situation comedy?
✓ Few people would be interested in yet another situation comedy.

8. COMBINE SHORT SENTENCES TO REDUCE WORD LENGTH.

Example   ✗ In the beginning of the twenty-first century, more unrelated people are living together under the same roof. These people may be joined together for love. They may be joined for convenience. Or, they may be joined out of necessity. Whatever the reason, choosing a roommate is one of the most important decisions you will make. If two people are united for love, then choosing a roommate is a very personal decision. If two or more people are going to live together for convenience, or out of necessity, then choosing roommates is an important decision. This decision must be well thought out because choosing the wrong roommate could cost you financially, physically, and mentally. Choosing a roommate is difficult, but the process you use in choosing a roommate is as important as the roommate you choose, because the process you choose will lead to your roommate, and your new roommate will have a significant effect on your life.

✓ In the beginning of the twenty-first century, more unrelated people are living together under the same roof, for love, for convenience, or out of necessity. If two people unite out of love, then the choice of a roommate is personal; however, if you live with someone for convenience or out of necessity, you must choose cautiously. The wrong roommate could cost you financially, physically, and mentally. Choosing a roommate, though difficult, is crucial because the roommate chosen will have a powerful effect on your life.

Writing the précis

1. Write out in your own words the main points in the passage.
2. Check that words you substitute are appropriate to their new context. Check the precise meanings of words.
3. Keep the original paragraph structure unless the piece is short.
4. Try to keep the tone and style of the original intact.
5. Do not add anything as you interpret the passage.
6. Keep the word length to approximately one-third of the original, unless otherwise instructed, but don't cut out essentials.
7. Read the passage again and revise carefully.

The Informal Essay

All writing is communication; creative writing is communication through revelation—it is the self escaping into the open. No writer long remains incognito.
—E. B. WHITE

In most cases, the essays you write as part of your course work will be formal in tone. When you are allowed the luxury of writing an informal essay, follow these basic suggestions:

1. Be yourself.
2. Choose a comfortable subject.
3. Experiment with style and subject.
4. Shop around.

The Role of the Informal Essay

The informal essay affords you greater freedom and a more casual approach than the formal essay. Although the same writing process is demanded in the informal essay—it too needs a thesis statement, a typical essay shape, and a command of the mechanics of writing—what you say and how you say it are a matter of invention rather than convention.

AUDIENCE: friendly company who find your perspective stimulating
PURPOSE: to talk about anything that appeals to your imagination

Be yourself

The informal essay should let the reader learn about you and about your subject. Whereas you are obliged to keep a restrained and professional distance in the formal essay, you should maintain a casual and personal tone in the informal essay. Someone reading your paper will learn not only the facts and figures of your subject, but also some of your characteristics and your attitudes.

You will necessarily be more exposed: flaws in your arguments, biases in your attitudes, and unattractive aspects of your personality may show. The informal essay is by definition a face-to-face meeting between you and the reader. To pre-

12

vent excessive vulnerability, you must examine your attitudes scrupulously, and be prepared to face your reader's reaction—alone.

Choose a comfortable subject

Whereas a formal essay must be logical, objective, tight, and well supported, an informal essay allows you to be more subjective in your viewpoint, more personal in your selection of supporting material, and more idiosyncratic in your approach.

The formal essay may argue a life-and-death matter; the informal essay is, by contrast, an intellectual exercise for its own sake. This characterization does not mean that the informal essay cannot be heartfelt or deeply important—but its tone is less public, its argument closer to your personal interests, and its value less dependent on knowledge of facts than on grace and eloquence.

Experiment with subject and style

You must draw the material and the viewpoint from your own sense of the subject, rather than looking to authorities for defence.

In an informal essay, your object is to keep your reader interested in what you have to say. You cannot assume that the subject is intrinsically appealing to the reader from a professional standpoint, as you do in the formal essay. Since the material you choose in the informal essay reflects you and your personal understanding of the matter, you must appeal to your reader personally and share your opinions enthusiastically.

The informal essay allows you the opportunity to experiment with language in a way that would not be appropriate in a formal or research essay. Try writing as you speak—without lapsing into grammatical and structural errors. For example, in an informal essay, you can use contractions (don't, can't, etc.), which are generally not acceptable in a formal essay.

Shop around

Make an effort to read some personal essays, whether newspaper editorials or in magazines or the "collected works" of a classmate. Here are some choices for stylistic study:

Barbara Amiel	Michele Landsberg
Russell Baker	Fran Lebowitz
Harry Bruce	Joey Slinger
Allan Fotheringham	Lewis Thomas
Ellen Goodman	James Thurber
Peter Gzowski	Jan Wong

CHAPTER 12 EXERCISES

Read the following informal essay and answer the questions that follow. (Essay reprinted with permission by Jeremy Cooper.)

Some say that television cannot teach me anything about real life, and that is the reason why I am currently engaged in a staring competition with my set. So far the tube has won best three out of five, but as Dr. Schuller says, "If it's going to be, it's up to me." That TV has to blink sometime. So, while I wait for sweet victory against the naysayers of educational TV, I will set my mind to learning and become a couch potato.

Channel 57, Women's Television Network, will be the genesis of my education. This week's Friday night "Girl Movie," *Indiscretion of an American Wife*, launched me into a convertible Mercedes and down the streets of Rome to rendezvous with the heroine's Italian lover, Matteo. He is a splendid chap with dark, mysterious eyes, lusty eyebrows, and a 5 o'clock shadow that never grows. He owns a vineyard, a gorgeous location where he and Julia make love under the warm stare of an Italian sun.

I quickly realize that if I am ever going to get the girl who drives the Mercedes and never have to shave again, then I better learn how to grow grapes. Where to go? Where to go? I know, Channel 39, Home and Garden Television. Here, Bob Vila, with his endless endorsements of Sears' paraphernalia, will not only reveal the secrets of a rigorous vineyard, but also the wonder that accompanies the satisfaction of building my own Italian villa. I will stand back in amazement as three or four of my neighbours' lonely and ignored housewives come to comment on my earthiness.

But wait, that home wrecker, Matteo, was a marvellous lover. He wooed Julia. She felt special. He fed her grapes. They lived happily ever after. Where does a fellow learn those kinds of sensitive manoeuvres?

Channel 60, of course. If such a gentleman is so inclined, he may stay up far into the wee hours of Saturday morning to watch the Showcase Late Revue. They always show second-rate low-budget porn with frequent nudity and gratuitous sex. Add in The Learning Channel's (TLC) objective and mechanized educational program *The Sex Files*, and a fellow will be well on his way to developing some top-notch manoeuvres. The sensitivity part is easy: a season of *Oprah* (ABC, Channel 10) and *I Dream of Jeannie* reruns (Family Channel, 37) is enough to earn any boy scout his sensitivity badge.

Now the next logical step is to apply all of this wonderful learning in the real world. Not so. Upon rousing himself groggily at one in the afternoon, the aspiring Matteo plunks himself back on the couch. Victory is mine. The television begs permission to be allowed to answer all of life's pressing questions.

How am I going to propose?—Life, Channel 56, *A Wedding Story*. What about divorce?—NBC, Channel 8, *Ally McBeal*. What if my indiscreet housewife gets pregnant and goes into labour in a taxicab?—TLC, Channel 41, *Paramedics,* or perhaps *Trauma: Life in the ER.* What if she sleeps with my brother?—Global, Channel 5, *Jenny Jones,* or TNN, Channel 17, *WWF.* Gosh, I am set. I have got the answers to the world and to a woman's heart right here at my fingertips. Now it is really time to put my research to work.

Blink.

I uprooted my tubers from the fertile furrow of my couch and headed out into the real, non-televised world. What a shock. Can you believe that no one wants to hire a paramedic whose primary work experience is eight hours per week watching TLC, and whose best reference came from the cable company? And did you know that not a single construction company would apprentice me, not even when I showed them my autographed portrait of Bob Vila? Frankly, I was stunned.

I was so bewildered, in fact, that I even stopped to talk with some of the other folks in the unemployment line. Trade tickets and diplomas and bachelor degrees and hours upon hours of work experience came flying out from under hats and pocket flaps. They weren't the send-away kind of certificates either; they were the real thing. Just about every person in the line had gone to school and bled over exams or term papers. What an epiphany. (I learned that word from *Spelling Bee*. Do you think those kids got so smart by watching TV?)

Apparently, asides and interior monologues do not work off-screen: someone was shaking me and slapping me in the face. The girl with the plumber, pipe fitter, butcher, and hairdresser tickets was pulling her hair out and yelling in my face, "No! Get a grip, man. Get a life. Kids don't learn that stuff from watching TV. They have to internalize their knowledge and put it to use; television just puts *it* out." (*It*? Is *it* like how a fire extinguisher puts fires out, so too television puts kids' ability to learn out, or, like how evangelists disseminate tracts, so too television puts knowledge into the minds of kids?) She was very enigmatic.

I changed the channel on her, set my mind to vineyards, and started to crawl toward the curb, out from under the unemployed, enraged ex–television junkies. By the time I struggled to my knees, the crowd was chanting, "Books, man, books. You gotta read books." It was very Gregorian. (Those monks were on Vision, Channel 16, last night.)

For some reason, maybe the rhythm, the chant stuck with me, or maybe I felt compelled to solve the butcher's riddle. I lack faith in the written word, but I decided to allow a few books my meagre reverence. I discovered Arnold Bennett has some interesting things to say about books:

> Study is not an end, but a means. I should blush to write such a platitude, did I not know by experience that the majority of readers constantly ignore it. The [person] who pores over a manual of carpentry and does naught with it is a fool. But every book is a manual of carpentry, and every [person] who pores over any book whatever and does naught else with—deserving an abusive epithet. (118)

The plumber's words came flooding back to me. I imagined that she and Bennett were like a diamond ring lodged in a sink's drainpipe waiting to be recovered. If they are right, I can watch all the Home and Garden Television I want, but if I do not swing a hammer, then I will never get my Italian villa. Internalizing began to sound like a lot of work, so I read on.

Bruce Hutchison wrote a short essay entitled "The Shadows," which uses Plato's Simile of the Cave to illustrate what has happened to the couch potato. Hutchison argues that television "is the great current illusion. The shadows are mistaken as things" (143). Indeed, as a sofa spud, I would sit in my cave and watch the shadows being emitted from the screen. I interpret the images as reality not knowing that I am actually separated from true life, a spectator behind a "gaudy curtain," and unable to see, never mind make love under, an Italian sun. I had the slightest urge to go get a pipe wrench and a hammer, but the thought of losing a fingernail made me turn another page.

Apparently, when a philosopher leaves the confines of the cave and steps into the sun, Plato calls this understanding. Hutchison agrees: "the grim inescapable fact of human understanding is that it must be private, must come from within. . . . Though [knowledge] is presented in a million different versions, the paramount problem of modern [people] is to find a satisfactory participation in modern life" (144).

Internalize? Participate? Philosophy? Understanding? I am going to have to watch some more *Spelling Bee,* but then again, why did that plumber slap me? Oh ya, those smart kids.

Children participate in the adult world through a sense of wonder. They wonder why the sky is blue, how babies are made, if the fridge light stays on when the door is shut; they wonder why wars start, how people die, and if all families have two fathers. Neil Postman, as quoted by Matthew Stevenson, states, "children must enter, through their questions, into the adult world. As media merge the two worlds the calculus of wonderment changes. Curiosity is replaced by cynicism, or, even worse, by arrogance. We are left with children who rely not on authoritative adults but news from nowhere" (3). And these cynical children grow up too. When they are eighteen, average American children have seen 17 000 murders, spent 20 000 hours mesmerized by the TV's glow, as compared to the 11 000 hours spent in front of a teacher; and, if they were watching during the 1996 prime time season, children will have 65 000 sexual references to discuss at the dinner table or across the TV tray (Stevenson 3).

Again, I was stunned. With children watching so much television, they do not have to wonder anything anymore. Television is putting it out, and by "it" I mean extinguishing wonder. When I was a kid, I used to wonder what it would be like to kiss a girl. Sure, my first kiss was not as graceful as the last kiss of *The Princess Bride,* and sure, there were no violins playing in the background, but if I may, I will quote a fitting piece of literature to describe the experience:

> A pear's a pear
> A plum's a plum
> But a kiss ain't a kiss
> If it ain't got the tongue.

Not even 65 000 sexual references could convince me to trade in that first kiss, even if she did throw up two minutes later.

With that, I closed my books, collected a tin can full of nails and a hammer, and headed outside. Now, there is bamboo lattice on my front lawn, but no grapes are growing yet; Bruce Hutchison is riding his garden tractor trying to put the fear of God into some stubborn cucumbers; Arnold Bennett is planting begonias in our new television planter box; I am dangling from the eaves of my very crooked house, but we are about to break for a barbeque. There are no lonely housewives banging down my door, and if they did, I am afraid they would knock the humble beginnings of my Italian villa over. If you want to drop in, I will have to ask you to do me a favour before you come over. Read Seamus Heaney's "Digging." It's about potatoes.

Bennett, Arnold. "Translating Literature into Life." *The Open Window: Essays and Short Stories.* Eds. W. F. Langford and Patrick J. Daniel. Toronto: Longmans, 1961. 117–120.

Hutchison, Bruce. "The Shadows." *The Open Window: Essays and Short Stories.* Eds. W. F. Langford and Patrick J. Daniel. Toronto: Longmans, 1961. 143–45.

Stevenson, Matthew. "America Unplugged: Giving Up TV Viewing." *The American Enterprise*. 8.5(1997) 30 Mar. 2001 <http://web4.infotrac.galegroup.com>.

1. How is word choice used to enhance the humour of this essay? Find examples to support your point.
2. How does the writer make the transition from TV to books to experience? By what techniques does the writer achieve these transitions?
3. Examine the introduction and conclusion. How is each of these made effective?
4. Find a copy of Seamus Heaney's poem "Digging." What is its relationship to the essay?

The Literary Essay

I find television very educational. Every time someone switches it on, I go into another room and read a good book.
—GROUCHO MARX

The Role of the Literary Essay

The literary essay requires you to read, to analyze, and to come to terms with the meaning of a piece of literature. Whether it demands secondary sources or simply focuses on the literary work itself, the literary essay demands that you show your understanding of how and why the work is put together the way it is.

Write the literary essay according to the following stages:

1. Formulate a thesis about the work.
2. Read the work closely.
3. Use secondary sources, if required.
4. Select only the best supporting evidence.
5. Quote often, but not at great length.
6. Write in the present tense.
7. Write with both the text and the argument in mind.
8. Revise with style.

AUDIENCE: someone who has read the novel or poem or short story, but who wants to understand more about how it works (for example, its structure, its themes, its techniques)

PURPOSE: to interpret the meaning of a work and the techniques by which that meaning is revealed

Formulate a thesis

The thesis of the literary essay should be something that helps the reader make sense of the work in question.

For example, in the essay that follows on p. 102, the reader needs to know how Yann Martel's novel *Life of Pi* succeeds in allowing both the reader and the writer to make the leap of faith that is demanded by magic realism. The thesis statement thus is that Martel demands a leap of faith from both narrator/writer and reader.

Find your thesis by asking yourself what the important questions are about the literary work you have in front of you. Sometimes these will be assigned, but sometimes you will have to find your own questions, based on class discussion and reading.

Remember that you cannot conclusively prove your thesis statement. All you are expected to do is to show that your reasons for it are based on the text itself.

Read the work closely

With your working thesis in mind, read the work carefully. Underlining or high-lighting the text as you go along is often a good idea (provided you own it, of course).

Note anything that might count as evidence for your analysis of the characteristics of a literary work. Don't, however, neglect passages that might support a contrary view. You will need to account for these as well.

Use secondary sources, if required

Maintain your balance when using secondary sources. Use them to get some critical perspective on the work in question, but remember that your own task is no different from theirs. The main reason for writing a literary essay is to show your own powers of analysis.

Keep track of the sources you have consulted. The ideas you find must be acknowledged to avoid charges of plagiarism. Keep track also of the basic line of argument set forth by each critic you consult: it is unfair to take ideas or phrasing if you intend to use them out of their original context. Note that if you copy and paste material from the Internet, it is wise to do so in a different font from the rest of your writing, in order to be able to differentiate at a glance between your words and another's.

Select only the best evidence

After close reading, you need to "back off" from the work somewhat. Your task is not to summarize the work, or to explain every detail of it, but merely to present a viewpoint that suggests what the work means and how it is put together.

Skim through the work, noting down the most prominent support you have found. Then, categorize the material into sections appropriate for discussion in your essay. Fit these into a rough outline, and you are ready to write.

THESIS STATEMENT: readers are asked to take a leap of faith to understand the meaning of the experience of the narrator in *Life of Pi*.   **Example**

A. Readers are asked to participate in a magic realism fable and suspend their disbelief accordingly.
B. Readers are encouraged to embrace a faith in the god of their choice, as the narrator does.

    C. Readers are asked actively to choose the better story between the two that are provided in the novel.

This essay accumulates evidence of how the reader is asked to make a leap of faith in ways similar to those made by the narrator. As you gather support, try not to include everything. Pick only those passages central to an understanding of the work's meaning and those that work best as illustrations of your thesis.

Quote often, but not at great length

The best illustration of a point in a literary essay is a quotation. Whereas paraphrase may be a useful way of reporting research, the quotation is the most precise way to examine meaning in literature. Exactitude is important.

Remember, though, that you must *use* your quotations. Don't just copy them and assume that your point has been made. Focus in on them to show exactly how they work as support for your thesis. Don't assume that the meaning of the quotations or your purpose in quoting them is self-evident.

Write in the present tense

When discussing a work of literature, stay in the present tense—treat the work as a living thing.

Example   When confronted by the priest, the pandit, and the imam when Pi is out walking with his parents, he explains, "Bapu Ghandi said, 'All religions are true.' I just want to love God" (*Life* 76).

History, on the other hand, and accounts of historical events, are written in the past tense.

Write with both text and argument in mind

Stay close to the text and to your argument at all times. But remember that you are not writing to record the plot or to state the obvious. Assume that the reader has read the work. Your job is to offer an interpretation of its meaning. Use the primary text to *demonstrate* your thesis and present your support for the argument at every step of the way.

Write an analysis, not an appreciation or a summary. Don't, for example, waste words admiring Sondheim's skill as a lyricist or Martel's gifts as a novelist. Instead, show how a particular literary work is put together and explain why it has the effect it does.

Assume that the work has unity and coherence, unless evidence shows otherwise. Take the text apart and show how some features of it work. Your job is to show how its synthesis is achieved.

When you are not working with a literary text alone but are instead analyzing a phenomenon, such as musical theatre, remember to keep your focus on the argument and your support for it.

Revise with style

In a literary essay, style is crucial. Your grade will depend not only on what you say but also on how you say it. Check for grace in style. Aim at writing smoothly and confidently. Find a critic you admire and emulate his or her method of proceeding. Your argument, no matter how cogent, will not succeed unless your paper is written well.

CHAPTER 12 EXERCISES

1. Examine the introduction of any short story to show how it works. How does it introduce themes that are picked up later?

2. Look at the concluding section of a short story you are studying. How was the conclusion set up in the earlier part of the story? What feeling does it leave the reader with?

3. Discuss the use of repetitive words or images in any short story you have studied. Why does the author deliberately stress these elements?

4. In any short story or play you are studying, what techniques are used to create the sense of a unified body of work?

12

Sample Literary Essay—MLA Style

The following is a sample literary essay whose format conforms to the new MLA guidelines. Refer to Chapter 14, Documenting—MLA, APA, and University of Chicago Guidelines, p. 135, for more information. Study it carefully, noting the format and the method of documentation.

↕ 2.5 cm

↕ 1.5 cm

L. Phillips 1 ——— Pages are
numbered in
upper right-han
corner. There
no need for a
title page.

Lorna Stevens

Professor Desai

English 120

14 March 2004

Reading and Writing as a Leap of Faith: Yann Martel's *Life of Pi* ——— Underline or
italicize titles
published
books.

Double-space. ———

Indent 1.3 cm ——— When Canadian novelist Yann Martel won the Man Booker Prize in October
or five spaces.
2002, he thanked his readers for "having met his imagination halfway" ("Joyful").

Indeed, reading a magic-realist fable like *Life of Pi* involves something akin to a leap of

faith for readers, in several ways: first, the story tests the credulity of readers by

asking them to embrace a surreal parable; second, the story helps readers have faith

in the god of their choice; and third, the story reminds readers that reality is a story

we choose, and it is our responsibility, along with the writer, to pick the better story

between the two options provided for us.

Life of Pi, in Martel's words, is easily summarized:

Indent long ———
quotations
(more than four
lines) 2.6 cm or
ten spaces on
the left-hand
side, and do not
enclose them in
quotation
marks.

The novel is about an Indian family that runs a zoo in India. They decide to ↔ 2.5 cm

emigrate to Canada in the mid-70s because of the political situation in

India. They close down their zoo, sell their animals to zoos in the United

States and since they're all going to the New World, they decide to travel

on the same ship. Alas the ship sinks and there are only five survivors: Pi

Patel, a tiger, an orang-utan, a zebra and a hyena and they all end up on

the same lifeboat and quickly it's just the tiger. So most of the novel is

about the relationship between Pi Patel and the tiger as they drift across

the Pacific for 227 days. ("Ask")

↕ 2.5 cm

2.5 cm

Stevens 2

Martel explains the role of the reader in an interview conducted after he won the literary prize:

> When I started writing I didn't ever imagine that I would have readers. But once I met readers they are now essential. I think a book really comes alive only once it has met a reader. A book in that sense otherwise is 50%—the other 50% is what the reader brings to it—their imagination. ("Ask")

Use shortened title for Web pages if they are listed by title in the Works Cited.

For Martel, it is this interaction between readers and writer that is important. And the role of the writer in coming to grips with the story he is telling is similarly learning to leap into his or her own imagination. In an essay entitled "How I Wrote *Life of Pi,*" Martel describes the arduous journey by which he arrived at the novel as one in which he learned to blend the real and the imagined, the literary and the ordinary in a novel that transcends time and place, in the tradition of magic realism. Martel admits to finding the idea for the plot in a book review of *Max and the Cats,* a novel by Brazilian Moacyr Scliar, an idea which acted on him like "electric caffeine" ("How"). But in addition to this literary influence, Martel needed the inspiration of India, and the painstaking research he conducted in India and Canada, including interviews with zookeepers and zoological studies. For him, even the writing of a book begins first with the social and imaginative interaction of reading, as he recounts. Even though he claims that he began the day in the splendid imagination of asking "OK, what's happening today with my tiger?" ("Yann"), he also defines the work of the novel as fundamentally social.

The novel is a surreal parable that requires imagination on the part of the reader who makes the journey with Pi and Martel. Still, it is a journey grounded in two worlds: one real, the other literary. The real one is significant since Martel reported to interviewers that he "wanted to go against the maxim that writers should only tackle subjects they already know about" ("Martel's"). Besides that, Martel based his

28 cm

22 cm

Stevens 3

research on recognizable literary roots, running the gamut from the story of Noah's ark in the Bible through to *Robinson Crusoe* and *The Old Man and the Sea* and other stories of shipwreck and disaster, a combination that culminated in what Martel himself whimsically refers to as "Beckett in the Pacific" ("How"). Like Daniel Defoe's *Robinson Crusoe, Life of Pi* explores the journey of one soul towards God, a journey brought about through the catastrophe of shipwreck. Both Crusoe and Pi discover a kind of providence in the way they tell stories of their salvation. As Crusoe recounts,

> How wonderfully we are deliver'd when we know nothing of it. How when we are in (a *Quandary*, as we call it) a Doubt or Hesitation, whether to go this Way, when we intended to go that Way; nay, to go the other Way, yet a strange Impression from the Mind, from we know not what Springs, and by we know not what Power, shall over-rule us to go this Way; and it shall afterwards appear, that had we gone that Way which we should have gone, and even to our own Imagination ought to have gone, we should have been ruin'd and lost. (137)

References made in parentheses usually include page numbers. Omit authors' names if they are clear from the context.

Works of shipwreck and peril at sea, like Gerard Manley Hopkins' poem "The Wreck of the Deutschland," seem to lend themselves to explorations of doubt and despair and of the human being's place in the universe. The theme of faith is omnipresent in such literary precursors. Witness Hopkins' lines:

> Into the snows she sweeps,
>
> Hurling the haven behind,
>
> The Deutschland, on Sunday; and so the sky keeps,
>
> For the infinite air is unkind,
>
> And the sea flint-flake, black-backed in the regular blow,
>
> Sitting Eastnortheast, in cursed quarter, the wind;
>
> Wiry and white-fiery and whirlwind-swivellèd snow
>
> Spins to the widow-making unchilding unfathering deeps. (97–104)

Stevens 4

In his poem, Hopkins explores the mystery of suffering unleashed upon the faithful, who cannot escape the unfathomable wrath of the sea.

Martel's method may involve faith, but it is also his theme since he recounts his protagonist's conversion to Christianity, Islam, and Hinduism all at once, which Bryan Walsh, one reviewer of the novel, describes as "promiscuously religious." When confronted by the priest, the pandit, and the imam when Pi is out walking with his parents, he explains, " 'Bapu Ghandi said, "All religions are true." I just want to love God,' I blurted out, and looked down, red in the face" (*Life* 76). But in the course of researching his novel and reading the foundational texts of Christianity, Hinduism, and Islam, Martel himself arrived at something similar and made his own leap of faith: "I used to dismiss spirituality and religion as being mumbo jumbo for children. . . . However, there's more than just fundamentalism out there when you talk about religion. And that I'm more in tune to now" ("Yann"). Hence, the novel is itself profoundly ambitious and makes the claim that it is "a story that will make you believe in God" (*Life* viii). Indeed, the story of a boy fighting for survival in a lifeboat he shares with a tiger is one that reminds the reader of the importance of faith as a means by which to endure suffering and to understand one's place in the universe. Hence, the last part of Pi's inventory reads like this:

> 1 large bar of dark chocolate
>
> 1 survival manual
>
> 1 compass
>
> 1 notebook with 98 lined pages
>
> 1 boy with a complete set of light clothing but for one lost shoe
>
> 1 spotted hyena
>
> 1 Bengal tiger
>
> 1 lifeboat

Enclose short quotations (no more than four lines) in quotation marks, and include them in the body of the essay.

Use a period and three dots (with spaces between) to indicate words left out of the end of a sentence.

1 ocean

1 God (*Life* 162)

The inventory leaps from the mundane to the transcendent, but Pi is matter-of-fact in his approach to the list. There is in his view one God, even though he cries out in distress to "Jesus, Mary, Muhammad, and Vishnu" (*Life* 166).

Of course, the trouble with the leap of faith, even in the novel, is that not everyone is willing to make it. When Pi tells his fabulous story to Mr. Tomohiro Okamoto and Mr. Atsuro Chiba, they refuse to believe it, and they choose instead a "nasty, brutish and short" version that Pi makes up for their benefit. Pi challenges them with these words:

> "You can't prove which story is true and which is not. You must take my word for it." . . .
>
> "In both stories the ship sinks, my entire family dies, and I suffer." . . .
>
> "So tell me, since it makes no factual difference to you and you can't prove the question either way, which story do you prefer? Which is the better story, the story with animals or the story without animals?" (*Life* 352)

The animals, whether allegorical in intent or not, do, according to Martel, represent human traits: "the zebra, the hyena and the orang-utan . . . arose naturally, each one a function of a human trait I wanted to embody, the hyena cowardliness, the orang-utan maternal instincts and the zebra exoticism" ("How"). One can, if one wishes, subscribe to the view that the zebra is the Taiwanese sailor, the orang-utan is Pi's mother, and the cannibalistic cook is the hyena, but that is just one way of reading the story, and not, in Pi's view, the better story.

Although they agree that the story with animals is the better story, the last word is given to the other, worse story, minus the animals except for the incontrovertible Bengal tiger. The leap of faith, in Martel's estimation, requires that we

Stevens 6

choose the better story, select the one more aesthetically pleasing, perhaps the one easier to live with. This view of reality accords with something that Martel explains in one of his interviews: "To me a belief is something you cling to and faith is a letting go. Not only in religious terms—when you love someone, you let go, you trust them. When you love a system or anything, you let go—that's faith. When you have a belief you cling" ("Ask"). So Martel brings the reader round to the kind of faith that involves letting go, but to no particular system of belief. For him, as he explains in the same interview, each religious perspective is a kind of cuisine, any of which can sustain life, but all of which are very different.

In some respects, Martel's *Life of Pi* is the quintessence of Canadian fiction, if one sees Canada, as Martel does, as a mosaic rather than a melting pot, the image typically used of America. As Martel comments, "Canada is very open to other voices. . . . the world is in Canada. It's a country with two official languages but no official culture. So people from all over the world are welcome to come and tell their own stories" ("Ask"). His study of the boy in lifeboat demonstrates that all creatures from all cultures, everywhere, are in the same boat and use their imaginations to leap beyond the ordinary to tell their own stories of life, with luck, as imaginatively and courageously as Martel's does.

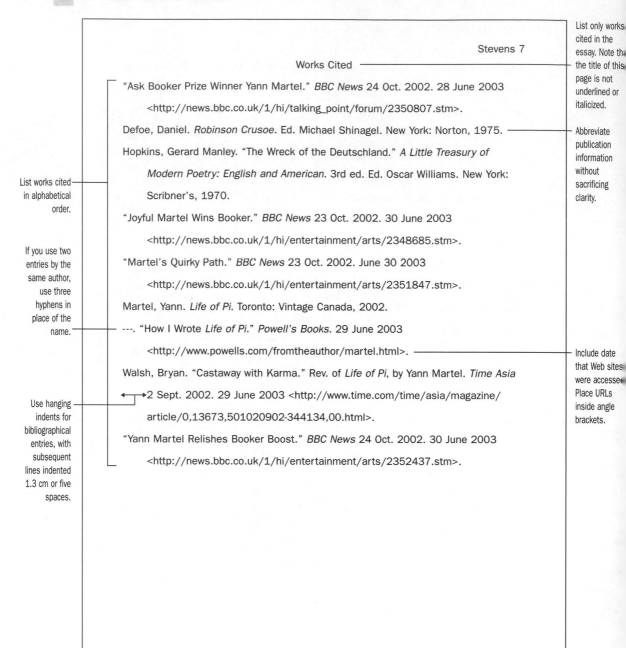

Stevens 7

Works Cited

"Ask Booker Prize Winner Yann Martel." *BBC News* 24 Oct. 2002. 28 June 2003

    <http://news.bbc.co.uk/1/hi/talking_point/forum/2350807.stm>.

Defoe, Daniel. *Robinson Crusoe*. Ed. Michael Shinagel. New York: Norton, 1975.

Hopkins, Gerard Manley. "The Wreck of the Deutschland." *A Little Treasury of*

    Modern Poetry: English and American. 3rd ed. Ed. Oscar Williams. New York:

    Scribner's, 1970.

"Joyful Martel Wins Booker." *BBC News* 23 Oct. 2002. 30 June 2003

    <http://news.bbc.co.uk/1/hi/entertainment/arts/2348685.stm>.

"Martel's Quirky Path." *BBC News* 23 Oct. 2002. June 30 2003

    <http://news.bbc.co.uk/1/hi/entertainment/arts/2351847.stm>.

Martel, Yann. *Life of Pi*. Toronto: Vintage Canada, 2002.

---. "How I Wrote *Life of Pi*." *Powell's Books*. 29 June 2003

    <http://www.powells.com/fromtheauthor/martel.html>.

Walsh, Bryan. "Castaway with Karma." Rev. of *Life of Pi*, by Yann Martel. *Time Asia*

    2 Sept. 2002. 29 June 2003 <http://www.time.com/time/asia/magazine/

    article/0,13673,501020902-344134,00.html>.

"Yann Martel Relishes Booker Boost." *BBC News* 24 Oct. 2002. 30 June 2003

    <http://news.bbc.co.uk/1/hi/entertainment/arts/2352437.stm>.

List only works cited in the essay. Note that the title of this page is not underlined or italicized.

Abbreviate publication information without sacrificing clarity.

List works cited in alphabetical order.

If you use two entries by the same author, use three hyphens in place of the name.

Use hanging indents for bibliographical entries, with subsequent lines indented 1.3 cm or five spaces.

Include date that Web sites were accessed. Place URLs inside angle brackets.

The Book Review

Having been unpopular in high school is not just cause for book publication.
—FRAN LEBOWITZ

Most of the book reviews you will be asked to write have a more specific purpose than the kind you see in newspapers and magazines. You will be asked not only to report on the content of a book and to evaluate it, but also to analyze it in terms of its contribution to the discipline. A book review gives you a chance to examine one potential source in a given area, often as a prelude to writing a research essay. Like any other essay, it demands a thesis statement that clarifies your reaction to the book.

If you are asked to review a book as part of a course requirement, select a book with a subject matter that appeals to you and with which you feel comfortable. Proceed according to the following stages:

1. Describe or summarize the contents of the book.
2. Describe and evaluate its tactics.
3. Consider its contribution.
4. Illustrate your argument.
5. Maintain your critical balance.

To write a focused book review, remember your role as a fair-minded and helpful critic.

The Role of the Book Review

Like other essays, the book review's form is determined by its readers and its function.

AUDIENCE: someone who has not read the book, but who is interested in its subject matter and has some background in the discipline

PURPOSE: to summarize, analyze, and evaluate a book, and to show your critical acumen in so doing; then, to recommend, to criticize, or to dismiss the book according to careful judgment

Describe the book

1. Determine the thesis of the book (if it is a critical text), the theme (or general meaning) of the book (if it is not), and the audience for whom the book is intended.
2. Summarize the book's contents briefly, without giving the show away.
3. Use the book's preface, introduction, and table of contents as a rough guide for your discussion of the work.
4. Discuss the general purpose of the book, without getting caught up in too much detail.

Example   Neil Postman, in his book *Teaching as a Conserving Activity* (1979), argues that the function of formal education should be to counteract the biases of the culture, rather than to reinforce them. To illustrate this point, he focuses on the pervasive influence of television and other media and recommends that education teach society to be more critical of the media. Postman intends this book to be a modification of his earlier work, *Teaching as a Subversive Activity* (1969), in which he advocated innovation. In this book, his argument is that education must work against the unthinking forces of change that prevail in the culture as a whole.

Describe and evaluate the book's tactics

1. If the book is a critical text, describe its method of argument. If it is not a critical text, describe the techniques by which the material is presented.
2. Note how well the book does what it sets out to do.
3. Note what else might have been done or what might have been done differently.
4. Note why you liked (or disliked) the book.

Example   The book sets out to show how television has affected our way of seeing the world. It argues that television has made us less conscious of the past, that it has lowered our attention span, and that it has made us more susceptible to "quick-fix" solutions to problems—as a consequence of too much exposure to television commercials, which reduce life to shallow and easily remedied problems.

Postman insists that the way to counter this problem is to teach people about the media and about how the media alter our perceptions of things. He argues that the development of strong critical-thinking skills will put a stop to the passivity and superficiality of the cultural attitudes provoked by television viewing.

The chief flaw in Postman's approach is his own lack of sources. Given that he advocates critical appraisal of the means by which information is conveyed, the onus is on him to show that some of the effects of television that he lists are, in fact, present.

Consider the book's contribution

1. Compare the book to others you have read with a similar thesis or theme.
2. Ask yourself what you learned from the book.

Example   *Teaching as a Conserving Activity* seems to present a useful corrective to the problems of value in education today. Postman points to some real dangers created by the commercialization of the media and emphasizes the role that education must play in maintaining old values in society as well as espousing new ones.

Illustrate your argument

1. At every step of the way, use snippets from the book to back up your position and to give the reader a taste of the work.
2. Include both positive and negative illustrations, unless, of course, your review is entirely positive or negative (rarely the case).
3. Be sure to integrate your illustrations from the book as part of your argument, and not simply as decoration.

Although some of the charges Postman makes about the negative effects of television are justified—such as its invasion of privacy and its stress on seeing things from the outside, superficially rather than analytically—some of his charges are exaggerated. When he claims that television is not analytic because it is "picture-centered,"[1] he argues that we cannot prove a picture true or false the way we can a proposition. But Postman here is comparing apples and oranges. Words are not always used to create propositions either; sometimes they tell stories, just as pictures do, and these stories cannot be categorized as being true or false either. The fault, if there is one, does not lie with the medium, but instead, perhaps, with the use to which it is put. In other words, television in itself does not automatically lead to a deterioration in critical-thinking skills.

Example

Maintain your critical balance

1. Don't be intimidated by ideas just because they are in print. Your object is to assess the merits of the book in question.
2. Don't be too harsh in your judgments. Remember that the author deserves mercy as well as justice.

Ultimately, Postman's position that education should move to counteract some of the biases of the culture is a valid one: some of his arguments for it, however, need more support and closer critical scrutiny than he has given them.

Example

CHAPTER 12 EXERCISES

Read the following book review and analyze its structure, using the questions that follow.

Moonbeam on a Cat's Ear by Canadian author/illustrator Marie-Louise Gay is a highly recommended addition to any collection of children's literature. In 1987, it was awarded a well-deserved Amelia Frances-Howard Gibbon Medal from the Canadian Library Association. Aimed at the preschool audience, the text is sparse and characterized by slight rhyme, and the illustrations are rounded, colourful, lively, and detailed. Specifically, *Moonbeam on a Cat's Ear* is the ideal bedtime book for children, and the illustrations and text are integrated with this purpose in mind.

Like the large-bodied, broad-faced, tiny-limbed characters in her other books (*Lizzy's Lion*, *Rainy Day Magic*, *Angel and the Polar Bear*) who embark on amazing journeys before returning to reality, Rosie and Toby Toby awake from their beds and journey through the sea and sky on the moon with a cat and a mouse before they return to their beds and sleep.

All of the action in the story is carried by the illustrations. The pictures show a strong substory not necessarily indicated by the text. The story begins by describing the illustrated scenes of the sleeping cat, then switches as Toby Toby enters Rosie's room and entreats her to go on an adventure. As Toby Toby begins musing about their plans with increasing excitement, the pictures show the characters actually doing the things he describes. This process escalates to the point of the characters being in the sky surrounded by lightning bolts, when Rosie says, "Oh Toby Toby it's so frightening!" The next page shows them both asleep on the bed. At this point, the text asks a direct question of the child:

> Was it a dream
> or did they really try
> to steal the moon right out of the sky?

As the illustrations show a stronger story than the text (just as the imagination is sometimes stronger than reality), the question posed is answered for the child by the final illustration of the cat and mouse still seated on the moon in the sky. Flipping back to the previous page confirms the animals' absence from the bedroom.

Through her use of such ambiguities, Gay reveals great insight into the minds of children. She omits adults from the story and focuses directly on the problems facing a child being put to bed. Children's bodies are relatively still (like the text), but their imaginations are alive and travelling (like the pictures). When the characters return to earth and are shown sleeping, a sense of calm is produced, but the last picture and teasing question allow something for children to think about as they fall asleep.

The author uses colours and techniques conducive to sleep. The predominant colour in *Moonbeam on a Cat's Ear* is blue. This, combined with a margin of white space surrounding each page, creates, even in the most active scenes, a quiet mood appropriate for bedtime. Marie-Louise Gay, in an interview with Marie Davis, speaks of the story as a "moon book": "The quietness, the serenity in *Moonbeam* is also due to the contrast between the bluish light and the stark white light. Everything seems to float in space." She speaks of other ways in which she invokes this mood: "I had tiny little borders, but they're not too intrusive. They have little things happening in them, but they're much calmer, like little paintings" (Davis 81). In painting the scenes, Gay has used a somewhat unusual technique that, while still using bright colours and distinct lines, produces a soft, dreamlike quality. By putting a white paint mixture on the gesso board and letting it dry with brush strokes in it, Gay achieves a ridge-like texture when she adds ink and watercolour on top.

Gay's use of perspective is cinematic in some respects. The book opens with a close-up of a cat's ear against a night sky, and then on the next page, the viewer sees the cat sleeping on the bed inside underneath a window. The third picture backs off even further, showing the mouse of which the cat is dreaming and Rosie in bed. Next, with a knock on the door, comes a shot of a previously unseen corner of the room, with a close-up of Rosie's startled face on the facing page. The next page shows the distanced darkened shadow of Toby Toby in the open doorway, contrasted in the next frame with a lightened close-up revealing Toby Toby with his flaming red hair and red pyjamas to match. The following two-page frame shows the joined shadowed backs of the figures of Toby Toby and Rosie as they exit out the front door into the night. In order not to disturb the flow, Gay shows the open door of Rosie's bedroom with the emerging figures of the cat and the mouse. The remaining pictures are shown at a middle range. The ninth picture is interesting since it is drawn looking down on Toby Toby as he reaches up from the top of the apple tree toward the unseen moon while the diminished figures of Rosie, the cat, and the mouse look upward. The final picture of the sleeping cat and mouse on the moon is from a distance and is in contrast to the opening close-up of the cat's ear.

Frames are used interestingly in this picture book. Gay's frames span the length of two pages for peaceful scenes and scenes in which the two characters are together. Single-page frames are used for abrupt actions, like the knock on the door, Rosie's startled face, or Toby Toby's darkened shadow. When Rosie becomes afraid in the storm, the picture is continued on two pages, but is split down the middle by the white of the inside margins.

Overspill is also used to dramatic effect. In overspill, illustrators extend drawings beyond their usual confines to provide viewers with a sense of parallel stories and/or additional dimensions. In *Moonbeam on a Cat's Ear*, the amount of overspill parallels the amount of action in the illustration. The quiet scenes in the beginning contain only a minimal amount of overspill, such as the butterfly wings, the tip of the moon, or the edge of the pillow. The extension of Toby Toby's hair over the border emphasizes the text below the picture, "with the bright red hair." As Rosie and Toby Toby go outside, their shadows in the doorway extend outside the frame to the bottom of the page. Change in lighting in Gay's work represents a change in the tempo of a story, a graphic depiction of what is happening inside the mind of a child. Because of the importance of the shift of the pictures away from the text in this story, a high degree of overspill exists. The overspill becomes more frequent as the action continues outside, for example, with the top of the apple tree (to emphasize height), the tips of the grounded moon boat (to emphasize length), the top of the sail, and then the lightning bolts, until the children are back in bed, when the overspill diminishes.

The amount of detail in the text serves many functions. It creates a sense of immediacy or realism. Examples from *Moonbeam on a Cat's Ear* include the shadows of moonlight, the messy state of the toys, scarves, coats, and shoes, and the open scissors beside bits of paper on the table top. Detail also helps create a sense of movement. In Gay's story, movement is always present, whether in the slight blowing of curtains, the flying of moths or the leaping of fish, the falling off of a slipper, or the streaks of movement behind the lightning bolts or the children as they fall.

The details also enhance the sense of flow and connection in the pictures. The cat and the mouse are present on every page, if one looks hard enough. (So is Toby Toby's frog until it wisely jumps off when they leave the water.) The moon appears on almost all the pages, whether it's in the sky, on Rosie's pyjamas, in the margins, or on the picture hanging on the bedroom wall. Even the mouse, dreamed by the cat, dreams himself of little cheese moons. Likewise, lightning bolts accompany the knock on the door; they are on the wallpaper, in the margins, and in the sky. The airplanes on Toby Toby's pyjamas are also found in the margins; the bed sheet turns into a sail, then back into the bed sheet again. Detail can enhance the flow of the story in even subtler ways, such as in the repetition of the shape of the cat's ear in the curtains or in the butterfly wings.

12

The detail in the borders has a more formalized structure. The tiny pictures help the flow of the words and alert the viewer to related details in the bigger illustration. When Toby Toby is high in the tree, there are images of rockets and kites in the margin. When the moon-boat leaves the sea for the sky, fish are shown leaping amongst clouds. The borders reinforce, but they also foreshadow. On the first page, the sequence of the phases of the moon is shown in the border. Apples are shown on the border of the page before the apple tree is shown. The cat and the mouse peek around the picture in the border of the page before they are shown sleeping on the moon on the last page.

This examination of *Moonbeam on a Cat's Ear* suggests some criteria for deciding a book's place in a collection of children's literature. One may want to consider Canadian content or medals awarded. One may also want to ponder intended audience, purpose, or message, and how well that purpose is achieved. The colour and quality of illustrations are important. As well, the integration between a text and its illustrations is vital to the coherence of a story intended for children. Here, technical issues like detail, style, innovation, consistency of scale, arrangement of text and pictures, flow, length, and readability come into play. The author's understanding of children and their interests is crucial if a picture book is to reach its intended audience.

1. How does the essay show the integration of text and illustrations?
2. What kinds of support does the essay writer use?
3. Analyze the strengths of the introduction and conclusion.

The Research Essay

I write in order to attain that feeling of tension relieved and function achieved which a cow enjoys on giving milk.
—H. L. MENCKEN

A research paper is a formal essay based on your exploration of other people's ideas, rather than simply an analysis of your own thoughts. Although both the expository essay and the persuasive essay may use source material to some extent, the research essay is unique. Its purpose is to formulate a thesis based on a survey and assessment of source material.

The following steps are essential to the development of a research paper:

1. Mapping out the area of exploration
2. Finding and using library resources
3. Going through the research process
4. Drawing up an outline
5. Recording source material
6. Writing and documenting your essay

The Role of the Research Paper

A research paper must be modified to suit its readers and its special aims.

AUDIENCE: an informed, curious reader, whom you address on a professional level

PURPOSE: to demonstrate your skill in exploring, evaluating, and recording source material in a manner that shows how you have synthesized it

Mapping out the area of exploration

Before you begin to explore the library, you must find a subject area that is appropriate for investigation. A good research topic will have the following characteristics:

1. SCOPE. Your subject should be neither too broad nor too narrow in its focus.

sleep—too broad

why we sleep—not enough research material available

what we now know about sleep and sleep disorders—more focused

Example

12

2. SUPPORT. Your subject must be treated in written sources that are available to you. For example, a recent subject may not be a good choice because there may not yet be enough written about it. Also, remember that your sources must be treated objectively, so that the final paper reflects what is known about a subject, rather than just what you believe to be true about a subject. For example, your discussion of sleep must attempt to integrate the reader's questions about sleep with what advances the research has made.

You can also find support for your arguments by conducting a search of Internet resources. Remember, though, that the Internet is best used as a supplement to your use of written sources. Overreliance on the Internet may lead to a bibliography that is current but that does not take into account the history of your subject matter. Also, the Internet, as an unregulated source of information, does not always provide you with the landmark studies in a particular field. Don't assume that everything you need to know is online.

3. SIGNIFICANCE. Find something that you want to explore and that needs exploration. It would not, for instance, be enough to announce that you were going to show what new understanding scientists have reached in the study of brain chemicals affecting sleep. You must explain how these chemicals operate.

Finding and using library resources

While the Internet is a very useful resource, libraries are indispensable for the exploration of your research topic. Make sure you know where these items are in your educational institution's library:

1. the circulation and reference desks
2. reference books
3. periodicals and their indexes
4. the card catalogue and computer card catalogue
5. CD-ROMs, microform, and online databases

6. sources available through library terminals
7. government documents

If you don't know where all of these items are in your library, take a tour, or make an appointment with a reference librarian and find out. If you are well-acquainted with your library, reference works like encyclopedias and bibliographies will be easy to find, as will periodicals, particularly if you begin your search by looking at these volumes:

The Reader's Guide to Periodical Literature. New York: Wilson, 1900 to date. (Also available on CD-ROM and online.)
Magazine Index
Academic Index
Business Index
Humanities Index (scholarly articles from 1974 to date)
Social Sciences Index (scholarly articles from 1974 to date)

Online information services include items like the following, to name just a few of the available options:

ERIC: educational materials from the Educational Resources Information Center
Historical Abstracts: abstracts of periodicals in history
MLA International Bibliography: index of books and articles published about modern languages, linguistics, and literature
Philosopher's Index: a guide to books and periodicals in philosophy

GATHERING LIBRARY SOURCES: CHECKLIST OF ACTIVITIES

1. Check reference works about research materials, such as the *Readers' Guide to Periodical Literature, Essay and General Literature Index,* and others specific to subject areas, such as *Business Periodicals Index, Social Sciences Index,* and *Humanities Index.*
2. Check bibliographies specific to your field of study, for example, *MLA International Bibliography* for research into language and literature.
3. Check guides to abstracts, such as *Periodical Abstracts,* or those that are field-specific, such as *Historical Abstracts, Humanities Abstracts,* or *Sociological Abstracts.*
4. Look for specific guides to research, such as James L. Harner's *Literary Research Guide,* or similar guides devoted to particular areas of study.
5. Read general articles in general or specialized encyclopedias, like *The Film Encyclopedia,* or related reference works, like English-language dictionaries or dictionaries in specialized areas of research like *The Dictionary of Art.*
6. Depending on the nature of your research, investigate biographies, such as *The Canadian Who's Who,* almanacs, such as *The World Almanac and Book of Facts,* and statistical reference works, such as those published by Statistics Canada.

7. Seek out print reference works in the library's reference room, or take advantage of online and CD-ROM databases. The latter allow simple electronic searches through many volumes at once and tend to be updated at subscribing libraries, so they are more current. In addition, you can print information you find or download it without the need for painstaking copying. Many electronic sources not only find names of works but also allow you to access full-text electronic versions, often from home as well as in the library. You can search online by author, by title, by subject, or in more detail, a convenience that will allow you to narrow your focus as you go along.

8. Do a search of the card catalogue or the online catalogue of your particular library. This step will allow you to find local materials immediately, without recourse to inter-library loans.

9. Find available journals in your library or online periodicals and newspapers to which your library subscribes.

10. Investigate subscription services, such as InfoTrac, to which your library may subscribe. InfoTrac, an online library subscription service from Thomson Learning, is available with a password at < http://www.infotrac-college. com > and provides access to many full-text articles from journals, newspapers, and magazines.

11. Photocopy or print articles or book title pages related to your topic, noting their sources completely for inclusion in your bibliography later.

12. Find non-print material, such as microform, on your topic. Microform is a good source for back issues of journals, newspapers, and magazines stored in your library.

13. Request interlibrary loan books or articles as needed.

14. Conduct your own search of the World Wide Web, paying special attention to gateway sites, such as Voice of the Shuttle and The Social Science Information Gateway, which you may find using a search engine such as Google or Yahoo! to direct you. Similarly, these sites will help you break down a larger subject area into its component parts. Remember to bookmark or otherwise record sites that you use for inclusion into your bibliography later.

KEEPING TRACK OF SOURCES

1. Record everything you need to find a source again, including page numbers.
2. Note what you found useful and why.
3. Keep track of your reading, quoting, and paraphrasing.
4. Put sources in alphabetical order for easy entry into a bibliography.

Doing research on the Internet

The sheer convenience of the World Wide Web makes it a desirable research tool. It is often more up-to-date than printed sources, and is able to combine many different media. It also has a broad range, including popular items as well as scholarly ones. There are, of course, disadvantages to the Internet as well. For one thing, materials are fluid there; they may change without warning or disappear altogether, or they may look different on different browsers. Because they allow anyone to publish, without the intervention of gatekeepers such as publishers, they are more democratic and broader in their range. Everyone from expert to amateur may be on the Web, so be aware that many resources are not in any way subject to peer review to set standards for the work that is produced. This, of course, means that it is up to you to decide how you evaluate the materials that you encounter on the Web.

You must, of course, also take your instructor's preferences into account. If he or she does not want you to use the Web for a particular assignment, respect that request. Most instructors, however, are open to the Internet as a possible resource, provided that you keep good track of what you found and where you found it, and that you apply certain standards to your use of source material. Don't neglect online library resources! The library pays subscription fees for a number of authoritative, up-to-the-minute resources that can answer your questions more reliably than a mere cursory personal search on the Internet. Remember, too, that the Internet is best for very current, popular topics, but less likely to provide definitive information for more traditional areas. And unless you know a good deal about your subject before you engage in an Internet search, you could be easily misled.

EVALUATING WEB SOURCES. Here are some questions you might ask of a site you are considering as a source for your research:

1. Who is the author? How well known is he or she?
2. Does the site or the author have a professional or academic connection?
3. Is the site sponsored by an academic institution?
4. Is the site objective, or does it have obvious bias?
5. Is the site well designed?
6. Is the site updated?
7. Have articles on the Web been peer reviewed?

CONDUCTING WEB SEARCHES. Many search engines are available on the Internet. Yahoo! and Google are among the best because they are directories organized in a hierarchical index by humans who provide descriptions and reviews of the listed sites. Other search engines, like AltaVista, may produce more hits because they attempt to catalogue every known site. To narrow down a search on AltaVista, however, it is possible to choose a particular domain—say, for example, only sites that end in ".edu" to focus especially on educational sites.

Advanced Web searches demand more than simple keywords if you need to keep the search focused. If you use three keywords, such as "apples oranges bananas," you will get all the sites that have any one of those words in them. If you type the word AND between them, the engine will select only those sites that contain all three words. If you type the word NOT between "apples" and "oranges," you will get sites with the word "apples" but not those that contain the word "oranges." If you want a search engine to look for three or four words exactly as they appear together, you should put them in quotation marks, as in "deep dish apple pie." When you conduct a name search, on the other hand, most search engines assume that two capitalized words together (Winston Churchill) will appear in that order and are, in fact, a name. You may need to experiment, however. Every search engine has its own approach to advanced searches.

KEEPING TRACK OF WEB SOURCES. You need to collect the following information, if it is recorded on the Web site: the author's name, the title of the page, the title of the larger work that the Web page comes from, the publication date of the page, the URL or Web address, and the date that you accessed it.

You can, of course, bookmark relevant files—or save bookmarked files to a diskette if you are working at a public computer—but that may not save all the relevant information if the page happens to undergo changes or be removed from the Web altogether. You can also copy and paste the relevant information to your word-processing program, to be printed later. Another option is to save the entire page to a diskette for safekeeping, something that guarantees that you will find it again, should you need to.

It's not a bad idea to keep a written log of what sources you consulted on the Web. One safeguard against the charge of plagiarism is a written record of your thinking at every stage, from brainstorming through to first and second drafts. Many instructors ask to see this record as a verification of your participation in the writing process.

STAYING HONEST. Remember that, even though you can easily copy and paste someone else's words from the Internet directly into your paper, you must acknowledge them. It is a good idea to use a different font for words that you have pasted into your paper, so that you are always clear about which words you are borrowing and which words are your own. Remember that if it is easy for you to find material on the Web, it is also relatively easy for an instructor to find out if the words are really yours. Search engines can be quite useful for that purpose.

For materials to be published on the Web

If you will be publishing your work on the Web, be prepared to ask permission if you feel you need to use materials from a source that constitute more than what is considered "fair use." A small citation is usually considered acceptable fair use, but if you want to quote something in its entirety—say, a song—it may well require copyright permission. You don't need to request permission for excerpts in papers submitted to an instructor.

Going through the research process

Read widely at first to locate the best sources. Then read deeply in order to get at the heart of the matter. Explore the topic with your tentative thesis in mind, revising it as you go along. A good researcher moves from the general to the specific.

1. Find general information in an encyclopedia, dictionary, or other reference book, either in print or online. Remember, though, that these general sources only scratch the surface.

2. Find information in the library computer system, microfiche, or card catalogue. Look under the subject heading or use the names of authors or titles that you have found in any of the encyclopedias you consulted.

3. Consult periodical indexes for further information. Often periodicals, particularly those online, will give you more current material than is available in books. *The Canadian Periodical Index (CPI)* lists all articles published in Canadian journals for a given year.

4. Examine your sources with your specific topic in mind. Check the table of contents and the index of the books you find to search for suitable material.

5. Note down bibliographical information for any of the sources you consult. Small note cards (7.6 cm × 12.7 cm) (3″ × 5″) are useful. Record the library call numbers for your sources.

6. Follow the rules of documentation that apply to your discipline at this stage, and you will save time and trouble toward the end. Check to see which style of documentation your instructor prefers (whether APA, MLA, University of Chicago, or other style) and make your notes accordingly.

SAMPLE BIBLIOGRAPHY CARD

Gibaldi, Joseph.
<u>*MLA Handbook for Writers of Research*</u>
<u>*Papers.*</u> *6th ed. New York: Modern Language*
Association, 2003.

LB 2369.M57

Drawing up an outline

An outline for a research essay takes its direction from your preparatory reading. Follow the instructions in Chapter 4 on how to design an outline with these precautions in mind:

1. Your outline must be flexible enough to accommodate all the information pertinent to your thesis statement.

2. Your outline must be fair and must reflect an objective approach to the material.

3. Your outline must be firmly established in your mind so that it does not attempt to include more material than can be adequately handled within the limits of the assignment.

4. Your outline is designed to be used. In the case of a research essay, the outline dictates the direction of your note-taking. It should help you stay on track in your explorations and help you limit yourself to what is possible.

Recording source material

Like an explorer, you must accurately record the steps of your journey. You need a system. Here are some suggestions to simplify the task:

1. Take notes on large index cards (10.2 cm × 15.2 cm [4″ × 6″] should do).
2. Identify the source on each card as briefly as possible. Usually, a last name and a page number will do.
3. Quote or paraphrase as the occasion demands (remember that too much quotation is dull). In addition, paraphrasing as you read will help you make sense of the material.
4. Limit yourself generally to one note per card to make sorting easier. This tactic will keep you from unconsciously relying too heavily on any one source.
5. Sort through your material at intervals to decide where it will fit into your working outline. If it won't fit, revise the outline or throw the irrelevant information out—no matter how attractive it is.
6. Copy accurately. If the passage is very lengthy, photocopy it to ensure precision, but be aware of copyright laws.

WHY BOTHER? Note-taking is such a painful chore that it is tempting not to do it. Don't succumb to the temptation. Note-taking is an essential part of research. It will help you determine the value of your sources. Ask these questions as you take notes:

1. Are the sources reliable?
2. Are they recent?
3. Are the sources themselves respected and well reviewed by others?
4. What are your own reactions to the sources?

This last point shows the need to record your own reactions to source material as you proceed. Add these ideas to your note cards to help you develop ideas later. You can differentiate them from source material by adding your initials.

Remember, the object of research is not to record facts, but to evaluate and synthesize your findings about an unsettled matter according to the viewpoint or thesis of your paper.

Writing and documenting your essay

Prepare an outline, complete with intended patterns of argument, as suggested in Chapters 4 and 5 of this text. Then, write the first draft of your essay's introduction, body, and conclusion. This time, however, you must make sure to acknowledge your debt to any source as you write. One good way to do so is to include an abbreviated version of the source in parentheses immediately following the quoted matter in your essay.

Example   Ward Churchill, for example, writes about the disservice done to Native Americans who are obliged to tolerate the trivialization of their heritage, when confronted by names of sports teams like the "Braves," the "Chiefs," or the "Indians." He dismisses the view that these names and symbolic representations are just harmless and argues instead that they are offensive to the people in question. Just as we would not tolerate "nicknames" used in a trivial way for other groups, so we should not accept sports' appropriation of these names to mere games. The names are important, and they demonstrate a level of injustice that cuts deep in North American culture. As Churchill claims, indigenous groups "have the right to expect—indeed, to demand— . . . that such practices finally be brought to a halt" (1993, p. 43).

This example shows abbreviation in the APA style of documentation. It is also an example of the benefits of good preliminary note-taking.

For more information on documentation in MLA, APA, and traditional footnote style, see Chapter 14.

Maintaining Control

The special challenge of the research paper is to handle your source material in a controlled way. To control your research essay, remember these guidelines:

1. KEEP IT LIMITED. Qualify the aim of your essay and stay within the limits of the thesis and the assignment.

2. KEEP IT CONCISE. Avoid pretentious diction. (See Chapter 3 for more information.)

3. KEEP IT FORMAL. This suggestion may even mean that you should not use the pronoun "I," in order to maintain objectivity (although it is often acceptable to do so). Ask your instructor for specific advice on this point.

4. KEEP IT CLEAN. Small errors reduce the essay's credibility as an accurate record of research.

5. MAKE IT YOURS. Don't lose yourself in assembled bits of research. Assimilate the material. Learn from it. What you include and how you use it determine your success as a researcher. Passing off information as your own constitutes plagiarism. Whether intentional or not, it is a serious academic offence to be avoided at all costs.

6. AVOID PLAGIARISM.
   - Distinguish between a paraphrase and an exact quotation as you make notes, to avoid using instances of exact wording without acknowledging the source.
   - Make sure to list sources and to present materials in differing fonts as you copy and paste from the Internet.

- Be sure to acknowledge someone else's wording.
- Be sure to acknowledge someone else's thinking.
- Be sure to acknowledge the source of any facts that are not unarguably public knowledge.
- Keep separate your ideas, your notes on others' ideas, and exact words and phrases that you borrow.
- Check with your instructor when in doubt.

Sample Research Essay—APA Style

The following is a sample research essay whose format conforms to the new APA guidelines. Study it carefully, noting the format and the method of documentation.

12

Use abbreviated title as page header throughout essay.

Multiculturalism 1

Number all pages in the top right corner of the page.

Multiculturalism and the Hyphenated Canadian

David Bharaj

Sociology 100

Professor Woodman

2.5 cm

Multiculturalism 2

Multiculturalism and the Hyphenated Canadian ——————

The title of the paper should be typed at the top of this page, below the page header, centred, and double-spaced.

   Multiculturalism has become increasingly seen as the best approach to dealing with the diversity of populations that make up Canada. Canadians frequently see this "mosaic" approach to diversity of race, religion, and culture as a more acceptable way of dealing with diversity than what is commonly characterized as the "melting pot" of American culture. Canadians consequently often pride themselves on this stress on uniqueness rather than on the hierarchical perspective of cultures that assume superiority over other groups.

   It is a convention of journalism that supports this attitude toward cultural diversity to identify members of certain racial, religious, or other minority groups as unique. They are typically described in Canadian newspapers as "Asian-Canadians" or "Irish-Canadians" to mark their uniqueness, without, it is hoped, any attempt either to assimilate or to stereotype them. But does this conventional way of naming particular groups of others actually contribute to the removal of stereotypes or, in some ways, contribute to them? The notion of hyphenated identity, in some respects, seems to

2.5 cm lead to stereotyping certain groups and to creating false barriers between individuals, 2.5 cm

at least as many of the affected members of these groups themselves report.

   Much of the question of identification depends on the individuals themselves. If one is perceived as an "insider" or member of a particular group, then that person is free to identify him or herself; others, however, may not be so empowered. Similarly, attitudes toward a group ought to be in the control of the group itself. Labels and perceptions ought to remain in the control of such "insider" members, rather than being appropriated by others. An example will make this position clearer:

Indent long quotations 1.3 cm or five spaces.

        The writers of the CBC Radio program Dead Dog Café, a program representing native culture in a humorous fashion, mentioned that the show

2.5 cm

Multiculturalism 3

often receives letters from listeners saying that if this show is written by non-natives, it is offensive; however, if it is written by natives, it is damn funny. Therefore, we can see how in the minds of many viewers the question of who is undertaking the representation is closely related to the issues surrounding the art object. (Baillargeon, 2000, p. 2) ——————————— Use the abbreviation "p." for page and "pp." for pages.

Many argue that undue focus on race, religion, or unique culture draws unnecessary attention to the differences between people rather than to their similarities. This is one of the claims of Neil Bissoondath in his discussion of what it means to be marginalized. He comments that conversations typically go like this:

"What nationality are you?"

"Canadian."

"No, I mean, what nationality are you *really*?" (1994, p. 111)

Jan Wong reinforces this opinion by relating comments of her schoolmates when she was younger.

Growing up in Montreal in the 1960s, I once called myself a Chinese-Canadian. Perhaps because my classmates always asked me where I was born.

Montreal, I'd reply.

Where were you *really* born? they'd persist.

The Montreal General, I'd say. (1999, p. A22)

Wong's point, like Bissoondath's, is that they are not, and do not want to be considered, "hyphenated Canadians." To hyphenate themselves, they believe, is to acquiesce in a kind of special segregated identity that actually does not accurately describe their identity. Wong reasons that "hyphenating is natural for the first generation, who are still rooted in the old country. It's optional for the second. But by the

Multiculturalism 4

Include page references with direct quotations.

third generation, we're definitely Canadian" (p. A22). Her point is that assimilation in Canada goes on just the same as it does in America, though being part of the melting pot here is clearly a slow process.

Many members of distinct racial, religious, and cultural groups argue that assimilation is the best way for members of particular groups to get a share in the benefits that accrue to the dominant culture. Richard Rodriguez, for example, defends the position in his essay, "Aria," that learning English for a Hispanic child like himself was key to finding a position of authority and power in the dominant English culture of America. Without developing his English to a high degree (and for the most part abandoning his own language), he would have been denied access to the public life of the country to which he and his family had emigrated. In Rodriguez's words,

> Today I hear bilingual educators say that children lose a degree of "individuality" by becoming assimilated into public society. . . . But the bilingualists simplistically scorn the value and necessity of assimilation. They do not seem to realize that while one suffers a diminished sense of *private* individuality by becoming assimilated into public society, such assimilation makes possible the achievement of *public* individuality. (1983, p. 141)

List author's last name and date of publication after the quotation unless one or the other is clear from the context.

What, of course, is essential in all these cases is granting the members of particular groups the right to label themselves and define their own identity. Despite the childhood rhyme's assumption that names are not as dangerous as sticks and stones, one of the problems of visible minorities in Canada and elsewhere is the acquisition of names and labels that are neither suitable nor welcome. Ward Churchill, for example, writes about the disservice done to Native Americans who are obliged to tolerate the trivialization of their heritage, when confronted by names of sports teams like the "Braves," the "Chiefs," or the "Indians." He dismisses the view that these

Multiculturalism 5

names and symbolic representations are just harmless and argues instead that they are offensive to the people in question. Just as we would not tolerate "nicknames" used in a trivial way for other groups, so we should not accept sports' appropriation of these names to mere games. The names are important, and they demonstrate a level of injustice that cuts deep in North American culture (1993, p. 43).

APA encourages writers to include page numbers in this case.

And the problem goes beyond names alone. Many members of visible minorities of race, religion, and culture tell stories of the discrimination they encounter on a regular basis, and their struggle to become accepted as part of the fabric of North American society. In films such as *Masala* (1993), for instance, director Srinivas Krishna recounts the story of a young Indian man's attempts to fit into the culture of Canadians in Toronto, all the time aware that his family does not really belong. The film shows that the family has lost touch with its roots in Indian religion, but that the gap that this deracination has created has not been filled by anything else. The film shows too that mainstream members of Canadian culture are slow to allow the integration of Indian families and individuals into their midst. The hero's family is caught between two conflicting cultures: one that dictates arranged marriages and one that tolerates sex without marriage, neither of which works to the benefit of the new group. The hero, a child of parents killed in the Air India crash, becomes himself a victim of Canadian prejudice and is stabbed in the back by some hoodlums on the street, though his only crime is his attempt to protect a younger member of his family from being hurt. Ironically, his family finds its way into Canadian mainstream culture when his uncle makes a deal with the Canadian government to sell a stamp he collected; he becomes, as a result, the curator of a museum as part of the deal, even though the government had originally tried to swindle him out of his property.

Attempts to accept "mosaic" concepts of different cultures often lead to failure, it seems, if only because some aspects of the immigrant culture are not truly

Multiculturalism 6

accepted; others are condemned immediately as not compatible with North American notions of equality and democracy. Take, for example, the treatment of women in many of the minority cultures. Many argue that the goals of multiculturalism and feminism are doomed to clash. Susan Moller Okin, for instance, argues that "many culturally based customs aim to control women and render them, especially sexually and reproductively, servile to men's desires and interests" (1999). Okin then proceeds to cite a number of practices considered abhorrent in North American culture, and certainly counter to women's rights. These include clitoridectomy, polygamy, the forced marriage of girl children to men selected by their families, and the forced marriage of women to their rapists, practices that continue today in many parts of the world. Unlike some cultural practices, these are unenlightened practices that endanger human rights, though still it is often the pattern of governments not to intervene in some of these customs, in the name of multiculturalism.

Obviously, the notion of multiculturalism is complicated by conflicting attitudes toward women. Issues that relate to human rights, in particular, are not simply matters of cultural tradition that should not be tampered with. Although there is a tendency to welcome a variety of cultures in the name of multiculturalism, it is important to recognize that all practices of different races, religions, and cultures are not as simple as an international smorgasbord of dishes. Some cultural practices, such as those that endanger the lives and rights of women, should not be welcome at the table.

The acceptance of different customs in the name of multiculturalism is evidently a more complex issue than current attitudes of "political correctness" would seem to suggest. Canadians need to respect the rights of individuals as a priority, rather than simply the rights of groups, even multicultural groups, if they are to build a society that honours human rights and embraces the best (and widest) definition of what it is to be human.

Multiculturalism 7

References

Baillargeon, A. (2000, May 4). Who are the myth makers? Multiculturalism and material culture. Retrieved August 21, 2000, from http://www.suite101.com/article.cfm/multiculturalism/38544

Bissoondath, N. (1994). Marginalization. In *Selling illusions: The cult of multiculturalism in Canada* (pp. 111–122). Toronto: Penguin.

Churchill, W. (1993, March). Crimes against humanity. *Z Magazine, 6,* 43–47.

Krishna, S. (Director). (1993). *Masala* [Video]. C/FP Video.

Okin, S.M. (1999, May). Is multiculturalism bad for women? *Boston Review, 22*(5). NJ: Princeton University Press. Retrieved August 20, 2000, from http://bostonreview.mit.edu/BR22.5/okin.html

Rodriguez, R. (1983). Aria. In *Hunger of memory: The education of Richard Rodriguez.* New York: Bantam.

Wong, J. (1999, July 2). Jan Wong wants to see Canadians de-hyphenate themselves. *The Globe and Mail*, p. A22.

Note that references may be listed like paragraphs for ease in word processing. Indent the first line, but not the rest.

Note differences in capitalization of books and periodicals.

Note that the authors' first names are reduced to initials.

The best sourc for up-to-the-minute information on Web citation is APA on the Web: www.apa.org.

Note that all page numbers need to be included in a reference to a article in a periodical.

Include date c retrieval for Web sites.

Part Five

DOCUMENTING AND DELIVERING YOUR PAPER

Chapter 13
PLANNING YOUR PAPER'S LAYOUT

Even if you are on the right track, you will get run over if you just sit there.
—WILL ROGERS

When you organize your final printed manuscript for submission to an instructor, you need to be careful to meet the specifications demanded for the paper's presentation. The paper should be easy to read, neat, and presented in a style consistent with a standard form of documentation. The specifications you follow depend, in large part, on whether you are using the MLA, APA, or University of Chicago style of documentation. Each of these styles requires certain things of the manuscript. For the sake of consistency, follow these guidelines as closely as you can.

The Layout of a Paper in MLA Style

You will likely follow MLA guidelines if you study English, philosophy, classics, or visual arts.

1. Use letter-quality medium-weight paper, 22 cm × 28 cm (8 ½″ × 11″).
2. Make sure the print quality is sharp, and the font is commonly accepted, such as Times New Roman in 12-point font. Do not use decorative fonts. Keep the right margin unjustified.
3. Double-space everything, including quotations, notes, and Works Cited, and use one side of the page only.
4. Leave 2.5-cm (1″) margins. Do not justify the right margin. Indent paragraphs 1.3 cm (½″) or five spaces. Indent long quotations an additional 1.3 cm (½″) or five spaces with a normal right margin.
5. Place page numbers in the upper right-hand corner beside your last name (without a page abbreviation or a comma).
6. On the first page, place your name, your instructor's name, the course name, and the date in the upper left corner. Double-space between the date and the title, centre the paper's title, without underlining, italicizing, or quotation marks. Note that a title page is not required.

7. Use a paper clip to attach the pages, or staple if your instructor prefers.
8. Keep a copy for your own protection.
9. Refer to the sample MLA essay on p. 102.

The Layout of a Paper in APA Style

When you use APA style for a manuscript, you are probably preparing a paper in the social sciences, where the date of publication is particularly important. Follow these guidelines for the proper preparation of a paper in APA style:

1. Use heavy-weight white bond paper, 22 cm × 28 cm (8½″ × 11″).
2. Use a clear font or typeface. Times Roman and Courier are preferred. Use underlining or italics to indicate titles of published books within your essay.
3. Double-space everything, including quotations and References.
4. Use 2.5-cm (1″) margins. Indent paragraphs 1.3 cm (½″) or five spaces. Indent long quotations an additional 1.3 cm (½″) or five spaces.
5. Use a shortened version of the paper's title as a header in the upper right-hand corner of each page. Number pages, starting with the title page, without an abbreviation for page or any punctuation.
6. Make a separate title page. The top line will be the header and the page number. Centre the title and capitalize major words. Include other identifying information, centred, and then centre the page vertically.
7. Use headings to separate sections of the paper, if desired. Centre main headings, all in capitals; type the next level of headings flush left, with ordinary capitalization; indent the next level of headings with only the first word capitalized, and follow these headings with a period, with the text continuing after one space.
8. Use a paper clip to attach the pages, or staple if your instructor prefers.
9. Keep a copy for your own protection.
10. Refer to the sample APA essay on p. 124.

The Layout of a Paper in University of Chicago Style

The University of Chicago style is often used in disciplines like history, where notes are extremely important. There are some major differences between the look of a manuscript in MLA or APA and University of Chicago style. The following list should make the changes clear:

1. Use heavy-weight white bond paper, 22 cm × 28 cm (8½″ × 11″).
2. Use a clear, standard font, like Times Roman or Courier, in pica (12-point size) or elite (10-point size). Letter-quality print is preferred. Use either italics or underlining for titles of published books in your essay.
3. Double-space most of the paper. Footnotes, endnotes, indented quotations, and visual elements are single-spaced, though separated by double-spacing.
4. Use a 3.8-cm (1½″) margin on the left. On the first page, the top margin must be 5 cm (2″); subsequent pages must be 2.5 cm (1″).
5. Number pages either at the top right corner or at the top centre of each page. The first page of a section has a page number at the bottom, centred.

6. Make a separate title page, centred vertically and horizontally. Do not count the title page in your numbering.
7. Centre the title of your paper 5 cm (2″) from the top of the next page. Leave three line spaces and begin the text.
8. If you use headings, make sure the first-level headings are centred, underlined, with important words capitalized; the next level should be centred and with ordinary capitalization, but not underlined; the next level should begin at the left margin, underlined and with ordinary capitalization.
9. Use a paper clip to attach pages, or staple if your instructor prefers.
10. Keep a copy for your own protection.

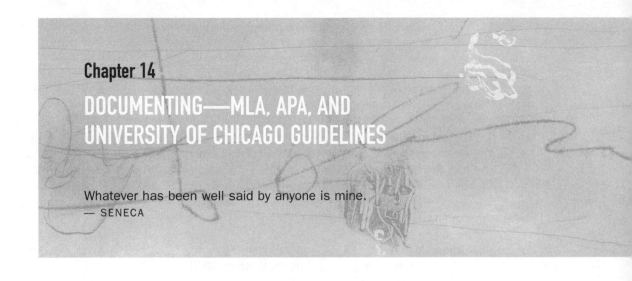

Chapter 14
DOCUMENTING—MLA, APA, AND UNIVERSITY OF CHICAGO GUIDELINES

Whatever has been well said by anyone is mine.
— SENECA

Your bibliography should list all items that you quote, paraphrase, or use as source material. Three basic styles of documentation will be covered in this section: MLA style, most commonly used in the humanities; APA style, often used in the social sciences; and University of Chicago style, often used in history and other disciplines that prefer a traditional footnote (or endnote) style.

To create entries for a Works Cited page in MLA style, you need to consult the copyright information available on the title page of any book that you used.

Gathering Publication Information from a Book

To find publication information, it is best to check the title page and copyright page of the actual book, rather than a library catalogue or another source. In the case of this book, these are on the first page and its reverse.

To create an entry for this book in a Works Cited page (though usually you don't need to include reference books such as this one), do the following.

Find the author's name on the title page, and reverse it.

Buckley, Joanne.   **Example**

Follow it with the title and a colon with the subtitle, if there is one, after it. These should be underlined in MLA style.

Buckley, Joanne. <u>Fit to Print: The Canadian Student's Guide to Essay Writing</u>.

Follow this with the edition number that appears on the title page.

Buckley, Joanne. <u>Fit to Print: The Canadian Student's Guide to Essay Writing</u>. 6th ed.

Then follow that with the place of publication as listed on the copyright page (usually the reverse of the title page) and a shortened version of publisher's name along with the date of publication.

> Buckley, Joanne. Fit to Print: The Canadian Student's Guide to Essay Writing. 6th ed. Toronto: Nelson, 2004.

If this book also had an editor, you would include that information, found on the book's title page, which would appear in your entry after the book's title and edition. Normally, you would list the book under the author's name on your Works Cited page, unless you used the book primarily because of the contributions made by the editor (a foreword or notes, perhaps). A translator also would appear in the same form as that shown for the editor.

> Buckley, Joanne. Fit to Print: The Canadian Student's Guide to Essay Writing. 6th ed. Ed. Katherine Goodes. Toronto: Nelson, 2004.

Use the first place of publication that is listed on the title page, if there is more than one office listed for publication. If the publisher has an imprint, such as Anchor Books for Doubleday or Vintage Books for Random House, use a shortened version of the imprint, followed by a hyphen, and then the publisher's shortened name.

> McEwan, Ian. Atonement. Toronto: Vintage-Random, 2001.

Use the most recent date, except where a work has been republished in a different version. For example, for a work like *Anne of Green Gables,* you would use the original date first after the title, and then the publication information with the most recent date of publication.

> Montgomery, Lucy Maud. Anne of Green Gables. 1908. Toronto: McGraw-Hill, 2003.

Sample Bibliographical Entries in MLA Style

The examples that follow show how certain entries would appear in a bibliography, if you follow the guidelines of the Modern Language Association. These entries should serve as models when you prepare your own bibliography page. In MLA style, this page is called "Works Cited." If you need further information, consult Joseph Gibaldi's *MLA Handbook for Writers of Research Papers*, 6th ed. (New York: Modern Language Association, 2003).

Books

ONE AUTHOR:

Frazer, James George. <u>The Golden Bough: A Study in Magic and Religion</u>. New York: Macmillan, 1922.

Use a shortened version of the publisher's name (in this case, Macmillan Publishing Company), making sure that your label for the company is still recognizable. Include complete subtitles in bibliographical entries, and italicize or underline the title and subtitle continuously.

TWO AUTHORS AND EDITION (IF NOT THE FIRST EDITION):

Strunk, William, Jr., and E. B. White. <u>The Elements of Style</u>. 4th ed. New York: Pearson Allyn & Bacon, 2000.

THREE AUTHORS:

Jardine, David W., Patricia Clifford, and Sharon Friesen. <u>Back to the Basics of Teaching and Learning: Thinking the World Together</u>. Mahweh, NJ: Erlbaum, 2003.

MORE THAN THREE AUTHORS:

Bonsanti, Georgio, et al. <u>La Basilica di San Francesco ad Assisi</u>. Modena: Panini, 2002.

CORPORATE AUTHOR:

Imperial Oil Limited. <u>The Review</u>. Toronto: Imperial Oil, Spring 2003.

EDITOR:

Chong, Woei Lien, ed. <u>China's Great Proletarian Cultural Revolution: Master Narratives and Post-Mao Counternarratives</u>. Lanham, MD: Rowman & Littlefield, 2002.

GOVERNMENT PUBLICATION:

Canada. Minister of Supply and Services Canada. <u>Canada Year Book 2002</u>. Ottawa: Statistics Canada, 2003.

STORY OR ARTICLE FROM AN ANTHOLOGY:

Davies, Robertson. "Stratford Forty Years Ago." <u>The Harbrace Reader for Canadians</u>. Ed. Joanne Buckley. Toronto: Harcourt, 2001. 28-32.

TRANSLATION:

Ringuet. <u>Thirty Acres</u>. Trans. Felix Walker and Dorothea Walker. Toronto: McClelland & Stewart, 1960.

REPRINT:

Montgomery, L. M. <u>Anne of Green Gables</u>. 1908. Toronto: McGraw-Hill, 2003.

The original hardcover edition was published in 1908. The paperback version appeared in 2003.

A WORK IN MORE THAN ONE VOLUME:

Rollins, Hyder Edward, ed. <u>The Letters of John Keats: 1814–1821</u>. 2 vols. Cambridge: Harvard UP, 1958.

14

A WORK IN A SERIES:
Woodman, Ross. <u>James Reaney</u>. Canadian Writers New Canadian Library 12. Toronto:
McClelland & Stewart, 1971.

The series number is given in Arabic numerals and without the abbreviation *vol.*

Magazines, Newspapers, and Journals

UNSIGNED ARTICLE:
"Terminator Set to Run for Governor in California." <u>Globe and Mail</u> 7 Aug. 2003, natl.
ed.: A1.

The names of months other than May, June, and July are usually abbreviated.
"A1" refers to the section and page number of the newspaper.

DAILY NEWSPAPERS:
Martin, Don. "World's Longest Undecided Border." <u>National Post</u> 5 Aug. 2003, natl.
ed.: A1+.

When not part of the newspaper's name, the city's name should be given in
brackets after the title, except in the case of a national edition. The + indicates
that the article continues on non-consecutive pages.

WEEKLY MAGAZINE OR NEWSPAPER:
Jonathon Gatehouse. "Iraq: The Price of Victory." <u>Maclean's</u> 28 July 2003: 20-22.

MONTHLY OR BI-MONTHLY MAGAZINE:
Simon, Barry, Dr. "Weighty Issues." <u>Canadian Living</u> May-Sept. 2003: 52-55.

JOURNAL—CONTINUOUS PAGINATION THROUGH THE YEAR:
Campbell, Jane. " 'Competing Towers of Babel': Some Patterns of Language in <u>Hard
Times</u>." <u>English Studies in Canada</u> 10 (1984): 416-35.

When the pages of a journal are numbered consecutively through the year, the
issue number and month are not included in your entry.

JOURNAL—SEPARATE PAGINATION FOR EACH ISSUE:
Davis, Marie. "Parable, Parody, or 'Blip in the Canadian Literary Landscape': Tom King
on <u>A Coyote Christmas Story</u>." <u>Canadian Children's Literature</u> 84.4 (1996): 24-36.

When the pages of a journal are numbered separately for each issue, an issue
number ("4" in this case) follows the volume number "84." They are separated by
a period.

EDITORIAL:
Robinson, Svend. "When It Comes to Immorality, Look Who's Talking!" Editorial. <u>Globe
and Mail</u> 7 Aug. 2003: A13.

BOOK REVIEW:
Miller, J. R. Rev. of <u>The Man from Halifax: Sir John Thompson, Prime Minister</u>, by P. B.
Waite. <u>Queen's Quarterly</u> 93 (1986): 646–48.

Encyclopedia

SIGNED WITH NAME OR INITIALS:
So[utham], B[rian] C. "Austen, Jane." Encyclopaedia Britannica: Macropaedia. 1974 ed. This article appears with the initials "B.C. So." appended to it. To identify it, you need only check the index of the encyclopedia and enclose the added information in brackets.

UNSIGNED ARTICLE:
"Literature." The Cambridge Encyclopedia. 1994 ed.

Government Publications

Canada. Royal Commission on Aboriginal Peoples. Restructuring the Relationship. Public Policy and Aboriginal People 1985–1992 Volume 2. Ottawa: Ministry of Supply and Services, Canada, 1996.
---. Standing Committee on Aboriginal Affairs. Minutes of Proceedings and Evidence of the Standing Committee on Aboriginal Affairs. 19 March 1990, Issue No. 22. Ottawa: Queen's Printer, 1990. 14-15.

The government agency is considered the author, unless the name of the author is given.

PAMPHLETS, BULLETINS, AND REPORTS:
Canada. Employment and Immigration Canada. Aboriginal Employment and Training Working Group. Ottawa: Government of Canada, 1991.

Unpublished Dissertations

DuBroy, Michael Thomas. "The Tale of the Folk: Revolution and the Late Prose Romances of William Morris." Diss. U of Western Ontario, 1982.

Micropublications

Books or periodicals in microprint form are documented as they would be in their original form.

Non-print Sources

TELEVISION OR RADIO PROGRAM:
"Killing Time." Cold Squad. CTV. CKCO-TV, Kitchener, ON. 12 Aug. 2003.

14

TELEVISION INTERVIEW:
Gowdy, Barbara. Interview with Vicki Gabereau. <u>Vicki Gabereau</u>. CTV. CFTO, Toronto.
5 Aug. 2003.

FILM:
<u>Atanarjuat: The Fast Runner</u>. Dir. Zacharias Kunick. National Film Board, 2002.

VIDEO:
<u>It's a Wonderful Life</u>. Dir. Frank Capra. 1946. Videocassette. Republic, 1993.

Include the title, director, distributor, and year. Note that the original year is
included before the distribution information. Include other information such as
writer or performers, if relevant.

PERFORMANCE OF STAGE PLAY:
<u>Troilus and Cressida</u>. By William Shakespeare. Dir. Richard Monette. Perf. David
Snelgrove, Claire Julllen. Tom Patterson Theatre, Stratford. 30 July 2003.

RECORDING:
The Tragically Hip. <u>Music@Work</u>. Universal Music, 2000.

SONG:
The Tragically Hip. "Putting Down." <u>Music@Work</u>. Universal Music, 2000.

LECTURE:
Gedalof, Allan. "Mystery Writing." U.W.O. Senior Alumni Series. Wesanne McKellar
Room, U of Western Ontario, London, Ontario. 14 Apr. 1987.

INTERVIEW:
Wiseman, Adele. Personal Interview. 15 Apr. 1987.

Sources from the World Wide Web

List any of the following that are relevant or available:

Last name of author, editor, translator, or compiler, followed by first name, if
author is given.
Title of article or short work in the site.
Title of book (underlined) in the site.
Name of editor, translator, or compiler.
Publication information for a print source, if there is one.
Title of site (underlined), or if untitled a description, such as "Home page."
Editor of site, with version number, or journal volume and issue number, if
applicable.
Date of latest electronic publication or update.
Name of subscription service, discussion list, or forum.
Total range of paragraphs or sections, if numbered.
Name of subscription service, and name and city of the library.

Name of any sponsoring institution of the Web site.

Date of your access to the site.

URL of site, or search page if simpler, in angle brackets.

SCHOLARLY PROJECT:

Orlando Project: An Integrated History of Women's Writing in the British Isles. 25 May 2000. U of Alberta. 1 Aug. 2000 <http://www.ualberta.ca/ORLANDO/>.

PROFESSIONAL SITE:

COCH/COSH: Consortium for Computers in the Humanities/Consortium pour Ordinateurs en Sciences Humaines. 1 Aug. 2000 <http://www.interchange.ubc.ca/winder/coch.htm>.

BOOK:

Braddon, M[ary] E[lizabeth]. Lady Audley's Secret. Vol. 1. London, 1862. Victorian Women Writers Project. Ed. Perry Willett. 20 June 2000. Indiana U. 1 Aug. 2000 <http://www.letrs.indiana.edu/cgi-bin/vwwp-query.pl?type=bibl&rgn= TEXT&idno=InU-ALB2585-1>.

POEM:

Johnson, Emily Pauline. "The Song My Paddle Sings." Flint and Feather. Toronto, 1912. The Pauline Johnson Archive. Sept. 1996. McMaster U. 1 Aug. 2000 <http://www.humanities.mcmaster.ca/~pjohnson/writings.html>.

ARTICLE IN A REFERENCE DATABASE:

"McLuhan, [Herbert] Marshall." Britannica Online. Encyclopedia Britannica Intermediate Version 1.0 2000. 1 Aug. 2000 <http://search.eb.com/bol/topic?tmapid= 125960000&tmaptyp=dx>.

ARTICLE IN A JOURNAL:

Brown, Susan, and Patricia Clements. "Tag Team: Computing, Collaborators, and the History of Women's Writing in the British Isles." Technologising the Humanities/ Humanitising the Technologies. Special issue of Computing in the Humanities Working Papers. Eds. R. G. Siemens and William Winder. Text Technology 8 (1998): 37-52. 1 Aug. 2000 <http://www.epas.utoronto.ca:8080/epc/chwp/orlando/>.

ARTICLE IN AN ELECTRONIC JOURNAL:

Miles, Adrian, et al. "I Link Therefore I Am." Kairos 8.1 (2003). 7 Aug. 2003 <http://english.ttu.edu/kairos/ 8.1/binder2.html?coverweb/vot/index.html>.

ARTICLE IN A MAGAZINE:

Joy, Bill. "Why the Future Doesn't Need Us." Wired. 8 Apr. 2000 <http://_www.wired.com/wired/archive/8.04/>.

ARTICLE IN A NEWSPAPER:

Lawlor, Allison. "Halifax Blast Forces 400 Residents to Flee." Globe and Mail. 7 Aug. 2003. 7 Aug. 2003 <http://www.theglobeandmail.com/servlet/story/RTGAM. 20030807.wgrain0807/BNStory/National/>.

WORK FROM A SUBSCRIPTION SERVICE:

"Marimba." <u>Compton's Encyclopedia Online</u>. Vers. 3.0. 1999. America Online. 12 July 2000. Keyword: Compton's.

POSTING TO A DISCUSSION LIST:

Scaife, Ross. "Trajan's Column." Online posting. 2 Aug. 2000. Humanist Discussion Group, Vol. 14, No. 144. Centre for Computing in the Humanities, King's College London. 3 Aug. 2000 <http://www.princeton.edu/~mccarty/humanist/>.

ELECTRONIC MAIL:

Rockwell, Geoffrey. E-mail to the author. 11 Aug. 2003.

CD-ROM SOURCE:

<u>The Oxford English Dictionary</u>. 2nd ed. CD-ROM. Oxford: Oxford UP, 1992.

Use the same order of information for a CD-ROM from a previously published source, if the information is given:

Last name of author, first name of author. <u>Title</u>. Place of print publication: Publisher, Date. CD-ROM. City of CD-ROM production: Producer, Electronic publication date. Access number is optional.

Citing Sources in MLA Style

Whenever you refer to material from another source, whether book, journal article, motion picture, or recording, you must acknowledge your source. Citing your sources no longer necessitates footnotes or endnotes. Instead, citations of sources are placed in the body of the essay in parentheses. A footnote or endnote is necessary only if you have supplementary material to add that does not properly belong in the text of the essay itself.

Simple citation

Include in parentheses after the citation only what is essential to guide the reader to the correct entry in the "Works Cited." Often, all that will be needed is the last name of the author followed by a page number. For example, if you were quoting from Margaret Laurence's *The Diviners*, the citation in the text would look like this:

Example   Morag's collection of photographs gives the reader insight into her own hidden past. As she says, "I keep the snapshots not for what they show but for what is hidden in them" (Laurence 6).

This citation refers the reader to the following entry on the "Works Cited" page:

Example   Laurence, Margaret. <u>The Diviners</u>. Toronto: Bantam, 2003.

If this is the only entry listed under Laurence, there is no confusion, and the reader knows that the quotation can be found on page 6 of the listed text.

Citation of more than one work by the same author

If, on the other hand, there are references to two works by the same author, a more specific notation is required. Say that you referred in the same essay to Margaret Laurence's earlier novel, *A Jest of God.* You might, perhaps, make the following reference:

> Rachel discovers her own capacity to hide the truth from herself. As she explains, "There is room enough in anyone's bonehouse for too much duplicity (Laurence <u>Jest</u> 182).

Example

This reference makes it clear that more than one book by Laurence is listed in the "Works Cited."

Citation of a work in more than one volume

If, in an essay about Keats's poetry, you decide to quote from the two-volume collection of Keats's letters, the citation would read as follows:

> Keats, in the composition of the odes, dedicates himself to the search for "the true voice of feeling" (<u>Letters</u> 2: 167).

Example

14

Here the Arabic numeral 2 refers to the second volume of the letters. A colon is used to separate the volume number from the page number.

Similar adjustments must be made to clarify abbreviated citations. Always remember to ask yourself what the reader needs to know in order to find the reference easily.

Citation of poetry and of long or short quotations

Avoid redundant citations. If the body of your essay already explains the source adequately, do not restate the information in parentheses. For example, you might write the following analysis of Keats's poetry:

> The poet speaks of the lure of death in "Ode to a Nightingale":
>
> > Darkling I listen; and, for many a time
> > I have been half in love with easeful Death,
> >
> > Call'd him soft names in many a mused rhyme,
> > To take into the air my quiet breath. (51-54)

Example

Here only the line numbers are listed in parentheses, since the title of the poem is given in the body of the essay itself. Note, too, that a long quotation is double-spaced, indented, and written without quotation marks. Because the quoted matter is poetry, the lines are given as they are in the text. If the quotation were fewer than four lines, it would be written in the body of the essay in the following way, using quotation marks:

Example   The poet speaks of the lure of death in "Ode to a Nightingale": "Darkling I listen; and, for many a time / I have been half in love with easeful Death" (51-52).

Citation of poetic drama

A reference to a play must refer to act, scene, and line numbers, as in the following case:

Example   In Shakespeare's <u>A Midsummer Night's Dream</u>, Titania, enchanted with Bottom, sees the world around with romantic eyes. As she says, "The moon methinks looks with a watery eye; / And when she weeps, weeps every little flower, / Lamenting some enforced chastity" (3.1.202-04).

Note that as many as three lines of poetry may be cited without indentation; four lines or more, however, do require indentation.

Citation of a Web site

Identify the author or the Web site's title in a sentence that introduces the quotation. To make finding the citation in the source material easier for your reader, use any Internet text divisions as substitutes for page numbers.

Example   Miles writes in "I Link Therefore I Am" that

> [I]n a screen literate world where print and the page are no longer exemplars for the expression of knowledge we remain hesitantly standing at the cusp of new academic genres. Hence, to use these works you need to be an active reader, at times you must do things with the text or digital artifacts for anything to happen, yet at other times the work will insistently run of its own accord. (Introduction)

Punctuation of citations

Note that for citations within the text, punctuation appears *after* the parentheses. In quotations set off from the text, citations *follow* the final punctuation. To make citations as unobtrusive as possible, try to place them at the end, rather than in the middle, of sentences.

For more detail, see Joseph Gibaldi, *MLA Handbook for Writers of Research Papers,* 6th ed. (New York: Modern Language Association, 2003), or consult the Internet at < www.mla.org/ >.

Sample Bibliographic Entries in APA Style

The following entries are arranged according to the style of the *Publication Manual of the American Psychological Association*. In this case, the bibliography is given the heading "References." The APA uses an author–date system of citation. Here are some guidelines to citations in the reference pages. See also the References page of the APA model essay on p. 130, and for more details consult this text: American Psychological Association. (2001). *Publication Manual of the*

American Psychological Association. 5th ed. Washington: American Psychological Association; or on the Internet at < www.apa.org/ >.

Information needed for APA references

1. List alphabetically by last name. Use initials instead of first or middle names.
2. Include the year next, in parentheses. Include the month or day if given.
3. List complete titles and subtitles.
4. Include these items in the following order: translator, edition number, volume number, issue number if the journal is paginated by issue, and inclusive pages.
5. Take publication information from books in this way: use an abbreviated form of the publisher's name, the first city listed, and the most recent date. From periodicals, get this information: the volume number, issue number (if relevant), and date.

APA format in references

1. For "unpolished" manuscripts, indent the first line five to seven spaces (the default tab setting on your word processor is acceptable). For finished manuscripts, "hanging indents" are used, as illustrated in the following examples. The latter format is recommended. However, the APA guidelines defer to your professor's style preference; you should clarify this before submitting your paper.
2. List authors by last names and initials. If a work is co-authored, invert the names of all the authors and use an ampersand (&) to join the final name.
3. For books, capitalize the first word of the title and of the subtitle as well as proper names; everything else is lower case. For periodicals, use both upper and lower case as usual, a comma, and a volume number. Underline or italicize titles and volume numbers. Underline both title and volume number with a continuous underline.
4. Abbreviate names of commercial publishers by using only the main elements of the name. Cite names of university publishers in full.
5. Separate sections of entries with periods, even the words in parentheses. But separate the place of publication from the publisher's name by a colon and one space.
6. Use only one space between items in APA citations.
7. For articles, list the complete page range (211–214) and introduce it with the abbreviation pp. (for pages) or p. (for page).
8. The examples shown below are single-spaced to save paper. When you submit your paper, all entries should be double-spaced.

Books

ONE AUTHOR:
Selye, H. (1956). *The stress of life.* New York: McGraw-Hill.

TWO AUTHORS:
Klug, B. J., & Whitfield, P. T. (2003). *Widening the circle: Culturally relevant pedagogy for American Indian children.* New York: RoutledgeFalmer.

Journals

ONE AUTHOR:
Turner, J. (1981). Social support as a contingency in psychological well-being. *Journal of Health and Social Behavior, 22,* 357–367.

MULTIPLE AUTHORS IN A JOURNAL WITH SEPARATE PAGING:
Blanton, S., Robin, B., & Kinzie, M. (1991). Repurposing a feature film for interactive multimedia. *Educational Technology, 31*(12), 7–12.

NEWSPAPER ARTICLE:
Fowlie, J. (2003, August 16). People short of breath hard hit. *The Globe and Mail,* National Edition, p. A13.

A Review

Johnson, B. D. (2003, June 16). Whales of a time [Review of the film *Whale Ridery*]. *Maclean's,* 85–86.

A Film

Egoyan, A. (Director). (2002). *Ararat* [Film]. Toronto: Alliance Atlantis.

Electronic Publications

CITING E-MAIL COMMUNICATIONS:
S. Shaw (personal communication, July 31, 2000).

CITING A WEB SITE:
TEXT Technology has an archive of prepublication essays for discussion purposes: http://cheiron.humanities.mcmaster.ca/texttech.
American Psychological Association. (2000, September 5). *Electronic reference formats recommended by the American Psychological Association.* Washington, DC: Author. Retrieved November 12, 2000, from http://www.apa.org/journals/webref/html

Citing articles and abstracts from electronic databases

APA now recommends a retrieval statement that lists the date of retrieval (except in the case of a CD-ROM) and the source (e.g., DIALOG), followed in parentheses by the name of the database. For Web sources, a URL should be listed that points to the "entry page" for the database.

The following are examples of citations from electronic databases. (Note that square brackets below will be replaced by your specific information.)

FROM A CD-ROM:

The following information should now be added to each reference:

Retrieved from [source] database ([name of specific database], CD-ROM, [release date], [item no. if applicable]).

Geddes, J. (1999). Making babies: In the age of in vitro fertilization, does the state have a place in the test tubes of the nation? *Maclean's, 112*(49), p. 52. Retrieved from Canadian Business & Current Affairs database (CBCA Fulltext Reference, CD-ROM, 2000 release).

FROM AN ONLINE DATABASE:

The following information should now be added to each reference:

Retrieved [month, day, year], from [source] online database ([name of specific database], [item no. if applicable]).

Buckley, J. (1997). The invisible audience and the disembodied voice: On-line teaching and the loss of body image. *Computers and Composition, 14*(2), pp. 179–88. Retrieved November 12, 2000, from ERIC on-line database.

FROM A DATABASE ACCESSED VIA THE WEB:

This information should be added to the reference:

Retrieved [month, day, year], from [source] database ([name of specific database], [item no. if applicable]) on the World Wide Web: [URL]

Kerrigan, D. C., Todd, M. K., & Riley, P. O. (1998). Knee osteoarthritis and high-heeled shoes. *The Lancet, 251,* 1399–1401. Retrieved November 12, 2000, from DIALOG database (#457, The Lancet) on the World Wide Web: http://www.dialogweb.com

Citing Sources in APA Style

As with the MLA style of documentation, you may cite your sources in parentheses in APA style. In APA style, however, the year of publication is given with the author's last name; hence, the title of a work is not usually needed. Note details in the following examples:

SHORT QUOTATION: **Examples**

Social support is defined as "those relationships among people that provide not only material help and emotional assurance, but also the sense that one is a continuing object of concern on the part of other people" (Pilsuk, 1982, p. 20).

LONG QUOTATION:

Seligman (1975) argues that helplessness may lead to depression:

Those people who are particularly susceptible to depression may have had lives relatively devoid of mastery; their lives may have been full of situations in which they were helpless to influence the sources of suffering and relief. (p. 104)

Note that, in this passage, the author's last name and the date of publication are not included in parentheses because they are already given in the body of the essay. This use of a signal phrase provides acknowledgment even though page numbers are not necessary in this case.

Example   PARAPHRASE:

Cobb (1976) insists that stress, not social support, is the key to understanding changes in health. Social support only acts as a buffer.

Following these basic guidelines should help you assemble your notes and your bibliography with relative ease. Remember these guidelines as you prepare the documentation for your essay:

1. Be consistent.
2. Give your reader all the information needed to find a reference.
3. Check the sample research essay on p. 124 for a model of APA format.
4. Check the appropriate style guide for further details.

For more detail, see the *Publication Manual of the American Psychological Association*, 5th ed., and consult the World Wide Web: <http://www.apastyle.org/electref.html>. The Web version supersedes the text for online sources.

Web citations in text

For specific parts of a document on the Web, cite the chapter, figure, table, or appropriate section. For quotations, give page numbers or paragraph numbers where available (using the abbreviation "para." for "paragraph"). Omit them if they are not available. See examples of these citations on p. 140.

For materials you publish on the Web

Be aware of copyright permission requirements, and seek permission where necessary. Permission is not necessary for extracts in papers submitted to an instructor.

References may appear in block style rather than with hanging indents, to accommodate browser limitations. Italics may be used instead of underlining, if they are used consistently. References may be single-spaced to allow for limitations of browsers.

Sample Bibliographic Entries in University of Chicago Style

Some disciplines, in particular history and political science, prefer a traditional footnoting style. The best sources of information about this style are Kate Turabian's *A Manual for Writers* and *The Chicago Manual of Style*.

If your instructor advises you to use this traditional style, rather than the parenthetical forms just outlined, refer to this section.

Since bibliographic listings can be complex, try to include as much information as possible in each entry. Remember that you are trying to help your reader locate the sources.

Books

ONE AUTHOR:

Miller, J. S. *Skyscrapers Hide the Heavens: A History of Indian–White Relations in Canada.* Toronto: University of Toronto Press, 1989.

TWO AUTHORS AND COMPONENT PART IN A LARGER WORK:

Rogers, E. S., and Flora Tobobondung. "Parry Sound Farmers: A Period of Change in the Way of Life of the Algonkians of Southern Ontario." In *Contributions to Canadian Ethnology*, edited by David Brez Carlisle. Ottawa: National Museums of Canada, 1975.

MORE THAN THREE AUTHORS:

Martin, Nancy, Pat D'Arcy, Bryan Newton, and Robert Parker. *Writing and Learning Across the Curriculum 11–16.* Upper Montclair, N.J.: Boynton/Cook, 1976.

Note that it would be permissible to shorten the note form of this entry to read:

1. Nancy Martin and others, *Writing and Learning Across the Curriculum 11–16* (Upper Montclair, N.J.: Boynton/Cook, 1976), 50.

EDITION AFTER THE FIRST:

Barker, Larry L. *Communication.* 4th ed. Englewood Cliffs, N.J.: Prentice-Hall, 1987.

ASSOCIATION AUTHOR AND REPRINT:

Nin.Da.Waab.Jig. *Minishenhying Anishnaabe-aki Walpole Island: The Soul of Indian Territory.* Windsor: Commercial Associates/Ross Roy Ltd., 1987; reprint, 1989.

This book is by a Native community, and the title is in Ojibwa. The name of the community is listed first.

It is important to list information about a reprint, in case changes have been made to the pagination.

EDITOR:

Storr, Anthony, ed. *The Essential Jung.* Selected and introduced by Anthony Storr. Princeton, N.J.: Princeton University Press, 1983.

TRANSLATION:

Pushkin, Alexander. *Eugene Onegin.* Trans. by Charles Johnston with an Introduction by John Bayley. Harmondsworth, Middlesex: Penguin, 1977.

A WORK IN MORE THAN ONE VOLUME:

Campbell, Joseph. *The Masks of God.* 4 vols. New York: Viking Press, 1960–68.

A WORK IN A SERIES:
Stanley, George F. G. *The War of 1812: Land Operations*. Canadian War Museum
    Historical Publication No. 18. Toronto: Macmillan, 1983.

COMPONENT PART BY ONE AUTHOR IN A WORK BY ANOTHER:
Purvis, Jane. "The Experience of Schooling for Working-Class Boys and Girls in
    Nineteenth Century England." In *Defining the Curriculum: Histories and
    Ethnographies*, edited by Ivor F. Goodson and Stephen J. Ball, 89–115. London:
    Falmer Press, 1984.

Magazines, Newspapers, and Journals

ARTICLE IN A POPULAR MAGAZINE:
Mohr, Merilyn. "The Evolutionary Image." *Equinox*, March/April 1989, 80–93.

ARTICLE IN A SCHOLARLY JOURNAL:
Creighton, D. G. "The Economic Background of the Rebellions of 1867." *The Canadian
    Journal of Economics and Political Science* 4 (1937): 322–34.

NEWSPAPER:
"Feminists Demand Legal System Review." *London Free Press*, 10 February 1990, D1.

BOOK REVIEW:
Rugoff, Milton. "The Feminine Mystic." Review of *Spiritualism and Women's Rights in
    Nineteenth Century America* by Ann Braude. *The New York Times Book Review,* 14
    January 1990, 19.

Non-print Sources

MOTION PICTURE:
Phillips, Robin. Dir. *The Wars*. Toronto: Spectra Films, 1983.

TELEVISION OR RADIO PROGRAM:
CBC. "The Nature of Things." 7 February 1990. "Thirty Years of Discovery." David
    Suzuki, narrator.

PUBLISHED INTERVIEW:
Davies, Robertson. "Interview with Robertson Davies: The Bizarre and Passionate Life
    of the Canadian People." Interview by Silver Donald Cameron (9 November 1971).
    Conversations with Canadian Novelists. Toronto: Colbert Agency, Inc., 1973.

UNPUBLISHED INTERVIEW:
Beedle, Merle Assance. Interview by author, March 1989.

Special Forms

UNPUBLISHED MATERIALS:

Crown Attorney's Case Book for Cases Prosecuted Under the Liquor Control Act (1927) in Middlesex County. Regional Room, D. B. Weldon Library, University of Western Ontario, London.

DISSERTATIONS:

Rockwell, Geoffrey. "A Unity of Voices, A Definition of Philosophical Dialogue." PhD diss., University of Toronto, 1995.

Government Publications

Here are some basic rules to follow when citing government documents.

1. List name of country, province, state, city, or district first in bibliographies. In notes, however, this information may be left out because it will be obvious from the text.
2. Next, list the name of the legislative body, department, or board. Use the name of the office rather than the name of the officer.
3. Follow with the name of the division or commission, if any.
4. Give the title of the document, underlined or italicized.
5. Include any additional information needed to find the document.

Use the following bibliographical format for a government publication:

Issuing Body. *Title*. Personal Author. (Report number; medium). Edition. Place: Publisher, Date. (Series title, number).

Ontario. Commission on Planning and Development Reform in Ontario. *New Planning for Ontario: Final Report*. John Sewell. (Chair). Toronto: Queen's Printer for Ontario, 1993.

CANADIAN DOCUMENTS:

List Canadian documents according to the executive department that issued them. Identify them by calendar year. The note would also include the chapter number.

Canada. House of Commons. *Order Paper and Notices*. 16 February 1972.

The note form would be:

1. House of Commons, *Order Paper and Notices*, 16 February 1972, 6.

AMERICAN DOCUMENTS:

U.S. Congress. Senate. Committee on Foreign Relations. *Aid Programs to Developing Countries*. Washington, D.C.: GPO, 1989.

Here "GPO" stands for Government Printing Office. The note form would be:

1. U.S. Congress, Senate, Committee on Foreign Relations, *Aid Programs to Developing Countries* (Washington, D.C.: GPO, 1989), 7.

14

BRITISH DOCUMENTS:

U.K. Board of Education. *Report of the Committee on the Position of Natural Science in the Educational System of Great Britain.* London: HMSO, 1918.

Here "HMSO" stands for Her (His) Majesty's Stationery Office. The note form would be:

1. Board of Education, *Report of the Committee on the Position of Natural Science in the Educational System of Great Britain* (London: HMSO, 1918), 6.

For more help in citing government documents, refer to the following:

Turabian, Kate L. *A Manual for Writers of Term Papers.* 6th ed. Chicago: University of Chicago Press, 1996.

Garner, Diane L., and Diane H. Smith. *Complete Guide to Citing Government Information Resources.* Rev. ed. Bethesda, Md.: Congressional Information Service, 1993.

Listing Electronic Sources

The Chicago Manual of Style has recently published its 15th edition and presented detailed information on how to document electronic sources. It recommends either the system suggested by MLA or the author–date system suggested by APA, and its accompanying rules on electronic documents.

ON THE WEB:

Modern Language Association

<www.apastyle.org/elecref.html> American Psychological Association

<www.ifla.org/I/training/citation/citing.htm> Library and Information Science: Citation Guides for Electronic Documents

<www.nlc-bnc.ca/iso/tc46sc9/index.htm> International Organization for Standardization

BOOKS ON CITING ELECTRONIC SOURCES:

Li, Xia, and Nancy B. Crane. *Electronic Styles: A Handbook for Citing Electronic Information.* 2nd ed. Medford, N.J.: Information Today, 1996.

Harnack, Andrew, and Eugene Kleppinger. *Online! A Reference Guide to Using Internet Sources.** 4th ed. New York: St. Martin's Press, 2003.

*Or check its more current Web site at < http://bedfordstmartins.com/online/ >.

Citing Sources in University of Chicago Style

Although notes can be used both for commentary and for reference, this section will concentrate on their use in making reference to particular works. Remember, though, that a note is often a good place to include supplementary commentary that does not belong in your paper proper, but that needs to be included.

In the University of Chicago style of documentation, you include notes compiled at the bottom of pages (footnotes) or in a list compiled at the end of the paper (endnotes). Each entry in your notes should correspond to a number in the text of your paper. The note numbers should appear a half line above your text at the end of the passage you are quoting or paraphrasing. The first line of each note is indented eight spaces from the left margin.

When you use this traditional style of documentation, always single-space your notes, and leave a space between each one.

The first note should contain complete information about the location of the source. Be sure to include everything that your reader will need to find it. Take your information from the title page of the work in question. The order of information for the first note follows this format:

For a first complete note, in this case a book

Note number, followed by a period
Name of author(s), editor(s) or organization(s) in normal order
Title and subtitle, if any, underlined or italicized
Name of editor or translator, if listed on title page
Name or number of edition, if not the first
Total of volume numbers (if multivolume work) or individual volume, if applicable
Series title and volume number if series is numbered
Facts of publication, enclosed in parentheses: (place of publication: name of publisher, date of publication)
Page number
URL for Internet sources or an indication of the medium (CD-ROM, DVD, etc.)

Sometimes some of these things will not apply to the text you are citing. Occasionally, too, some of the facts of publication may be missing. These may be supplied in square brackets, if you know them, or they may be indicated by these abbreviations:

n.p. meaning "no place" or "no publisher" or both
n.d. meaning "no date"

A first full reference to a book would look like this:

6. Northrop Frye, *The Great Code: The Bible and Literature* (New York: Harcourt Brace Jovanovich, 1982), 117.

For a first complete note, in this case an article

Follow this order for an article in a magazine or periodical:

Note number, followed by a period
Name of author(s)
Title of article in quotation marks
Name of periodical underlined or italicized
Volume number or issue
Publication date in parentheses
Page numbers, inclusive (These normally are not preceded by "p." for page or "pp." for pages, unless confusion is possible.)

A first full reference to an article would look like this:

3. Peter Elbow, "Embracing Contraries in the Writing Process," *College Composition and Communication* 35 (1984): 161.

Note that long quoted passages in University of Chicago style are single-spaced and indented five spaces.

Note too that there are some significant differences between the format of notes and that of bibliographic entries:

1. Notes are listed consecutively by number; bibliographic entries are listed alphabetically by last name of author. Hence, authors' names are not inverted in notes, though they are in bibliographies.
2. In notes, items are usually separated with commas; in bibliographic entries, items are separated with periods.
3. Notes include facts of publication in parentheses; bibliographic entries do not enclose this information in parentheses.
4. Notes include the specific page references of the citation; bibliographic entries do not, though they do include the page range of journal articles, inclusive.

Notes after the first full reference to a work

The best way to cite something after the first full reference is to include the following:

Author's last name
Shortened title of the work, maintaining key words without changing word order
Page number
Note that the use of Latin abbreviations such as *Ibid.* is now discouraged. The second references to the book and article listed above would look like these:

7. Frye, *Code*, 133.
8. Elbow, "Embracing Contraries," 163.

Some instructors may allow you to dispense with a shortened version of the title and use just the author's last name and the page number. This method is used only if you are citing no more than one work by an author. In any case, check with your instructor first.

Part Six

FIT, FORM, AND FUNCTION

Chapter 15
THE SENTENCE SIMPLIFIED

Any fool can make a rule and every fool will mind it.
—HENRY DAVID THOREAU

Some fundamental understanding of the way a sentence is put together will help you analyze your style, eliminate grammatical errors, and punctuate more accurately. First, learn to differentiate the parts of a sentence. When analyzing a sentence, always find the verb first. The verb is the part of the sentence that describes the action or the state of being. Next, find the subject: ask *who* or *what* performed the action or is being described. Note that, usually, the subject appears before the verb.

Example   The German shepherd chased the raccoon.

What is the verb? (chased—an action)
What is the subject? *Who* or *what* chased the raccoon? (the German shepherd)

Example   Her sunglasses look sophisticated, like something out of *The Matrix* movies.

What is the verb? (looks—a state of being)
What is the subject? *Who* or *what* looks sophisticated? (her sunglasses)
    The most common English sentence is made up of a subject, a verb, and an object, usually in that order.

Examples   Sweetiepie, the chimpanzee, refused to eat the banana.
                 S   V   O

It threw its food on the floor of the cage.
S   V   O

It gave the zookeeper a nasty look.
S   V   O

Even chimpanzees lose their temper.
        S   V   O

In each of these cases, the first noun or pronoun in the sentence is the subject, which performs the action. What follows the subject is the predicate, made up of the verb, which describes the action, and the object, which receives the action.

    Another common simple sentence pattern is subject, verb, and complement, sometimes called a "subjective completion." Here the verb must be a linking verb that describes a state of being, rather than an action.

Vladimir is a brilliant Web designer.   **Examples**
   S   V   C

His work seems elegant and contemporary.
S   V   C

Knowing how to use all the latest software is the key.
S   V   C

Some people are gifted that way.
         S   V   C

A sentence is a grammatical unit that can stand alone. It must be composed of a subject and a verb and is usually accompanied by an object or a complement.

Parts of Speech

A knowledge of the roles parts of speech play will help you understand how your sentences are constructed.

Nouns

Nouns name something: a person, place, or thing. They may be abstract or concrete. As a general rule, something may be classified as a noun if you can put an article ("a," "an," or "the") or a possessive pronoun ("my," "her") in front of it.

advertising	corset
philosophy	computer
doctor	giraffe

Examples

Pronouns

Pronouns stand in the place of nouns. There are many kinds of pronouns.

PERSONAL: I, you, he, she, we, they (subjective)
                me, you, him, her, us, them (objective)
                my, your, his, her, our, their (possessive)
                mine, yours, his, hers, ours, theirs (absolute possessive)

15

Example **I** never should have lent **her my** notes from yesterday's class.

REFLEXIVE OR INTENSIVE: myself, yourself, and so on

Examples Frankenstein's creature was shocked when he looked at **himself** in the mirror. (reflective)

I did it all by **myself**. (intensive)

RELATIVE: who, which, that, whose, whoever, whomever, whichever, and so on

Example The best friends are those **who** remain loyal to the end.

These pronouns connect subordinate clauses to main clauses.

INTERROGATIVE: who, whom, which, what

Example **Who** do you think you are?

These pronouns begin questions.

DEMONSTRATIVE: this, that, these, those, such

Example **Such** is life.

These pronouns point to someone or something.

INDEFINITE: any, some, each, every, few, everyone, everybody, someone, somebody

Example **Everybody** loves **somebody** sometime.

These pronouns stand for an indefinite number of people or things.

RECIPROCAL: each other, one another

Example Scott and Zelda loved and hated **each other** intensely.

These pronouns express a reciprocal relationship.

Verbs

A verb is an action word or a word that describes a state of being. It may have many forms and tenses. It also may be composed of an auxiliary verb and a main verb. Verbs may be transitive or intransitive (some verbs may be either), or linking.

A transitive verb needs an object to be complete.

Winston **shut** his mouth.   **Example**

An intransitive verb is complete without an object.

Hayden **sneezed.**   **Example**

A linking verb connects the subject to a state of being.

Anne **is** pregnant.   **Example**

Adjectives

Adjectives describe or modify nouns.

delicious	wooden	**Examples**
handsome	abstract	
devilish	superstitious	

Adverbs

Adverbs describe or modify verbs, adjectives, and other adverbs. They often end in "ly."

soon	too	**Examples**
devilishly	now	
often	generally	

Prepositions

The preposition is a linking word that is always followed by a noun or a pronoun (and its modifiers, if any).

on the wagon	according **to** her	**Examples**
in your mind	**by** all accounts	
to the lifeboats	**from** me **to** you	

Prepositions are used to link objects to verbs or nouns and to form a phrase that shows place, time, position, or manner. These phrases usually function as adjectives or adverbs in a sentence.

I'll get back **to her** as soon as possible.   **Examples**
Two players **on my team** were taken **to hospital**.

15

Conjunctions

Conjunctions are used to join two words, phrases, or clauses.

Examples   The office sent invoices to those **who** owed money **and** greeting cards to those **who** did not.

After the war was over, Ashley returned to Melanie.

Love is **as** strong **as** death.

Interjections

Interjections are exclamatory words or phrases that interrupt a sentence.

Examples   **No**, I don't want to go to the dentist.

My word! I simply don't believe what you say.

Note: Keep the following definitions in mind as you read the next chapter.

Phrase

A phrase is a group of words.

Examples   playing doctor

in the tree house

Clause

A clause is a group of words with a subject and a verb.

Example   We were playing doctor in the tree house.

Chapter 16
COMMON SENTENCE PROBLEMS

What is written without effort is in general read without pleasure.
—SAMUEL JOHNSON

A well-structured sentence tells its readers where to start and where to stop. The sentence, if it is correctly formed, constitutes a complete thought. It contains a main subject and a main verb connected to the subject.

Sentence Structure: Fragments, Run-ons, Comma Splices

Avoid fragments

A sentence fragment lacks either a subject or a main verb. Or, sometimes, it ignores the connection between them.

> ✗ Ramona did not follow the cheesecake recipe. But added cheddar instead of cream cheese.

Examples

(missing subject: she)

> ✓ Ramona did not follow the cheesecake recipe. She added cheddar instead of cream cheese.

> ✗ Wilhelm enjoyed many forms of relaxation. Practising tai chi, doing origami, and baking cookies.

(no connection to the subject: he)

> ✓ Wilhelm enjoyed many forms of relaxation: practising tai chi, doing origami, and baking cookies.

> ✗ Norrie didn't bring his homework. Because Fido ate it.
> ✓ Norrie didn't bring his homework because Fido ate it.

Note: A fragment may, on rare occasions, be used for rhetorical effect. Deliberate fragments must, however, be used sparingly. It is also a wise idea to use a dash (two hyphens in typing) before a deliberate sentence fragment to indicate its purpose to your reader.

Example
Should colleges and universities have the right to charge foreign students higher tuition than Canadian students?—Under no circumstances.

Avoid run-on sentences

A run-on sentence is actually two sentences that run together without any punctuation to indicate where one ends and the next begins.

Example
✗ Hedda couldn't sleep on the new waterbed she always felt seasick.
✓ Hedda couldn't sleep on the new waterbed. She always felt seasick.

Avoid comma splices

A comma splice is similar to a run-on sentence. It occurs when two main clauses are "spliced," or incorrectly joined, by a comma. The comma splice fails to show the relationship between two clauses.

Examples
✗ Graeme had too much to drink, he got the hiccups.
✗ His mother was the designated driver, she took him home.

A comma splice, like a visible seam, is a sign of faulty workmanship. There are several methods by which it may be corrected. Run-ons may also be treated the same way:

1. JOIN THE TWO IDEAS WITH ONE OF THE FOLLOWING COORDINATING CONJUNCTIONS: "AND," "OR," "NOR," "FOR," "BUT," "YET," "SO."

Examples
✓ Graeme had too much to drink, and he got the hiccups.
✓ His mother was the designated driver, so she took him home.

2. JOIN THE TWO IDEAS WITH A SUBORDINATING CONJUNCTION.

Examples
✓ Because Graeme had too much to drink, he got the hiccups.
✓ Since his mother was the designated driver, she took him home.

3. FORM TWO SEPARATE SENTENCES.

Examples
✓ Graeme had too much to drink. He got the hiccups.
✓ His mother was the designated driver. She took him home.

4. JOIN THE TWO IDEAS WITH A SEMICOLON.

Use this method of correction only if the two ideas in question are logically connected. Note that sometimes a word may be used as a conjunctive adverb to join two sentences with a semicolon. Such words as "however," "therefore," and "hence" frequently serve this function. For more information, see page 176.

✓ Graeme had too much to drink; he got the hiccups.   **Examples**
✓ His mother was the designated driver; she took him home.

CHAPTER 16 SENTENCE STRUCTURE EXERCISE A

Correct the comma splices, run-ons, and fragments in these sentences. Some may be fine as they are. Answers begin on p. 219.

1. My friend Anne is always asking to go to the Ardmore Tea Room in Halifax, she likes to eat fish cakes there.

2. Kraft Dinner is not a Canadian product nevertheless, it seems to be a staple among Canadian students.

3. Outdoor markets are much admired in Canada, well-known examples include Toronto's Kensington Market, Vancouver's Granville Market and The Forks in Winnipeg.

4. If you would like to visit a great Irish pub, go to Edmonton the one I recommend is called O'Byrne's.

5. Michael Smith has owned very successful restaurants in Prince Edward Island and New Brunswick however, he is best known for a television program on the Food Network.

6. Graham Kerr, though born in England, produced his show "The Galloping Gourmet" in Canada, he lived in this country for some time when the show was on the air.

7. Toronto's most celebrated chef is probably Susur Lee his cuisine is a clever fusion of Western and Asian that is original and mouthwatering.

8. Canada has its share of cookbook authors. Which include Jeanne Benoit, Jean Paré and Edna Staebler.

9. The best Japanese restaurant I have visited is Tojo's in Vancouver many tourists flock there for fabulous sushi.

10. Some would say that Canada does not have its own unique cuisine nevertheless, it has produced both great chefs and great authors of cookbooks.

CHAPTER 16 SENTENCE STRUCTURE EXERCISE B

1. Canadians are often unaware of their famous fellow citizens and even of the tourist attractions in their own country perhaps we just need to be reminded.

2. Guy Lombardo, a famous band leader, was born in London, Ontario, a bridge in that city was constructed in his honour.

3. Linda Evangelista, a Canadian from St. Catharines, Ontario, has become an instantly recognizable supermodel her face is reproduced on magazine covers throughout the world.

4. Among historical figures, Nellie McClung being famous as a woman's rights activist in Canada though more Canadians would recognize Carry Nation or Susan B. Anthony, who are Americans.

5. Louis Riel, a leader of his people in their resistance against the Canadian government, possibly the most controversial figure in Canadian history, many Canadians still would not know much about him.

6. Places in Canada are sometimes not instantly recognizable to audiences either hence, cities like Vancouver and Toronto pass for American cities.

7. Toronto, sometimes called Hollywood North, is often used as a film location these days films can be shot more inexpensively there than in New York City.

8. In fact, a watchful audience member might notice that the CN Tower appears behind Jennifer Lopez's shoulder in *Angel Eyes*, however, the film is supposed to take place in Chicago!

9. Films like *My Big Fat Greek Wedding* were shot, in part, in a Greek section of Toronto, this phenomenon accounts for the appearance of many Canadian actors in that film, including Fiona Reid.

10. Keep an eye out for Canadiana many historical and contemporary Canadian people and places need to be better known in their own country!

Modifiers

Modifiers are descriptive words or phrases. A modifier may be a simple adverb or an adjective, or a more complex adverbial phrase or adjectival phrase. A modifier should describe clearly and unambiguously. To do so, it must be as near in the sentence as possible to the thing described.

Avoid misplaced modifiers
A modifier, whether a word or a phrase, should be placed next to the word it describes.

Examples   ✗ Rotting on the vine, the farmers could not sell the grapes to wineries.
✓ The farmers could not sell the grapes rotting on the vine to wineries.

✗ Licking each other fondly, the children admired the kittens.
✓ Licking each other fondly, the kittens were admired by the children.

Watch the position of limiting modifiers
A limiting modifier is a word that qualifies part or all of the statement. Consider carefully the placement of the following modifiers (and others): "only," "just," "nearly," "almost," "hardly."

Only Gilbert brought a case of beer.

(No one else brought one.)

Gilbert brought only a case of beer.

(He brought only one case.)

Gilbert brought a case of beer only.

(He didn't bring a case of wine.)

Avoid squinting modifiers

A squinting modifier is ambiguously placed in the sentence, so that the writer's intention is unclear.

The suspect confessed that he had served time **later**.
The suspect confessed **later** that he had served time.

Avoid dangling modifiers

A modifier dangles when what it is meant to describe is accidentally left out of the sentence. To figure out what it does describe, ask *who* or *what* is being described.

✗ After vacuuming the living-room rug, the cat tracked mud all over it.
✓ After vacuuming the living-room rug, I saw that the cat had tracked mud all over it.

or

✓ After I vacuumed the living-room rug, the cat tracked mud all over it.

Dangling modifiers that end in "ing" are usually easy to spot. Remember, however, that a dangling modifier may also involve a prepositional phrase or an infinitive form. A dangling modifier may also occur at the end of a sentence.

✗ As a weightlifter, my muscles are in tremendous shape.
✓ As a weightlifter, I believe that my muscles are in tremendous shape.

✗ To get a high-paying job, education is essential.
✓ To get a high-paying job, you need education.

✗ Fernando's travel bills were expensive, being used to flying first class.
✓ Being used to flying first class, Fernando had expensive travel bills.

or

✓ Since Fernando was used to flying first class, his travel bills were expensive.

Note that some modifiers apply to the entire sentence rather than to any one word or phrase within it. These constructions, called "absolute modifiers," include phrases such as "To make a long story short" and "All things considered."

CHAPTER 16 MODIFIERS EXERCISE A

Correct problems with modifiers in the following sentences. Some may be correct as they stand. Check your answers on p. 220.

1. Declan has almost stopped speaking to all his former business associates.
2. After checking your e-mail, the computer should be turned off.
3. As the designated driver, drinking at this party is not acceptable for me.
4. Most of the textbooks purchased, after spending hundreds of dollars on them, wound up in the used bookstore.
5. Alone at the cottage, the forest seemed dark and forbidding.
6. After investigating a number of exciting new jobs, Deepa's old job seemed tedious and underpaid.
7. In hot weather, the fan should be run continuously before turning on the air conditioner.
8. Unless they are Persians, most cat owners do not need to worry about grooming.
9. As a forty-six-year-old man, Stats Canada calculates that he has lived 58% of his life.
10. Buying exercise equipment, my birthday was passed peacefully.

CHAPTER 16 MODIFIERS EXERCISE B

1. Once loaded, the gardener should move the wheelbarrow carefully.
2. Sticky toffee pudding is enjoyed by many diners, especially when covered in hot rum sauce.
3. Just like you, my student loan is enormous.
4. Being tired all day long, the bed looks inviting.
5. Barking loudly at any intrusion, the owners of the bichon frise were awakened from a sound sleep.
6. Khiet heard that there were more divorces this year on the television news.
7. By forwarding your e-mail to another account, less time will be wasted reading ads for herbal medication and weight-loss cures.
8. When planning to build a fish pond, raccoons and other wildlife who like to eat fish need to be discouraged.
9. My finding the parakeet dead at the bottom of the cage led to a search for the cats.
10. Keen on hunting, the best wife for Gaston would be someone like Annie Oakley.

Pronoun Reference and Agreement

A pronoun, as the name suggests, acts for a noun or in the place of a noun. A pronoun should almost always refer to a specific noun in the sentence itself. The noun to which it refers is called an "antecedent." When a pronoun does not refer clearly to its antecedent, confusing or ambiguous writing is the result.

A Guide to Proper Pronoun Usage

Make sure your pronoun matches its antecedent. A pronoun must agree in gender: it may be masculine (he, him, his), feminine (she, her, hers), or neuter (it, it, its). A pronoun must also agree in number: it may be singular or plural.

In gender

> Nancy named **her** dachshund Simon.
> Nancy named **him** Simon.

Example

In the second sentence, "her dachshund" has been replaced by the masculine pronoun "him."

In the past, the masculine pronouns ("he," "his," "him") were used to refer generally to nouns that were not specifically feminine.

16

> The reader must make up **his** own mind.

Example

Although the masculine pronoun is still, strictly speaking, grammatically correct, many people now find its general use offensive. It is now more common to find such cases phrased as

> The reader must make up **his or her** own mind.

Example

For those who find the use of "his or her" cumbersome, the best solution is to use the plural pronoun, and an accompanying plural noun, of course.

> Readers must make up **their** own minds.

Example

The determination of gender in English does not pose much of a problem, apart from this dispute. Problems do arise, however, with the number of pronouns.

In number

1. BE SURE TO LOCATE THE CORRECT ANTECEDENT FOR THE PRONOUN IN QUESTION.

Example   Chloë is one of those students **who** skip their classes regularly.

"Students" is the antecedent of the relative pronoun *who*. Both the verb "skip" and the pronoun "their" are plural. Note that "one of those" takes the plural, but "one of these" is singular, as in "One of these gloves is lost."

2. BE ESPECIALLY CAREFUL WITH COLLECTIVE NOUNS AND THEIR PRONOUN REPLACEMENTS.

When a collective noun is considered as a unit, the pronoun that stands for it is singular.

Example   The jury has reached its decision.

Here the jury acts as a unit.

When the component parts of a collective noun are considered individually, the pronoun that stands for it is plural.

Example   The jury have expressed their differences of opinion.

Here the jury acts individually; each member has his or her own opinion.

3. BE CAREFUL OF IMPRECISE USE OF SOME INDEFINITE PRONOUNS.

"Anyone," "anybody," "someone," "somebody," "everyone," "everybody," "each," "either," "neither," "nobody," and "no one" are indefinite pronouns, all of which generally take singular verbs.

Example   Nobody wore his or her bathing suit.

Ideally, "his or her" should allow an indefinite pronoun, if the construction is to avoid charges of sexism. In conversation, many people would get around this problem by saying,

Example   Nobody wore their bathing suits.

This form, despite its regular occurrence in spoken English, is still considered imprecise grammatically. It should properly be replaced by the following:

Example   None of us wore our bathing suits.

The best approach is to use the plural form.

In case

Pronouns, besides being masculine or feminine, singular or plural, also have different forms, depending on their case. They may be used as subjects ("he," "she," "they"), objects ("him," "her," "them"), or possessives ("his," "her," "their").

1. USE THE SUBJECTIVE FORM IF THE PRONOUN IS THE SUBJECT OF A VERB (STATED OR IMPLIED).

The police officer stated that it was **she** who had reported the theft of the painting.

Example

"She" is used here because a verb is implied.

It was **they** who had masterminded the heist.

Example

"They" and not "them" is used here because it functions as the subject of the verb "had masterminded."

   This precision is essential in writing English, but in informal speech, by contrast, "It's me" or "It was her" is considered acceptable.

2. MAKE SURE TO USE THE OBJECTIVE FORM OF THE PRONOUN IF IT IS THE OBJECT OF A VERB.

The poodle gave his master fleas.
The poodle gave **him them**.

Example

In the second version, the objective forms for both pronouns—objects of the verb "gave"—have been substituted.

The poodle gave **his master and me** fleas.

Example

Although you might be tempted to write "The poodle gave his master and I fleas," it becomes obvious that the objective pronoun "me" is correct when you remove the words "his master and." When the pronoun case is a problem, try taking out part of a compound subject and reading the sentence. The correct pronoun should then be obvious.

3. MAKE SURE TO USE THE OBJECTIVE FORM OF THE PRONOUN AFTER A PREPOSITION.

Between **you** and **me**, I think you should use deodorant.
It's important for **you** and **me** to wear clean underwear every day.

Examples

4. AFTER "THAN" OR "AS," USE THE FORM OF THE PRONOUN THAT WOULD BE REQUIRED IN THE COMPLETE IMPLIED CLAUSE.

A sloth is harder working than **he** [is].
A monkey can communicate as well as **she** [can].

Examples

Note the difference in meaning in the following examples:

I love you as much as **he** [does].
I love you as much as [I love] **him**.

Examples

16

Pronoun Problems in Essay Writing

Use personal pronouns with discretion

Too few personal references in an essay may be as awkward as too many. Few instructors disallow the use of "I" entirely. Its occasional use should prevent needless circumlocution and impersonality. Never stoop to cold and formal constructions like "It is the opinion of this writer," or the overly polite "myself." "We" is sometimes acceptable, though its overuse may sound pompous. "One" may serve as an alternative, though it runs the risk of sounding too distanced and impersonal.

You are writing your paper: its words and thoughts are yours. Avoid "I" and "in my opinion" only when a personal perspective might make your point seem weak or merely a matter of personal idiosyncrasy.

Check to see that your pronoun references are present and accounted for

Examples
UNCLEAR: In small towns, they do not lock their cars.
CLEARER: Residents of small towns do not lock their cars.

UNCLEAR: Esther changed the baby's diaper, and it screamed.
CLEARER: When Esther changed its diaper, the baby screamed.

UNCLEAR: Robert hates studying floristry, but he intends to become one anyway.
CLEARER: Robert hates studying floristry, but he intends to become a florist anyway.

Avoid broad pronoun references

A broad pronoun reference occurs when "this," "which," or "that" is used to refer to an idea rather than to a specific word in the sentence. Some broad references may be tolerated, if the meaning is generally clear. Be careful of raising unanswered questions in the reader's mind, however.

Example
UNCLEAR: Dexter stays up all night watching reruns of "Leave It to Beaver," which is why he falls asleep on the job so often.
CLEARER: Dexter stays up all night watching reruns of "Leave It to Beaver," a habit which causes him to fall asleep on the job often.

"Which" does not clearly refer to any specific noun in the preceding sentence. Add a noun before "which" to clarify the point.

"This" too is a broad reference. Although its usage is gaining ground, many instructors still do not find it is precise enough. Look at the following example:

Example
UNCLEAR: Using vague pronouns makes reading difficult. This should not be accepted.
CLEARER: Using vague pronouns makes reading difficult. This practice should not be accepted.

"This" is best accompanied by a noun that makes its reference clear. It should refer to a specific, easily identifiable noun.

CHAPTER 16 PRONOUNS EXERCISE A

Find and correct problems with pronouns in the following sentences. Some may be correct as they are. Check your answers on p. 221.

1. If a customer is not satisfied with the products, they should complain to the store manager, and they can be returned.
2. In this book it says that Sister Wendy is a well-known authority on art history.
3. When you are summoned for jury duty, one is expected to respond quickly.
4. Even if you don't have a membership to the fitness club, you don't need to be one to benefit from this special trial offer.
5. Everything you thought about we professors is sadly true.
6. Between you and I, you should know better than to believe everything you see on the Internet.
7. In David's apartment, he has lots of dust bunnies under the bed.
8. Everyone who answered the advertisement was looking for ways to improve their income without actually having to work.
9. When I pulled the cat's tail, it meowed fiercely.
10. Kim bought clothes from the Salvation Army just like her.

CHAPTER 16 PRONOUNS EXERCISE B

1. She wondered who's job it was to empty the garbage, which had been neglected for at least a week.
2. When a student hands in their paper late, the instructor is likely to give them a reduced grade.
3. One might enjoy long vacations if you didn't worry about work piling up at home.
4. The actor who we saw backstage was handing out autographs to the adoring throngs.
5. Each of us has our own reasons for attending the support group, and they do not want publicity.
6. Whom would you say is the culprit?
7. Everybody is entitled to their own opinion when they discuss politics or religion.
8. They are closing down the cod fisheries in Newfoundland.
9. Nobody hates grammar more than me.
10. Do you intend to join Tammy Faye and I?

Subject and Verb Agreement

The subject and verb in a sentence are closely connected. In order for the sentence to express itself clearly, the subject and the verb must agree.

Most problems with agreement between subject and verb result from difficulties in locating the subject of a verb. Solve these problems by locating the verb in each clause. Remember, first, that a verb describes either an action or a state of being. Next, ask *who* or *what* is performing that action or is being described. The answer to the question *who* or *what* is the subject of the verb. Having located the subject and verb, you may then check to see that they match.

Example   Big Brother is watching you.

Who is watching?
—Big Brother (the subject of the verb "is watching")

How to Match Subjects and Verbs Correctly

Check to see that verbs agree in number with their subjects. In other words, singular subjects take singular verbs; plural subjects take plural verbs.

Problems to watch for:

1. THE NOUN THAT IMMEDIATELY PRECEDES THE VERB MAY NOT BE THE SUBJECT.

Example   Not one of these science-fiction writers has ever seen an extra-terrestrial creature.

The correct subject is "one."

2. SUBJECTS JOINED BY "AND" ARE USUALLY, BUT NOT ALWAYS, PLURAL.

Example   My friend and guardian angel has come to my rescue.

"My friend and guardian angel" refers to one person.

3. SINGULAR SUBJECTS THAT ARE JOINED BY A PHRASE OTHER THAN "AND" ARE NOT MADE PLURAL. SUCH PHRASES AS "AS WELL AS," "IN ADDITION TO," AND "ALONG WITH" HAVE NO EFFECT ON THE AGREEMENT OF THE VERB SINCE THEY ARE NOT PART OF THE SUBJECT.

Example   A hamburger, along with french fries, is Dee's typical dinner.

"Along with french fries" is not part of the subject.

4. SUBJECTS JOINED BY "OR" OR "NOR" ARE EACH CONSIDERED SEPARATELY. THE VERB AGREES WITH THE SUBJECT CLOSEST TO IT.

Neither tears nor litigation moves Scrooge to act fairly toward his employees.   **Example**

"Tears" and "litigation" are each considered separately; since "litigation" is closer, the verb is singular.

5. THE FOLLOWING SUBJECTS ALWAYS TAKE SINGULAR VERBS: "EACH," "EITHER," "NEITHER," "ONE," AND WORDS ENDING IN "BODY" OR "ONE."

Neither of the twins eats turnip.   **Example**

6. SUBJECTS LIKE "SOME," "ALL," "MOST," "ANY," OR "NONE" MAY TAKE SINGULAR OR PLURAL VERBS, DEPENDING UPON THE NOUN TO WHICH THEY REFER.

Some of the guests refuse to eat parsnip.   **Examples**
All of us enjoy caviar.

(plural verb)

All of the caviar is gone.   **16**

(singular verb)

7. A COLLECTIVE NOUN, USED TO REFER TO A GROUP OF PEOPLE OR THINGS, TAKES A SINGULAR VERB WHEN THE COLLECTIVE IS CONSIDERED AS A UNIT AND A PLURAL VERB WHEN EACH MEMBER IS CONSIDERED INDIVIDUALLY.

Singular (considered a unit): The union is planning a strike.   **Example**

Plural (considered as individuals within the group): The union are voting on the new benefits package.

8. A LINKING VERB (A VERB DESCRIBING A STATE OF BEING) AGREES WITH ITS SUBJECT AND NOT WITH ITS PREDICATE.

The only thing Myrna ever buys is cigarettes.   **Examples**

"Thing" is the subject; hence, "is" is the appropriate verb.

or

Cigarettes are the only thing Myrna ever buys.

In this example, "cigarettes" is the subject; hence, the plural verb is correct.

9. A VERB STILL AGREES WITH ITS SUBJECT, EVEN WHEN THEIR ORDER IS INVERTED. THE SUBJECT FOLLOWS "THERE IS" OR "THERE ARE," "HERE IS" OR "HERE ARE," AND THE VERB IS SINGULAR OR PLURAL ACCORDINGLY.

Example   Here are the pizzas you ordered.

Here "pizzas" is the subject; hence, the correct verb is "are."

10. RELATIVE PRONOUNS ("WHO," "WHICH," "THAT"), ACTING AS SUBJECTS, TAKE SINGULAR OR PLURAL VERBS, DEPENDING ON THE WORDS TO WHICH THEY REFER (THEIR ANTECEDENTS).

Example   Harry is one of those people who cheat at Scrabble.

"People," the antecedent of "who," is plural; hence, the verb "cheat" is also plural. *But note:*

Harry is the only one of us who spells badly.

"One" is the antecedent in this case; hence, the verb "spells" is singular.

11. SOME NOUNS MAY LOOK PLURAL THOUGH THEY ARE ACTUALLY SINGULAR. EXAMPLES INCLUDE "PHYSICS," "ECONOMICS," "ETHICS," AND "NEWS." CHECK DOUBTFUL USAGE IN A DICTIONARY.

Example   News is big business on television today.

CHAPTER 16 SUBJECT AND VERB AGREEMENT EXERCISE A

Correct the agreement problems in the following sentences. Some sentences may be fine as they are. Check your answers on p. 222.

1. Either the lottery officials or the provincial government are going to have to make a decision about who will receive this month's prize.
2. The tornadoes that tear through this country every year has a disastrous impact.
3. Ana seems to forget that there is assignments to be submitted before she can graduate.
4. A high percentage of the student body are opposed to the tuition hikes.
5. A high percentage of the students are in favour of a year-round school year.
6. A number of reasons has been given for your behaviour at the barbeque yesterday.
7. Erika is the only one of my students who have already found a job in her field of expertise.
8. If the board of governors has the inclination, they can oppose the layoffs.
9. The main criteria of excellence in work is determination and doggedness.
10. The number of stars in the sky are infinite.

CHAPTER 16 SUBJECT AND VERB AGREEMENT EXERCISE B

1. Tessie's main worry as a new homeowner were squirrels getting into the chimney.

2. Tastes in furniture differs.

3. Every last one of those reports were proofread painstakingly before they were submitted.

4. A zebra and a tiger was lost in the flood.

5. The going rate for mortgages steadily increases as the dollar drops.

6. Economics were her chief concern as a provincial minister.

7. "Canadian Idol" and the Canadian version of "Who Wants to Be a Millionaire?" competes for viewers every weeknight.

8. Neither one of you know a thing about how to save your money.

9. Each of us have a date with destiny.

10. This cell phone and camera is easy to use, even if the screen is very small.

End Punctuation

1. Use a period after a statement, an indirect question, or a command.

I have something to tell you. (statement)
Don't look now. (command)
Penny asked me when I got my nose fixed. (indirect question)

Examples

16

2. Use a period after most abbreviations, unless they are easily recognized.

Note that some formal abbreviations, such as Mr., Mrs., and Dr., always end with a period in common usage.

Mr.	CBC
Mrs.	DVD
Dr.	CD player

Examples

3. Use a question mark after a direct question.

Who's been eating my porridge?
Whatever is the matter?
What's for supper?

Examples

4. Use exclamation marks sparingly to express emphasis in an informal essay. Use them in a formal essay at your own risk.

✗ Hugo did his homework!
✓ Amazingly, Hugo did his homework.

Example

The Colon

The colon (:) is used to introduce something. Remember the following rules for colon usage:

1. Use a colon only after a complete sentence (that is, after an independent clause).

Example   ✗ Delores loved: foreign vacations, fur coats, and cold cash.
✓ Delores loved three things: foreign vacations, fur coats, and cold cash.

2. Use a colon after a complete sentence to introduce ideas, lists, or quotations.

Examples   This report can mean only one thing: we are going to be parents.

Dorothy Parker makes this claim: "The two most beautiful words in the English language are 'Cheque enclosed'".

3. Use a colon to indicate amplification or further development of an idea.

Example   Thanatology is a branch of psychology: it deals with the subject of death and dying.

The Semicolon

A semicolon (;) is a heavier punctuation mark than a comma, but lighter than a period. Use a semicolon generally only where you might use a period instead.
    Semicolons are especially useful in the following cases:

1. Use a semicolon to join two closely related main clauses.
The use of a semicolon instead of a coordinating conjunction shows a close connection (or a sharp antithesis) between two ideas.

Example   Man proposes; God disposes.

2. Use a semicolon with a transitional word or phrase when it is used to join two main clauses.
Transitional words or phrases such as "however," "moreover," "furthermore," "hence," "as a result," and "consequently" may be used in this way.

Example   I won't accept charity; however, I will take cash or travellers' cheques.

The semicolon takes the place of a period in this sentence.
But note:

    I will not, however, accept charity.

In this case, "however" is not used to join two main clauses. Since the transitional word interrupts one main clause, commas are adequate punctuation.

3. Use a semicolon to separate items listed in a series if commas are already used as internal punctuation.

Maxwell always did three things before he went to bed: one, he put on his pyjamas; two, he drank warm milk; three, he fell asleep in the armchair in front of the TV set.

Example

CHAPTER 16 SEMICOLON AND COLON EXERCISE A

Add or remove semicolons and colons where appropriate. Some may be correct as they stand. Answers are on p. 223.

1. According to his partner, Nick is: lazy, sloppy, and irresponsible, however, the partner, if truth be told, is rigid and lacking in sympathy.
2. Having heard of your recent inheritance, I would like to request one thing: can I see the spreadsheet?
3. Buying a condominium in a large city like Vancouver or Toronto is costly, hence, I am planning to live in a cardboard box over a hot air vent.
4. There are only ninety-eight days left till my birthday, that's plenty of time for you to save up to buy me a two-week vacation in Milan.
5. The bestselling fiction writers in Canada in the past few years are; Margaret Atwood, Yann Martel, Alice Munro, and Carol Shields.
6. Summer movies are highly entertaining but not very deep, they replace sophisticated plot, character, and setting with car chases, sexy actors, and unbelievable stunts nevertheless, they succeed at the box office.
7. Two things are bothering me; my computer has a virus, and my hard drive needs defragmenting.
8. Your online business can be saved only if you marry money or inherit a fortune from a long-lost relative.
9. The incumbent politician had a goal in mind, to win back the shaken confidence of his constituents after the scandal.
10. Rico's dream was: to be a bronco buster at the Calgary Stampede.

CHAPTER 16 SEMICOLON AND COLON EXERCISE B

1. Kerry told Malo that it would be all right after five or six years presumably, everyone would forget what the quarrel had been about by then anyway.
2. Here is what I learned today from watching the Food Network; how to finish a dessert, using a blow torch, how to set fire to the kitchen curtains, using the same blow torch, and how to scare off my dinner guests, even before dinner is over.

16

3. The new parents considered these names for the twins, Ben and Jerry, Mick and Keith, or Mutt and Jeff.

4. If you have high blood pressure, you should avoid eating salt, gaining weight, and drinking alcohol.

5. Banff is a glorious tourist town it has beautiful mountain scenery it also has the highest rate of sexually transmitted disease in Canada, according to some sources.

6. The German shepherd was afraid of thunderstorms, his owner always drove home to keep him company during any weather disturbance.

7. Green vegetables are good for you, why can't we get lettuce on our sandwiches in this cafeteria?

8. The Shih Tzu next door would benefit from obedience school, he bites his owners' ankles every chance he gets.

9. Buying coffee in a Tim Hortons outlet is the number one Canadian pastime there are more doughnut shops than there are houses, it seems.

10. Ethel disliked her new living room furniture, hence, she decided to spend more time in the family room.

The Comma

A comma (,) is a light mark of punctuation. Some basic rules that govern its use are listed below. When in doubt about a particular usage, let ease in reading be your guide.

1. Use a comma before "and," "or," "nor," "for," "but," "yet," "so" if any of these words are used to join two independent clauses.

Example   Gunther doesn't normally snore, but tonight his dog needs earplugs.

But note:
A comma is not needed if a complete independent clause does not follow.

Example   Ivor hates school but loves recess.

In this case, "but" actually joins a compound verb, rather than two independent clauses.

2. You may use a comma after a word, a phrase, or a clause used to introduce the main subject and verb. The comma is essential if the sentence would be confusing without it.

Example   Bracing himself, Rocky applied for a job as a snake charmer. Because he had never seen a snake before, Rocky was different from the other candidates. Alas, the snake did not find him charming enough.

3. Use a comma after a word or phrase that modifies an entire sentence. To find out whether something is a sentence modifier, test to see if it can be moved elsewhere in the sentence without changing the meaning.

However, he did find work cleaning cages at the zoo.   **Example**

"However" can be shifted in the sentence; hence, it is a sentence modifier:

He did, however, find work cleaning cages at the zoo.

4. Use a comma if you would like to emphasize contrast.

Tracy attended school for the social life, not for the good of her mind.   **Examples**
Pee-Wee wanted precious antiques, but found worthless junk.

5. Use commas to separate elements in a series.

Cinderella invited Flora, Fauna, and Merryweather to her coming-out party.   **Example**

A comma before "and" at the end of the list is usually advisable to prevent confusion.

Ogden tells us that his old age begins, and middle age ends, and now his   **Example**
descendants outnumber his friends.

Here a comma is used to separate a series of independent clauses. Note, however, that two independent clauses together must normally be separated by a semicolon.

6. Put commas around words, phrases, or clauses that interrupt a sentence. Commas may be used around a word or a group of words if that part of the sentence might be removed and still leave a subject and predicate.

Frankly, my dear, I am indifferent.   **Examples**
Yes, Virginia, there is a Santa Claus.

7. Put commas around appositives, words that rename those that precede.

Jethro and Elly May, Melissa's pet gerbils, are on the loose again.   **Examples**

Madame de Pompadour said that Canada, then a colony of France, was useful
only to provide her with furs.

16

8. Put commas around interrupting phrases or clauses that are non-restrictive in meaning.

Example   My grandmother, who lives in Halifax, is getting a divorce.

Here the clause "who lives in Halifax" is non-restrictive, and it implies that the author has one grandmother; some incidental information about her is enclosed in commas.
But note:

My grandmother who lives in Halifax is getting a divorce.

Here the clause "who lives in Halifax" is restrictive and lacks commas. It implies that the author has two grandmothers and uses the clause to identify which one.

9. Commas should not enclose material that is restrictive, that is, essential to the sentence's meaning.

Example   ✗ People, who live in glass houses, shouldn't throw stones.

This sentence, because of the way it is punctuated, says that all people shouldn't throw stones.

    ✓ People who live in glass houses shouldn't throw stones.

This statement identifies those people who shouldn't throw stones. The modifier, because it performs the necessary function of identification or limitation, cannot be surrounded by commas.

10. Commas should not separate main sentence elements. Do not use a comma between a subject and verb or between a verb and an object or complement.

Example   ✗ Everything Zsa Zsa does, gets on my nerves.
    ✓ Everything Zsa Zsa does gets on my nerves.

PUNCTUATION CHECKLIST

Use a comma   when you begin a sentence with a subordinate clause
when you begin a sentence with a long phrase
when you want to set off interrupting words
when you are indicating a non-restrictive phrase or clause
when you divide two main clauses with coordinating
    conjunctions
when not to do so would make the meaning unclear

Use a semicolon	when you separate main clauses with a conjunctive adverb like "however" or "therefore" used to connect two main clauses logically
	between items that have commas in them
	when you connect two main clauses without a conjunction
Use a colon	when you introduce a word, a phrase, or a clause
	when you wish to amplify the meaning of something
	after a complete sentence *only*

CHAPTER 16 PUNCTUATION EXERCISE A

Correct errors in comma usage in the following sentences, by adding or removing punctuation as necessary. Some sentences may be correct as they are. Check your answers on p. 224.

1. The new townhouse was stylish yet there wasn't enough room to swing a cat.

2. Take your choice: you can come quietly or we can get tough.

3. June and Gwynneth did not go to bingo games nor did they enjoy psychic fairs.

4. Kurtis and Scott went to Rio de Janeiro last year and Sandy went to the south of Spain.

5. Impressed beyond words Gordon met his idol an actress from his favourite situation comedy "Gilligan's Island."

6. If there were any truth in advertising; my teeth would be as white as pearls.

7. Judging from what Aline buys, the people at Amazon must figure that she is an intellectual snob with a great deal of money; a taste for trendy fiction; no social life; and lots of time on her hands.

8. Ewan celebrated his fiftieth birthday by buying a kilt, and leaving his wife for someone twenty years his junior.

9. Rhonda displayed her new tableware; polished and shining as if they were her very own front teeth.

10. While elegant dishes may look splendid at picnics, I prefer paper plates that can be thrown away, and don't need to be washed.

CHAPTER 16 PUNCTUATION EXERCISE B

1. As the thunderstorm raged outside Faisal and Beenish ate their picnic in the backseat of the van.

2. When our guests left we gathered up the leftovers and realized we would be eating finger food for the next week; yet there wasn't a drop of gin left in the house.

3. Knowing that she probably would never see the money again reluctantly Maya agreed to grant Walter the loan.

4. The escaped Labrador retriever had a mission, you see, he was very attracted to an Akita hound, that he met in the park yesterday.

5. Axel drove her to the interview at 160 km an hour an action which resulted in his licence being suspended for a few days.

6. As age creeps up on you you can always resort to Botox; plastic surgery; or at the very least to clothes that conceal your stringy neck your flabby upper arms and your love handles.

7. After the parrot fell off its perch, Kathie who was sitting her friends' pets went into the house to count the cats to see if they were all still there.

8. Despite her best efforts to comfort her neighbours they did not seem to appreciate her references to a Monty Python sketch about a dead parrot.

9. It's my lucky day, today I was accepted into university.

10. The resort had been advertised as having twenty-four-hour room service but in reality the guests had to rely on expensive snacks and drinks from an overpriced mini-bar.

The Dash

Type a dash using two hyphens, with no spaces before or after.

Example   I won't drink—I want to know when I'm having a good time.

1. Use a dash for emphasis around parenthetical expressions.

Example   The show—though a huge success with the public—was panned by the critics.

Note: Commas are also correct in this sentence, but less emphatic.

2. Use a dash to introduce something with extra emphasis.

Example   Rob loved birthday cards—whether cheques were enclosed or not.

Note: A colon is also correct in this sentence but less emphatic.

3. Keep the dash in reserve for special occasions. Use it sparingly, especially in formal writing.

Parentheses

Parentheses are used to enclose incidental material. They (that is, the words they enclose) serve the same function as an aside in a theatrical production. Though they get the reader's attention, the material they enclose is presented as "inside information."

1. Use parentheses in formal writing to enclose the necessary definition of a term at its first appearance.

> The NFB (National Film Board of Canada) has won several Academy Awards for its productions.

Example

2. Use parentheses to enclose any part of a sentence that might be enclosed by commas or dashes, if the reader has only passing interest in it.

> In the next episode of "Degrassi Junior High" (Saturday night at nine), the twins seek a cure for acne.

Example

3. Use parentheses sparingly. Too many make the writing self-conscious and hard to follow.

> ✗ In this report (which is the product of months of arduous research), I will discuss various methods of sleep-teaching.

Example

The Apostrophe

Apostrophes are used after nouns and indefinite pronouns (e.g., "anyone," "somebody") to indicate possession. Note these general rules:

1. Add " 's" to form the possessive case if the owner is singular.

> monkey's uncle—the uncle of the monkey
> horse's mouth—the mouth of the horse
> pig's eye—the eye of the pig

Examples

Note that even when the word ends in "s," the ending is usually " 's," since that is how we pronounce it.

> James's novels—the novels of James
> Stevens's poetry—the poetry of Stevens

Examples

2. Add "s' " to the form of the possessive case if the owners are plural.

> workers' coalition—the coalition of workers
> boys' team—the team of boys

Examples

But note that words that do not form the plural with "s" are made possessive by the addition of " 's."

Examples   women's rights—the rights of women
people's court—the court of people
men's washroom—the washroom of men

3. Do not use an apostrophe with possessive pronouns.

Example   The villa is his, the Mercedes is hers, and the Swiss bank account is theirs.

Note that "its" (another possessive pronoun) also does not have an apostrophe. Do not confuse the possessive pronoun "its" with the contraction for "it is."

Examples   It's time to take you home. (it is time)
Its diaper wet, the baby fussed noisily. (possessive case)

CHAPTER 16 POSSESSION EXERCISE A

Correct the possessives in the following sentences. Some may be fine as they are. Turn to p. 225 for answers.

1. According to the stockbrokers prediction, the financial mistakes you made in the past few years will not affect next years earnings.
2. Rebeccas son now shops in the mens clothing department, but he still reads childrens books.
3. Ross vacation plans were cut short last year, but next years trip to Haifa should be glorious.
4. Yesterdays chaperone is todays cruise director.
5. To get a good nights sleep, you need to keep the cats from getting into the bedroom, for Petes sake.
6. My friends sister Carmen said that Santas elves had made her a present.
7. The actors talents were considerable, but his performance just was not enough to ensure the plays success when the critics reviews were so vicious.
8. Dickens novels and Shakespeares plays normally make up a secondary schools curriculum in Canada.
9. Mens and womens washrooms are conveniently located near the malls entrance.
10. I would make a citizens arrest if I thought the communitys by-laws had been violated.

CHAPTER 16 POSSESSION EXERCISE B

1. The bedrooms appearance was similar to that of an eldercare facility, in the housekeepers opinion.
2. Pearl Josephines mother thought her daughters name was appropriate, but her classmates teasing prompted Pearl to change it to P.J.

3. Johns idea of a birthday favour included asking if the lovers quarrel could be settled peacefully.

4. Abel watched the bank managers face when he tried to cash his travellers cheques.

5. Canadas history is full of unacknowledged heroes like Lionel Conacher, who won hockeys most prestigious award, the Stanley Cup and also won footballs most coveted prize, the Grey Cup, while being one of this countrys most accomplished track runners and a boxer who fought Jack Dempsey.

6. Tim Hortons success as a hockey player prompted him to start a business which has become a landmark among Canadian businesses; coffees pre-eminence as Canadas favourite drink is beyond question.

7. Mans best friend may be his dog, but in Rudyard Kiplings view, a womans best friend may well be a cat.

8. She enjoyed reading Horaces poetry for it's depth, Henry James novels for their sophistication, and Sears catalogue for it's sales.

9. Everything Ruth cooks looks like a dogs breakfast, but her familys appetite is powerful after a long days work.

10. Her purses contents included yesterdays credit card receipts, tomorrows theatre tickets, and todays unfinished lunch.

16

Chapter 17

ELEMENTS OF STYLE: STRUCTURING THE SENTENCES

Look and you will find it—what is unsought will go undetected.
—SOPHOCLES

Variety in your sentence structure will ensure that your reader pays attention, not only to what you say, but also to the way you say it. Try to develop an awareness of the subtle changes in emphasis and reading pace that occur when you modify the structure of a sentence. Such consciousness will enhance your style and impress your reader.

Sentence Variation

1. Vary your sentence structure.
The following are examples of different types of sentences.

SIMPLE SENTENCE: one independent clause

Example Catherine and Michael agreed to split their assets equitably in the prenuptial agreement.

COMPOUND SENTENCE: two independent clauses joined by one of the coordinating conjunctions ("and," "or," "nor," "for," "but," "yet," "so")

Example Donald kept his business empire, and Ivana kept her wardrobe and her cosmetics.

COMPLEX SENTENCE: one independent clause joined to one dependent clause

Example Marriage is a lottery in which couples stake their happiness and their worldly goods.

Note: Dependent clauses begin with a subordinating conjunction, such as one of the following:

after	because	however	that
although	before	if	though
as	how	since	

Subordinate, or dependent, clauses also begin with words starting with a "wh"— "when," "where," "why," "which," "who," "while," "whereas," "what"—except where these words introduce questions.

COMPOUND–COMPLEX SENTENCE: a compound sentence joined to a complex sentence

> They knew that a lot of people didn't expect their marriage to last, so they cele-brated their first anniversary six months early.

Example

2. Practise subordination by converting groups of simple or compound sentences you find in your writing into complex sentences.

> Joanne hated school. She quit and found a job behind a counter. Later she returned to college in a different program. This time the program was more suited to her talents and goals.
>
> REVISED: Because Joanne hate school, she quit and found a job behind a counter. Later when she returned to college, she entered a different program, which was more suited to her talents and goals.

Example

3. Practise joining simple sentences together using verbal phrases rather than subordinators. Start by changing the verb into a participle (usually ending in "ing" or "ed"). Then remove its subject, and connect it to the appropriate word in the following sentence.

> Joshua makes extra money. He plays piano in a restaurant downtown.
>
> REVISED: By playing piano in a restaurant downtown, Joshua makes extra money.

Example

4. Practise cutting tangled constructions down to size by using simple sentences where the reader might have difficulty in understanding or where you wish to place more emphasis.

> A factory job is superior to a job requiring postsecondary education. Some would argue the opposite. Still, the advantages of a factory job are numerous. Here are some of these advantages. A factory worker makes more money at an ear-lier age than a college student. Thus he can live on his own earlier. A factory

Example

17

worker also has more spare time to pursue other goals. There is also less stress placed on a factory worker. He is more likely to be happy and healthy.

REVISED: Although some would argue the opposite, a factory job is superior to a job requiring postsecondary education. Because a factory worker makes more money at an earlier age than a college student, he is able to live on his own earlier. In addition, because a factory worker has more time to pursue other goals and faces less stress than someone in a white-collar job, he is more likely to be happy and healthy.

5. Try converting some of the phrases and dependent clauses in your writing into absolutes (phrases with connecting words removed). Keep the subject of the clause and its accompanying participle; remove other words.

Example   Because his sports car was wrecked and his hopes of winning races gone, Mario decided to become a gas-station attendant.

REVISED: His sports car wrecked and his hopes of winning races gone, Mario decided to become a gas-station attendant.

6. Vary your sentences by making them more suspenseful. The typical English sentence moves directly from subject to verb to object or complement, a structure often called "loose." In other languages, the word order is often not so direct, placing subject or verb near the end of the sentence. This structure is called "periodic." Try making your own sentences periodic occasionally, so that the impact of the thought is delayed.

Example   LOOSE: Desmond gave Molly a diamond ring.

PERIODIC: Shyly, anxiously, and with tears in his eyes, Desmond gave Molly a diamond ring.

CHAPTER 17 SENTENCE VARIATION EXERCISE

1. Join these sentences, using verbal phrases. Answers are on p. 226.
   a. Vidia wanted to buy a notebook computer. She checked the advertisements on eBay every day, but a reliable notebook seemed too expensive.
   b. Bruce tried to keep the morale of the employees high. He provided incentives and collegial activities for employees. He instituted a yoga class and invited people to company picnics.
   c. The indolent student attends few classes. He refuses to complete homework assignments and avoids eye contact with the instructor when he does go to class.

2. Rewrite these sentences using absolutes, rather than dependent clauses or simple sentences.

   a. With her toes pointed, Karen executed the pirouette.
   b. The training session provided a wealth of information. It was attended by those who wanted practice in designing Web pages.
   c. When Hiram and Edwina's honeymoon was over, they decided to start a family.

3. Rewrite these simple sentences to form complex sentences. Use verbal phrases and absolutes where appropriate.

   John Keats was not a nobleman, but a member of the lower classes. He managed to become a surgeon with some financial assistance from his family. In those days, a surgeon was a tradesman rather like a barber. It was an honourable trade. Keats nevertheless wanted to be a poet. He wrote a small number of poems. His poetic development is amazing. Keats never became famous in his lifetime. He did, however, leave a small, brilliant body of work. It is still read today. In 1821 at the age of 25, Keats died. He succumbed to tuberculosis. His works are now much admired. He is considered one of the greatest English poets.

4. Take the following loose sentences and make them periodic. Make the subject or the verb more complicated, or change the word order to delay the impact of the sentence.

   a. The cat was lying in the basket on the shelf at the top of the wall unit.
   b. Although it has too much fat, Frances enjoys eating fried fish.
   c. These days young people in North America are eating more junk food.

5. Analyze an essay written by one of your classmates to determine what sentence patterns he or she uses most commonly. Make suggestions on how to rewrite some of the sentences, and examine the changes in emphasis that such revision creates.

6. Analyze some writing in a current newspaper or magazine you enjoy. Try to model some sentences on the structure of those you find.

Parallelism

Parallelism is one of the basic components of good writing style. The repetitive rhythm of parallel structure allows the reader to anticipate what comes next and to keep the overall construction in mind. Consider the following sentences:

> NOT PARALLEL: Dawn finished her essay by staying up all night, working without a break, and finally, she asked her mother to type the paper for her.

Example

> PARALLEL: Dawn finished her essay by staying up all night, working without a break, and finally, asking her mother to type the paper for her.

Making sentences that are logical, powerful, and easy to understand requires a developed sense of parallel construction. To sharpen this sense, you need to become aware of certain basic requirements of balanced sentence structure.

1. Make sure grammatical elements match.

To form a parallel construction, join nouns with nouns, verbs with verbs, participles with participles, adjectives with adjectives, and so on. Connecting words like "and," "or," "but," and "yet" are often signals of the need for a parallel construction.

Example   NOT PARALLEL: The actor was handsome, articulate, and he loved to look at himself in a mirror.

PARALLEL: The actor was handsome, articulate, and vain, loving to look at himself in a mirror.

Since the first two items are adjectives ("handsome" and "articulate"), the last item in the series should be an adjective too.

Example   NOT PARALLEL: People who are in debt should give up credit cards, borrowing money, eating out in expensive restaurants, and living above their means.

PARALLEL: People who are in debt should give up using credit cards, borrowing money, eating out in expensive restaurants, and living above their means.

The parallelism is improved when each of the nouns in question is preceded by an "ing" form.

Example   NOT PARALLEL: They divorced because the husband thought that no one should read while he was talking, and the wife thought that while she was reading, no one should talk.

PARALLEL: They divorced because the husband thought that no one should read while he was talking, and the wife thought that no one should talk while she was reading.

The balance is improved by maintaining the same word order in each clause.

2. Use parallel constructions after "than" or "as."

Example   NOT PARALLEL: It is better to light a candle than curse the darkness.

PARALLEL: It is better to light a candle than to curse the darkness.

What follows "than" should be parallel with what precedes. Hence, the word "to" should be repeated.

Example   NOT PARALLEL: My grades are just as good as Stephanie.

PARALLEL: My grades are just as good as Stephanie's.

or My grades are just as good as Stephanie's grades are.

The grades are being compared, not the grades and Stephanie.

3. Balance sentence elements connected by correlatives.

Correlatives come in pairs. They include "not only . . . but also," "both . . . and," "either . . . or," "neither . . . nor," "whether . . . or."

The grammatical constructions that follow the first coordinator should also follow the second.

> NOT PARALLEL: Derek didn't only apologize to her and admit that he had been wrong, he gave her a red rose and asked her forgiveness.
>
> PARALLEL: Not only did Derek apologize to her and admit that he had been wrong, but he also gave her a red rose and asked her forgiveness.

Example

Correlative conjunctions are used here to join two clauses.

> NOT PARALLEL: Whether you take the bus or if you go by plane, two days is not long enough for a trip to Disneyland.
>
> PARALLEL: Whether you take the bus or you go by plane, two days is not long enough for a trip to Disneyland.

Example

Correlatives are used here to join two main clauses. Note the revisions in the following sentences:

> NOT PARALLEL: Arnold was sound both mentally and in body.
>
> PARALLEL: Arnold was sound both in mind and in body.

Example

17

What follows "both" should be grammatically parallel to what follows "and."

> NOT PARALLEL: You either give Jason his toy back, or I'll tell your mother.
>
> PARALLEL: Either you give Jason his toy back, or I'll tell your mother.

Example

What follows "either" must be grammatically parallel to what follows "or." In this case, a subject and verb follow both items.

4. Parallel constructions may also be indicated by transitional signposts such as "first," "second," and "third."

> NOT PARALLEL: The sales clerk quit his job: first, the customers were rude; second, he was tired of minimum wage; and third, annoyed at having to work on Saturday nights.
>
> PARALLEL: The sales clerk quit his job: first, the customers were rude; second, he was tired of minimum wage; and third, he was annoyed at having to work on Saturday nights.

Example

5. Make sure that items in a list are grammatically parallel.

Example

NOT PARALLEL: This report makes four recommendations:
1. divers should be certified by an accredited school
2. they should wear appropriate equipment at all times
3. they should work in pairs
4. regular health checkups

PARALLEL: This report makes four recommendations:
1. divers should be certified by an accredited school
2. they should wear appropriate equipment at all times
3. they should work in pairs
4. they should get regular health checkups

In this case, the items listed have been changed so that they are all main clauses; in the incorrect example, the fourth item is a phrase.

Remember that parallel construction need not be confined to words and phrases; it may extend to subordinate clauses and to sentences. Effective use of parallel structure will enhance your writing by making it clear, balanced, and carefully structured.

Example

NOT PARALLEL: Every one of these buildings, public and private, restored or dilapidated, will share a similar fate: bought by a developer, or if the city expands, they will be destroyed.

PARALLEL: Every one of these buildings, public and private, restored or dilapidated, will share a similar fate: if a developer buys them, or if the city expands, they will be destroyed.

"Or" in the corrected sentence joins two subordinate clauses, both in the active voice.

CHAPTER 17 PARALLELISM EXERCISE A

Improve the instances of faulty parallelism in the following sentences. Some may be fine as they are. Check your answers on p. 226.

1. The dentist advised me to give up soft drinks and that I remember to floss.
2. Quickly and with grace, the dancer accepted the bouquet from the conductor.
3. Either I am overtired or suffering from an illness.
4. The piano is elegant, enormous, and it is out of tune.
5. My best friend has a new house in the country, an in-ground pool and has acquired a huge mortgage.
6. Either the dog is scared or upset; he normally does not growl at visitors.
7. The weak Canadian dollar affects the market, and tourists' buying power in other countries is severely reduced.

8. The money you spend on video rentals and snack food could be spent on tuition and books, and should be invested in your future.

9. My general practitioner is dedicated, hardworking, and has considerable knowledge of medicine.

10. You can end your speech with a snappy anecdote, by asking an intriguing rhetorical question or with a basic summary of your points.

CHAPTER 17 PARALLELISM EXERCISE B

1. Rover has fleas, is smelly and never obeys us, but he is ours.

2. Gord found shopping on eBay as addictive as cigarettes.

3. This movie is a box-office blockbuster: it is full of action, steamy sex, and there is gratuitous violence everywhere.

4. Vacations in exotic lands are relaxing, recreational, and they deplete one's bank account.

5. Canadians are polite, deferential, and they distrust Americans.

6. Animation films are becoming popular because they entertain every member of the family, artistic, and demonstrate surprising technological advances.

7. When I go to a wedding, I look forward to the banquet, the dance, and I enjoy the company of the other guests.

8. A good teacher has a sense of humour, is enthusiastic about work, and is strict.

9. Cars should be big enough to hold more than two people, impressive enough to show off to your relatives, and they should work even under difficult weather conditions on Canadian roads.

10. My grade in this course is better than Homer.

Active and Passive Voice

The voice of a verb tells you whether the subject acts or is acted upon. There are two voices: active and passive. In the active voice, the sentence takes this form: actor, verb, receiver. In the passive voice, the form is inverted: receiver, verb, actor, and the verb always includes some form of "to be." In an active sentence, the subject is the actor:

The zookeeper fed the lion raw meat.   **Example**

In a passive sentence, the subject is acted upon:

The raw meat was fed to the lion by the zookeeper.

Keep these points in mind when you decide which voice is more appropriate in a given context:

1. The active voice is more forthright and usually more concise.

2. The active voice emphasizes the actor; the passive voice emphasizes the receiver of an action. In the example above, the zookeeper is the subject in the active sample; the raw meat is the subject in the passive sample.

3. The active voice emphasizes action; the passive is best used to describe stasis.

Example

ACTIVE: The Chihuahua bit the mail carrier.

PASSIVE: The mail carrier was bitten by the Chihuahua.

4. The passive voice is awkward when it is used to avoid direct phrasing or when it results in unclear, lengthy constructions.

Examples

ACTIVE: Amos, the shifty used car dealer, sold 50 lemons last month. (direct)

PASSIVE: Last month, 50 lemons were sold. (indirect: This rather dishonest use of the passive voice is typical of writers who wish to avoid responsibility for something or who wish to keep things impersonal.)

ACTIVE: At Hallowe'en, Harry played a prank on his mother. (clear)

PASSIVE: At Hallowe'en, a prank was played on his mother by Harry. (unclear and lengthy)

5. The passive voice is occasionally useful to avoid overuse of the pronoun "I." Be wary of overusing the passive voice, however.

Example

ACTIVE: I based this study on interviews with computer operators across the country.

PASSIVE: This study is based on interviews with computer operators across the country.

6. Remember that the passive voice is useful when you wish to emphasize the receiver of the action, rather than the performer.

Example

ACTIVE: The spectators could see the fireworks from a great distance.

PASSIVE: The fireworks could be seen from a great distance.

Since it is unimportant who could see the fireworks, the passive is preferable here.

7. The passive voice is also the best choice when you wish to avoid being too personal.

> ACTIVE: You must obey this summons immediately.
>
> PASSIVE: This summons must be obeyed immediately.

Example

Since the summons is meant to be formal and impersonal, the passive is preferable here.

In general, instructors do object to the overuse of the passive voice when the active is more lively and more colourful. So beware of overusing "to be" verbs that are static and dull, when a stronger word can be found.

CHAPTER 17 ACTIVE AND PASSIVE EXERCISE A

Identify all the verbs in the following sentences as active or passive. Discuss which you would change and why. Answers are on p. 227.

1. Fifty million people across North America lost power within about nine seconds on August 14, 2003, at 4:11 p.m. Eastern Standard Time.
2. Not only was Ontario affected, but Michigan, Ohio, Vermont, Massachusetts, Connecticut, New Jersey, and New York.
3. Blackouts are seldom reported on such a large scale; those without battery-operated radios were not informed of how widespread the occurrence was until the next morning.
4. A state of emergency was declared in Ontario.
5. In most cases, no power was generated for at least ten hours.
6. The next day people were told to dispose of eggs, meat, fish, milk, and other perishables in order to prevent salmonella poisoning.
7. Governments in Canada and the United States immediately blamed each other for the problem.
8. No one, however, really knew the underlying cause for quite some time after the event.
9. Despite some panic, remarkably few crimes were committed, even in big cities such as New York.
10. By contrast, in previous blackouts, such as the one in 1977, a great many stores were looted.

CHAPTER 17 ACTIVE AND PASSIVE EXERCISE B

1. Most news stories recount a sense of community this time, fortunately.
2. Luckily, most schools were closed for the summer.
3. Rush-hour traffic, however, was adversely affected by the loss of traffic lights.

17

4. In this blackout, people helped each other, directing traffic and handing out cold drinks and food.

5. In case of blackouts, people are advised to have a radio with batteries, three days' supply of tinned food and bottled water, as well as flashlights and candles.

6. People are also advised to engage in familiar, calming pastimes, such as reading, playing board games, and going outside.

7. Fear of recurring blackouts led governments to advise people to shut off air conditioning and other non-essential drains on energy.

8. Most of us discovered how much we take electrical power for granted.

9. For some the blackout provided an opportunity to get to know their neighbours.

10. This blackout will also likely be followed by a baby boom as in past instances.

Chapter 18
REDUCING WORDINESS

It is my ambition to say in ten sentences what other men say in whole books—what other men do not say in whole books.
—FRIEDRICH NIETZSCHE

A wordy essay does not necessarily transgress the word limit of the assignment. Rather, it contains extraneous words that contribute nothing to the meaning and drain force from the essay's argument.

Wordy writing is often characteristic of a first draft. It is close to idle chat: though spontaneous and sometimes even fascinating, it lacks direction. It wanders, perhaps arriving eventually at meaning; it does not set out in orderly pursuit of it. A wordy essay is often a sign of poorly revised and overdressed thought.

Make every word fit. If you can make your writing more succinct, your work will be clearer, and your reader will be more attentive. A few suggestions for improving the conciseness of your writing are listed below.

A Perfect Fit

Avoid visible seams
When talking, we commonly join ideas together randomly. Speed is the goal, not beautiful construction. Consider the following example:

Emilio bought the book. **Example**

You decide to add a further detail:

Emilio bought the book, which was reputed to be steamy and sensational.

Your new thought shows an obvious seam. "Which" and "that" can often be removed to produce a more graceful line.

Emilio bought the book, reputed to be steamy and sensational. **Example**

Avoid frills

Often, a speaker describes something by using words accompanied by adverbs meant to accentuate their effect. Here are some examples:

Examples

✗ quite elegant   ✗ extremely upset
✗ very angry   ✗ altogether pleased
✗ rather uneasy   ✗ not true

Replace these with stronger, less wordy, expressions:

✓ splendid   ✓ distraught
✓ irate   ✓ ecstatic
✓ anxious   ✓ false

In writing, the search for impact is better served by a stronger word, rather than a modified word. And, in writing, there is time to search for it. Use that time to dress your thoughts appropriately.

The same advice holds true for redundant wording. Avoid phrases like these:

Examples

✗ past history   ✓ history
✗ triangular in shape   ✓ triangular
✗ the city of Saskatoon   ✓ Saskatoon
✗ personal opinion   ✓ opinion
✗ refer back   ✓ refer
✗ exactly identical   ✓ identical

In each case, the omitted words added nothing to the meaning.

Avoid baggy constructions

A baggy sentence often contains vague words intended to conceal vague thoughts. Such sentences invariably include the following all-too-common words and phrases. Some of these can be excised. Most can be replaced by a single word.

Examples

✗ due to the fact that   ✓ because
✗ during the time that   ✓ when
✗ with regard to   ✓ about
✗ being   (omit)
✗ previous to   ✓ before
✗ at which time   ✓ when
✗ in the very near future   ✓ soon
✗ in the event that   ✓ if

Tentative language and unnecessary compound verbs are another frequent cause of bagginess. Avoid phrases like the following:

✗ make assumptions about
✗ come to the conclusion
✗ exhibit a tendency to

✗ be in a position to
✗ make a recommendation
✗ take action on

Substitute:

✓ assume
✓ conclude
✓ tend

✓ can
✓ recommend
✓ act

Avoid the "grand style"

Writing in the "grand style" uses pompous phrasing to clothe humble ideas. Pompous introductions are a common source of the problem:

✗ It is this theory which needs . . .
✓ This theory needs . . .
✗ It was his view that . . .
✓ He thought that . . .

Avoid excessive formality

Just as you wouldn't wear evening dress to compete in a bowling tournament, so you should not use static language to describe active thoughts.

Where possible, keep sentences in their typical order—use the active voice, and move from subject to verb to object. "The Prime Minister gave the order" is a much more direct statement than the passive construction "The order was given by the Prime Minister."

✗ A decision was made by the committee to conduct further studies.
✓ The committee decided to conduct further studies.

While the passive mode has its uses (as discussed in Chapter 17), it *is* wordier, less forceful, and generally harder to understand. It is all talk and no action. When revising, keep a watchful eye on the number of times you resort to the static passive voice. It can occasionally serve as a tactful way of avoiding direct confrontation.

PASSIVE: This amount is owed. (what the bill says)

ACTIVE: You owe us this amount. (what the bill means)

Wordiness Analyzed

The preceding examples illustrate that wordiness is most often caused by speech habits not entirely abandoned in writing. To analyze the causes of your own wordiness, note especially any words you use to *warm up* as you begin to write, to *cover up* your insecurities and uncertainties as you proceed, or to *spruce up* a thought better left unadorned.

Preventive Measures

When editing, check to see that your sentences are designed for simplicity, concreteness, action, grace, and impact.

CHAPTER 18 WORDINESS EXERCISE

Improve the following sentences by removing or changing redundant words or phrases. Answers are on p. 228.

1. Amelia had not the tiniest bit of experience as a teacher of composition; for that reason, it was difficult to make a recommendation for her to use to apply for that position.

2. In the event that there is a thunderstorm, you should turn off your computer; we are not in a position to replace any of the equipment, so we have made the decision to be very careful.

3. Students who exhibit a tendency to work hard receive excellent grades according to my past experience.

4. In his opinion, it would not be wise for Gio and Carmen to collaborate together on the project; whenever they are in close proximity to each other, they do not accomplish much, due to the fact that they both have bad tempers.

5. One factor in my making the assumption that I will need to find a new job is that I received a pink slip.

6. Martin made a study of the basic fundamentals of the art of kung fu fighting, but his future plans for an action movie career were completely wiped out by his failure to work out on a regular basis.

7. In the view of the court, we owed the sum total of $2000 for refusing to pay the fine in a timely way; we reached the conclusion that tickets are not to be taken lightly.

8. Behaviour of a rude nature will not be tolerated by anyone in contemporary society today.

9. Another reason that taxes have been raised higher is that the government needs to find revenues to support the new programs before its term in office has finally ended.

10. Drivers who are inclined to talk on cell phones while driving are encouraged to remember that those who are paying close attention to one task are less likely to have to make calls to their insurance companies.

Part Seven
REVIEWING THE RESULTS

Chapter 19

PERFECTING THE ESSAY

1. Out of clutter, find simplicity.
2. From discord, find harmony.
3. In the middle of difficulty lies opportunity.
(Three rules of work)
—ALBERT EINSTEIN

Tips on Revising

The revision process involves more than fussing over a few typographical errors; it should ideally be a process that reconceives and reviews the entire essay: not only its mechanics, but also its structure and its thought. While it is usually valuable to proceed as this book recommends—from thesis to outline, to research (if required), to first draft—the first written draft you produce is unlikely to be the clearest version of your thinking on any given subject. Bearing in mind your own shortcomings as a writer, as you have come to know them in your writing experience, prepare yourself to judge your own work in its entirety. Much of your real writing will be done at this stage, now that you are free to put yourself in the reader's position and imagine your paper's impact on him or her.

Remember that an essay has a duty to be unified, clear, and coherent. Accordingly, judge your work by the relevance of the information you have provided, by its ability to explain itself fully and clearly, and by its ability to make connections in the reader's mind. Putting yourself in the reader's position means that you must re-examine your assumptions about the subject matter and the reader's knowledge of it, and you must be willing to query the things that strike you as doubtful or awkward as you read. Detachment is crucial here, as is the time to do a good job.

Word processors make revision a simple matter. It is usually best to print out a first draft and then make corrections on paper before making another pass through the paper. Compare the first draft at the top of p. 203 to the final wording of the essay on p. 106.

Even after all your hard work, some minor but significant details may affect the reader's perception of your paper. Often these errors are the most embarrassing ones, errors that undercut your effort and distract the reader's attention from the elegance of your essay's form and the substance of its content. Like the

Although they agree that the story with animals is the better story, the last word is given to the other, worse story, minus the animals except for the incontrovertible Bengal tiger. The leap of faith, in Martel's estimation, requires that we chose the better story, select the one more aesthetically pleasing, perhaps the one easier to live with. This view of reality accords with something that Martel explains in one of his interviews: "To me a belief is something you cling to and faith is a letting go. Not only in religious terms—when you love someone, you let go, you trust them. When you love a system or any-thing, you let go—that's faith. When you have a belief you cling" ("Ask"). It is in this way that Martel brings the reader round to the kind of faith that involves letting go, but to no particular system of belief. Explaining the point in the same interview, for him, each reli-gious perspective was a kind of cuisine, any of which could sustain life. All the possible cuisines, however, were very different.

spelling

shorten

combine

tense

19

emperor with no clothes, you and your work may be easily subjected to ridicule or to charges of arrogance if you neglect responsible proofreading and stringent self-criticism. To ensure the quality of your work, follow these steps:

1. Move from the whole to the parts.

Revising is complicated. The process involves more than superficial corrections of mechanical errors. It involves a careful reconsideration of every part of your draft. Try to follow this sequence, or one adapted to suit you, when you revise your papers.

a. Check your facts. Does anything need to be added or changed?
b. Rethink your scheme of organization. Does the order make sense?
c. Test the paragraph structure. Are your ideas developed and linked properly?
d. Read over your sentences. Are they clear, smooth, varied?
e. Examine your word choice. Is it accurate, suitable, effective?
f. Check your grammar and spelling. Is the paper free of errors?

2. Reflect on your image.

Just as you wouldn't buy an item of clothing without first looking to see if it suited you and fit properly, don't write a paper and then submit it without first assessing its immediate impact on its readers. Reread the paper, scrutinizing its details very carefully—preferably a few days after you have written it. Reading aloud will help you find any awkward instances of grammatical construction and style. If you *still* feel insecure, ask a friend to read it too.

3. If you can't be perfect, be careful.

Some errors, in this imperfect world, may still creep in. Make necessary corrections as unobtrusively as possible. Resist the impulse to redo the whole paper (possibly introducing new errors), and instead make the corrections neatly in black ink—above the line. Stroke out unwanted letters with a small vertical line, and remove repeated words by the judicious use of "white-out" (Liquid Paper) or the simple horizontal stroke of a pen.

4. Make your paper "easy on the eyes."

Don't allow your essay to offend the eye. Avoid a printout so faded that you develop eyestrain trying to read it. Make your handwriting bold, large, and neat. If you submit a computer printout, take special care in proofreading to avoid errors that may have been introduced in production. Submit the paper in a tidy folder, neatly stapled or paper-clipped (as your instructor may prefer). Even if neatness is not an acknowledged criterion of excellence, there is no question that first impressions have a lasting effect.

5. Tie up any loose threads.

Don't submit your paper without checking such details as page numbers, exact quotations, bibliographical information, doubtful spellings, word divisions, and grammatical constructions.

6. Follow the "dress code."

Make sure that your assignment adheres to any conditions explicitly stated by the instructor, however arbitrary or trivial such matters may seem to you. Check to see that the mechanical format of your paper conforms to the expected standards of the instructor. Such items as the treatment of abbreviations, bibliographical arrangement, and even the format of the title page and the position and form of page numbers need careful attention. Although you may have already invested considerable time in these matters, a last-minute check is a good idea.

7. Use every means at your disposal.

Don't hand in a word-processed paper that hasn't gone through the spell checking process. Spell checkers can't catch every mistake. Simple homonyms like "hear" and "here" are indistinguishable for them. American spelling is still the norm, and "our" at the end of words will be considered an error. For all that, computers are remarkably thorough in catching small errors that your tired eyes may miss. It is worthwhile to follow through on the advice of spell checkers and even of grammar checkers, though you may occasionally have good reason not to follow it. Not every use of the passive voice is reprehensible; not every fragment is unjustifiable. Still, word-processing spell checkers and grammar checkers do oblige you to look more closely at what you are saying and how you are saying it. Don't skip this step, and don't forget that a good Canadian dictionary is an important resource too.

Revision Checklist

The whole—The argument

Does your introduction tell your reader what he or she needs to know?

Can you find your thesis statement somewhere toward the end of the introduction?

Does every point you raise relate clearly to the thesis?

Is the point of every paragraph and its connection to your argument clear from its beginning?

Are there enough paragraph breaks (and not too many) for ease of reading?

Is your argument as persuasively ordered and worded as it can be?

Do you conclude by moving from the specific to the general?

Are there any fallacies in your reasoning or easy objections to be made?

The parts—The sentences

Do you avoid sentence fragments?

Do your sentences show variety in their structure?

Do you use passive voice sparingly and only justifiably?

Do you keep your sentence length manageable?

Do you use colons, semicolons, and commas correctly?

Have you checked to see that wordiness and redundancy are at a minimum?
Is your meaning clear without rephrasing—even when revised some time after the first draft?

The parts—The words

Do you use diction that is straightforward, clear, and unpretentious?
Do you avoid slang or excessive or unnecessary jargon?
Do you use terminology with expertise?
Do you avoid contractions?
Do you spell correctly?

General Advice

Does your essay read well, even aloud?
Can friends read it easily without questions or problems?
Have you checked specifically to eradicate the mistakes you typically make?

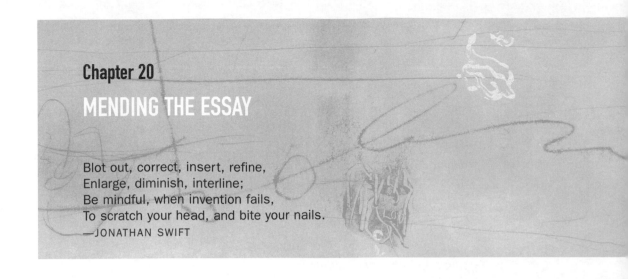

Chapter 20
MENDING THE ESSAY

Blot out, correct, insert, refine,
Enlarge, diminish, interline;
Be mindful, when invention fails,
To scratch your head, and bite your nails.
—JONATHAN SWIFT

If, when you get an essay back, you find that your work has been disappointing, there are still some things you can do to redeem yourself. It may be too late to get the kind of grade that you had in mind on this particular paper, but some of the tactics proposed below ought to make the next essay better.

First, don't throw the paper away in a fit of glee or gloom. You write essays not only to get grades but also to learn how to write. Long after you have forgotten the facts and figures involved in writing your paper, you will still have the writing skills that were developed in its preparation. Your reading, writing, and research skills are the most visible parts of your education long after you graduate.

Deciphering Comments

1. **Read the grader's comments when your essays are returned to you—regardless of the grade you receive.**
Don't read only the comments accompanying the grade at the end of the paper, but also any questions or hints dropped in the margins or within the text of the paper.

2. **Next, see that you understand what the comments and questions mean.**
The list below should help:

#	add a space
agr	error in agreement (subject/verb or antecedent/pronoun)
apos	indicate possession or add apostrophe

awk	awkward wording
bib	error in bibliographical form
⌒	close up space
⸗	correct letter case
case	error in pronoun case
coh	problem with coherence
cs	comma splice
d	problem with diction or usage
dev	inadequate paragraph development
div	incorrect word division
dm	dangling modifier
doc	error in documentation
frag	sentence fragment
gr	error in grammar or usage
log	logic
mm	misplaced or misrelated modifier
p	error in punctuation
par	problem with paragraphing
pass	overuse of the passive voice
?	unclear, doubtful, or unreadable
ref	problem with pronoun reference
rep	repetition
rev	revise or proofread
run-on	run-on sentence
shift	shift in verb tense or logic
sp	spelling error
ss	problem with sentence structure
stet	keep as it was
sub	faulty subordination
t	error in verb tense
trans	transition
ts	problem with thesis statement
//	faulty parallelism
∧	something missing
wdy	problem with wordiness
ww	wrong word
X	obvious error

3. Ask your instructor to explain a particular comment if you do not understand it.

4. When you have read through the comments, try to analyze the kind of mistakes that you make most frequently and determine that you will take steps to eliminate them.

5. Next, consult a reliable guide in order to correct your mistakes.

Such guides include a dictionary (for spelling errors and errors of usage), a writing/grammar handbook (such as this one), or a guide to proper format of notes and bibliography (such as the *MLA Handbook*).

Learning from Experience

1. Analyze the strengths and weaknesses of your style.

At first, this may seem a puzzling endeavour, but after a time you should be able to discern changes in your writing—not only in its mechanics, but in the development of its thought as well.

2. Analyze your writing habits.

Do you find that you have certain favourite expressions that crop up too often? Do your readers frequently comment that your sentences are too complex or too simple? Do certain tactics in your argument often meet with an unfavourable response? Paying attention to these trends in your collected essays will enable you to become more sensitive to your patterns of self-expression and more able to prevent problems in the future.

3. Keep a list of your most common spelling and grammar errors from past work.

Refer to this list when you are about to write the final draft of your next paper. It may help eliminate some pitfalls.

4. Exercise your writing skills.

Reading is probably not a strong enough remedy to cure you of some errors; writing is the recommended therapy. If possible, set yourself the task of completing some exercises aimed at a specific problem diagnosed by your instructor. If, for example, dangling modifiers are a persistent problem, consult the section in this book on their diagnosis and treatment. Your instructor may agree to check your answers afterwards.

5. Rewrite.

Rewriting is also a good way of curing some of the ills of essay writing. Try, for example, to recast a troublesome paragraph in clearer, smoother prose, incorporating your instructor's suggestions. Remember, though, that no writer ever developed a style mechanically; it is intimately related to thought. Rethink your thoughts as you rewrite. You will learn a great deal about the impact your writing has on its readers if you remember the grader's comments.

6. Work through appropriate sections of this book with an essay that has just been returned.

This exercise will help you in your next essay assignment.

7. Experiment.

Writing should not always be a chore. Sometimes, when you find yourself able to express something exactly the way you want to, writing becomes play. Allow yourself to become comfortable as you write. Remember that your real writing purpose, grades and completed assignments aside, is to say what you want to say. Practice will make writing a satisfying form of self-expression.

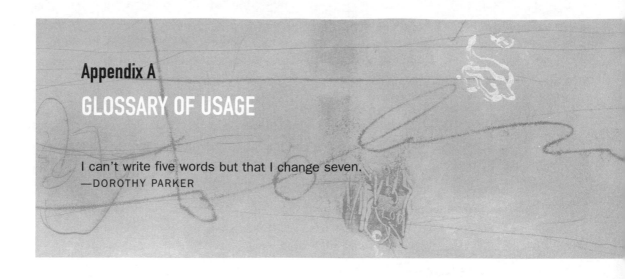

Appendix A
GLOSSARY OF USAGE

I can't write five words but that I change seven.
—DOROTHY PARKER

This glossary lists some words that are a common source of errors, either because they are confused with other words, or because they are not acceptable in standard usage. Check through this list if you are in doubt about a particular usage.

accept/except

"Accept" is a verb that means "to consent to"; "except" is a verb or a preposition that means "to exclude."

I would **accept** your proposition **except** for my husband and six children.

advice/advise

"Advice" is a noun; "advise" is a verb.

I **advise** you to follow your mother's **advice**.

affect/effect

"Affect" is usually a verb; "effect" is usually a noun. Note, however, that "effect" may occasionally be a verb, meaning "to bring about."

His breakup with his girlfriend **affected** his grades.

A broken heart may have a bad **effect** on scholastic achievement.

He thought that by writing a tear-stained letter he could perhaps **effect** a reconciliation.

all right/alright

The *first* is the correct spelling.

all together/altogether

The first means "in a group"; the second means "completely" or "entirely."

> **All together**, the students in the class decided that the teacher was **altogether** incompetent.

allude/elude

"To allude" means "to make indirect reference to"; "to elude" means "to escape."

> A lewd reference may **elude** you, but it may perhaps **allude** to another literary source.

allusion/illusion

The first is a veiled or indirect reference; the second is a deception.

> She found the poet's **allusion** to Shakespeare; her belief that the words came from Milton was an **illusion**.

a lot/allot

"A lot" is a colloquialism for "many" or "a great deal"; "to allot" is a verb, meaning "to divide" or "to parcel out." There is no form "alot."

> Each of the heirs had been **allotted a lot** of their grandfather's fortune.

among/between

"Among" involves more than two; "between" involves just two.

> **Among** his peers he is considered a genius; **between** you and me, I think he is overrated.

amount of/number of

"Amount of" is for quantities that cannot be counted and hence is followed by a singular noun; "a number of" is for quantities that may be counted and takes a plural noun.

> A **number** of students drink a large **amount** of alcohol.

as/because

"Because" should be used instead of "as" in a sentence meant to show cause and effect, since "as" or "while" may also refer to the passage of time.

> ✗ **As** he was awaiting trial, he refused to speak to the press. (ambiguous)
>
> ✓ **Because** he was awaiting trial, he refused to speak to the press.

aspect

Avoid this vague word. While not always incorrect, it often contributes to vagueness.

being/being as/being that

"Being" can almost always be eliminated. "Being as" or "being that" should be replaced by "because" or "since."

bottom line

This popular bit of financial jargon has no place in formal writing.

can/may

"Can" implies ability; "may" implies permission or possibility.

I **may** go shopping today since I **can** buy anything I want.

centre on/revolve around

Avoid "centre around," an illogical phrase.

comprises/comprised of

"Comprises" means "consists of." Do *not* use "is comprised of."

✗ Canada is **comprised of** ten provinces and three territories.

✓ Canada **comprises** ten provinces and three territories.

conscious/conscience

"Conscious" is an adjective meaning "aware"; "conscience" is one's inner sense of morality.

The jury became increasingly **conscious** of the criminal's lack of **conscience**.

continual/continuous

"Continual" means "repeated"; "continuous" means "without ceasing."

Her homework was **continually** interrupted by telephone calls from people selling vacuum cleaners.

The air conditioner was used **continuously** throughout the long, hot day.

could of/should of/would of

You mean "could have," "should have," "would have."

data/criteria/phenomena/media

All of these words are plural. Their singular forms are "datum," "criterion," "phenomenon," and "medium." Check the subject and verb agreement carefully with each.

Some people think the media **are** responsible for all modern ills.

disinterested/uninterested

"Disinterested" means "impartial"; "uninterested" means "bored" or "unconcerned."

The ideal referee is **disinterested** in the outcome of the game, but shouldn't be **uninterested** in the actions of the players.

due to

"Due to" is acceptable only after some form of the verb "to be." Use "because of" to imply a causal relationship.

The bus is **due to** arrive in fifteen minutes.

Because of his allergies, he had to give up Muffy, his Persian cat.

elicit/illicit

"To elicit" is a verb meaning "to evoke"; "illicit" is an adjective meaning "illegal."

> The questions at the press conference should **elicit** some response to the president's **illicit** behaviour.

enthuse/enthused

Avoid these words. Use "enthusiastic" instead.

> Shania Twain's fans were **enthusiastic** about her concert tour.

equally as

Do not use "equally" and "as" together. Instead, use one or the other.

> She and her brother are **equally** good at contact sports.

> She is **as** good as her brother at contact sports.

etc.

Avoid this abbreviation, which usually means that the author does not know what else to say.

the fact that

Avoid this wordy expression.

factor

This word generally adds nothing; leave it out.

farther/further

"Farther" refers to actual distance; "further" is abstract.

> The **farther** he walked, the more his feet hurt.

> She would not stand for any **further** shenanigans.

fewer/less

"Fewer" is used with plural nouns; "less" is used with singular nouns.

> The **fewer** the guests, the **less** liquor we will need.

firstly, secondly

"First" and "second" are all you really need.

hopefully

Replace this word with "It is hoped that," or more simply, "I (we) hope that."

> ✗ **Hopefully**, the paper will be finished tomorrow.

This sentence implies that the paper itself is hopeful.

> ✓ **It is hoped that** the paper will be finished tomorrow.

> ✓ **I hope that** the paper will be finished tomorrow.

impact on

"Impact" is a noun, not a verb. Replace it with "have an impact on."

The economy will **have an impact on** workers' salaries.

imply/infer

"To imply" means "to suggest"; "to infer" means "to conclude."

She **implied** that he was cheap; he **inferred** that he should have offered to pay her bus fare.

input

Avoid this word and other computer jargon, except when you are discussing computers.

in the case of

A wordy construction, best avoided.

✗ **In the case of** your mother-in-law, she means well.

✓ Your mother-in-law means well.

into

Avoid using this preposition to mean "interested in."

✗ He was **into** macramé.

✓ He was **interested in** macramé.

irregardless

The correct word is "regardless."

its/it's

"Its" is the possessive form, like "his" or "her." "It's" is a contraction for "it is" or "it has."

That dog's bark is worse than **its** bite.

It's certainly got big teeth, though.

-Ize

Avoid some of the newly created verbs with this ending. They are part of the growing and deplorable tendency to turn nouns into verbs, as in "prioritize." There is usually a simpler form.

✗ He **utilized** the facilities.

✓ He **used** the facilities.

lay/lie

"Lay" takes an object; "lie" does not.

The farmer made the hen **lie** on the nest to **lay** an egg.

like/as/as if

"Like" is a preposition and should not be used as a conjunction. Substitute "as" or "as if" if a clause follows.

✗ He looks **like** he's going to make it.

✓ He looks **as if** he's going to make it.

✓ He looks **like** a winner.

myself

"Myself" is not a more polite form of "I" or "me." It should be reserved for use as an intensifier or reflexive.

✗ The host introduced my wife and **myself** to the guests.

✓ The host introduced my wife and **me** to the guests.

✓ I, **myself**, solved the problem.

✓ I drove **myself** to the airport.

parameters/perimeters

Avoid the use of "parameters" except in its specific application to geometry. Use "perimeters" to mean "boundaries," or to refer to a length or distance.

parent

Do not use this word as a verb; "parenting" is also suspect. "Parenthood" is a perfectly acceptable substitute.

practice/practise

"Practice" is the noun; "practise" is the verb.

I know **practice** makes perfect, but I hate to **practise**.

presently

Substitute "currently" or "now." "Presently" actually means "soon."

principal/principle

The first means "chief" or "main" as an adjective, the head of a school as a noun; the second means "a basic truth."

His **principal** objection to her comments was that they were based on questionable **principles**.

quote/quotation

"Quote" is a verb, *not* a noun—"quotation" is the noun.

✗ This **quote** from Pierre Trudeau makes the point clear.

✓ This **quotation** from Pierre Trudeau makes the point clear.

relate to

Use this verb to indicate how one idea is related to another. Do not use it to mean "get along with."

✗ How do you **relate to** your new psychiatrist?

✓ This point **relates** directly **to** my argument.

suppose to

Use "supposed to," or better, use "should" or "ought to."

than/then

Use "than" in comparative structures.

Bill Gates makes more money **than** I do.

"Then" is an adverb that makes a reference to time or is used to draw a conclusion.

Then, it follows that I am not in the same tax bracket as he is.

that/which

Use "that" when what follows restricts the meaning. Use "which" in a non-restrictive case.

Here is the book **that** I told you about. (not just any book, but a specific one)

His fortune, **which** included stock certificates, bonds, and the first penny he had ever earned, was kept in an old shoebox under his bed. (the words surrounded by commas supply incidental, non-restrictive information)

their/there/they're

"Their" is possessive; "there" is an adverb or an expletive; "they're" is a contraction of "they are."

There ought to be a law against **their** foolishness. **They're** asking for trouble.

try and

Replace this phrase with "try to."

We must **try to** stop meeting like this.

unique

"Unique" means "one of a kind." It cannot be modified.

✗ Her sequined dress was **very unique**.

✓ Her sequined dress was **unique**.

who's/whose

"Who's" is a contraction of "who is" or "who has"; "whose" is the possessive form.

Who's been sleeping in my bed?

Whose bed is this, anyway?

-wise

Avoid this suffix.

✗ Timewise, the project is on schedule.

✓ The project is on schedule.

Appendix B

ANSWER KEY

Suggested answers to specific exercises

CHAPTER 3 EXERCISE 5A

1. Diana Krall and Avril Lavigne are well-known Canadian singers.
2. The perpetrator of the crime was in the country illegally.
3. Because he had polio, Lou used a scooter.
4. People with disabilities need your help.
5. The woman who works on the switchboard must be well-spoken.
6. Call firefighters if you smell smoke.
7. Sara Binks is a celebrated fictional Canadian poet.
8. Humans cannot live by bread alone.
9. Whenever he went to the variety store, he felt that he was cheated.
10. Lin Song was an Asian student.

CHAPTER 3 EXERCISE 5B

1. Native Canadians often choose to live on the reserve.
2. Because she has West Nile virus, Bette is paralyzed and uses a wheelchair.
3. There were many men in the office, along with the women at the reception desk.
4. People who are aged and infirm use this transportation system.
5. A man and a woman came in this morning to rent an apartment.
6. People with AIDS take special medications.
7. People with disabilities can apply for supplemental income.

8. Dodi was committed to a reform school for girls.

9. Gentlemen accompanied the ladies to the celebration.

10. May I speak to the head of the house?

CHAPTER 16 SENTENCE STRUCTURE EXERCISE A

Suggested answers

1. My friend Anne is always asking to go to the Ardmore Tea Room in Halifax. She likes to eat fish cakes there.

2. Kraft Dinner is not a Canadian product; nevertheless, it seems to be a staple among Canadian students.

3. Outdoor markets are much admired in Canada. Well-known examples include Toronto's Kensington Market, Vancouver's Granville Market, and The Forks in Winnipeg.

4. If you would like to visit a great Irish pub, go to Edmonton. The one I recommend is called O'Byrne's.

5. Michael Smith has owned very successful restaurants in Prince Edward Island and New Brunswick; however, he is best known for a television program on the Food Network.

6. Graham Kerr, though born in England, produced his show "The Galloping Gourmet" in Canada, and he lived in this country for some time when the show was on the air.

7. Toronto's most celebrated chef is probably Susur Lee; his cuisine is a clever fusion of Western and Asian that is original and mouthwatering.

8. Canada has its share of cookbook authors, which include Jeanne Benoit, Jean Paré, and Edna Staebler.

9. The best Japanese restaurant I have visited is Tojo's in Vancouver. Many tourists flock there for fabulous sushi.

10. Some would say that Canada does not have its own unique cuisine; nevertheless, it has produced both great chefs and great authors of cookbooks.

CHAPTER 16 SENTENCE STRUCTURE EXERCISE B

1. Canadians are often unaware of their famous fellow citizens and even of the tourist attractions in their own country. Perhaps we just need to be reminded.

2. Guy Lombardo, a famous band leader, was born in London, Ontario; a bridge in that city was constructed in his honour.

3. Linda Evangelista, a Canadian from St. Catharines, Ontario, has become an instantly recognizable supermodel, and her face is reproduced on magazine covers throughout the world.

4. Among historical figures, Nellie McClung is famous as a woman's rights activist in Canada, though more Canadians would recognize Carry Nation or Susan B. Anthony, who are Americans.

5. Louis Riel, a leader of his people in their resistance against the Canadian government, is possibly the most controversial figure in Canadian history, although many Canadians still would not know much about him.

6. Places in Canada are sometimes not instantly recognizable to audiences either; hence, cities like Vancouver and Toronto pass for American cities.

7. Toronto, sometimes called Hollywood North, is often used as a film location; these days, films can be shot more inexpensively there than in New York City.

8. In fact, a watchful audience member might notice that the CN Tower appears behind Jennifer Lopez's shoulder in *Angel Eyes*; however, the film is supposed to take place in Chicago!

9. Films like *My Big Fat Greek Wedding* were shot, in part, in a Greek section of Toronto. This phenomenon accounts for the appearance of many Canadian actors in that film, including Fiona Reid.

10. Keep an eye out for Canadiana. Many historical and contemporary Canadian people and places need to be better known in their own country!

CHAPTER 16 MODIFIERS EXERCISE A

Suggested answers

1. Declan has stopped speaking to almost all his former business associates.

2. After checking your e-mail, you should turn the computer off.

3. As the designated driver, I cannot drink at this party.

4. After spending hundreds of dollars on textbooks, most students sold them to the used bookstore.

5. Alone at the cottage, I found the forest dark and forbidding.

6. After investigating a number of exciting new jobs, Deepa thought his old job seemed tedious and underpaid.

7. In hot weather, the fan should be run continuously before you turn on the air conditioner.

8. Unless they are Persians, most cats do not require grooming.

9. As a forty-six-year-old man, he has lived 58% of his life, according to Stats Canada.

10. Buying exercise equipment, I passed my birthday peacefully.

CHAPTER 16 MODIFIERS EXERCISE B

1. The gardener should move the wheelbarrow carefully once it is loaded.

2. Many diners enjoy sticky toffee pudding, especially when it is covered in hot rum sauce.

3. Just like you, I have an enormous student loan.

4. Being tired all day long, I think the bed looks inviting.

5. Barking loudly at any intrusion, the bichon frise awakened its owners from a sound sleep.

6. Khiet heard on the television news that there were more divorces this year.

7. By forwarding your e-mail to another account, you will waste less time reading ads for herbal medication and weight-loss cures.

8. When planning to build a fish pond, one needs to discourage raccoons and other wildlife who like to eat fish.

9. CORRECT

10. Keen on hunting, Gaston needs a wife like Annie Oakley.

CHAPTER 16 PRONOUNS EXERCISE A

Suggested answers

1. If customers are not satisfied with the products, they should complain to the store manager, and the products can be returned.

2. This book says that Sister Wendy is a well-known authority on art history.

3. When you are summoned for jury duty, you are expected to respond quickly.

4. Even if you don't have a membership to the fitness club, you can benefit from this special trial offer.

5. Everything you thought about us professors is sadly true.

6. Between you and me, you should know better than to believe everything you see on the Internet.

7. In David's apartment, there are lots of dust bunnies under the bed.

8. All those who answered the advertisement were looking for ways to improve their income without actually having to work.

9. When I pulled the cat's tail, the cat meowed fiercely.

10. Kim bought clothes from the Salvation Army just as her friend did.

CHAPTER 16 PRONOUNS EXERCISE B

1. She wondered whose job it was to empty the garbage, a task that had been neglected for at least a week.

2. When students hand in their papers late, the instructor is likely to give them reduced grades.

3. One might enjoy long vacations if one didn't worry about work piling up at home.

4. The actor whom we saw backstage was handing out autographs to the adoring throngs.

5. Each of us has our own reasons for attending the support group, and we do not want publicity.
6. Who would you say is the culprit?
7. All people are entitled to their own opinion when they discuss politics or religion.
8. The government is closing down the cod fisheries in Newfoundland.
9. Nobody hates grammar more than I do.
10. Do you intend to join Tammy Faye and me?

CHAPTER 16 SUBJECT AND VERB AGREEMENT EXERCISE A

1. Either the lottery officials or the provincial government is going to have to make a decision about who will receive this month's prize.
2. The tornadoes that tear through this country every year have a disastrous impact.
3. Ana seems to forget that there are assignments to be submitted before she can graduate.
4. A high percentage of the student body is opposed to the tuition hikes.
5. A high percentage of the students is in favour of a year-round school year.
6. A number of reasons have been given for your behaviour at the barbeque yesterday.
7. Erika is the only one of my students who has already found a job in her field of expertise.
8. If the board of governors have the inclination, they can oppose the layoffs.
9. The main criteria of excellence in work are determination and doggedness.
10. The number of stars in the sky is infinite.

CHAPTER 16 SUBJECT AND VERB AGREEMENT EXERCISE B

1. Tessie's main worry as a new homeowner was squirrels getting into the chimney.
2. Tastes in furniture differ.
3. Every last one of those reports was proofread painstakingly before it was submitted.
4. A zebra and a tiger were lost in the flood.
5. CORRECT
6. Economics was her chief concern as a provincial minister.
7. "Canadian Idol" and the Canadian version of "Who Wants to Be a Millionaire?" compete for viewers every weeknight.
8. Neither one of you knows a thing about how to save your money.
9. Each of us has a date with destiny.
10. This cell phone and camera are easy to use, even if the screen is very small.

CHAPTER 16 SEMICOLON AND COLON EXERCISE A

Suggested answers

1. According to his partner, Nick is lazy, sloppy, and irresponsible; however, the partner, if truth be told, is rigid and lacking in sympathy.
2. CORRECT
3. Buying a condominium in a large city like Vancouver or Toronto is costly; hence, I am planning to live in a cardboard box over a hot air vent.
4. There are only ninety-eight days left till my birthday; that's plenty of time for you to save up to buy me a two-week vacation in Milan.
5. The bestselling fiction writers in Canada in the past few years are Margaret Atwood, Yann Martel, Alice Munro, and Carol Shields.
6. Summer movies are highly entertaining but not very deep: they replace sophisticated plot, character, and setting with car chases, sexy actors, and unbelievable stunts; nevertheless, they succeed at the box office.
7. Two things are bothering me: my computer has a virus, and my hard drive needs defragmenting.
8. CORRECT
9. The incumbent politician had a goal in mind: to win back the shaken confidence of his constituents after the scandal.
10. Rico's dream was to be a bronco buster at the Calgary Stampede.

CHAPTER 16 SEMICOLON AND COLON EXERCISE B

1. Kerry told Malo that it would be all right after five or six years; presumably, everyone would forget what the quarrel had been about by then anyway.
2. Here is what I learned today from watching the Food Network: how to finish a dessert, using a blow torch; how to set fire to the kitchen curtains, using the same blow torch; and how to scare off my dinner guests, even before dinner is over.
3. The new parents considered these names for the twins: Ben and Jerry, Mick and Keith, or Mutt and Jeff.
4. CORRECT
5. Banff is a glorious tourist town: it has beautiful mountain scenery; it also has the highest rate of sexually transmitted disease in Canada, according to some sources.
6. The German shepherd was afraid of thunderstorms: his owner always drove home to keep him company during any weather disturbance.
7. Green vegetables are good for you: why can't we get lettuce on our sandwiches in this cafeteria?
8. The Shih Tzu next door would benefit from obedience school: he bites his owners' ankles every chance he gets.

9. Buying coffee in a Tim Hortons outlet is the number one Canadian pastime: there are more doughnut shops than there are houses, it seems.

10. Ethel disliked her new living room furniture; hence, she decided to spend more time in the family room.

CHAPTER 16 PUNCTUATION EXERCISE A

Suggested answers

1. The new townhouse was stylish, yet there wasn't enough room to swing a cat.

2. Take your choice: you can come quietly, or we can get tough.

3. June and Gwynneth did not go to bingo games, nor did they enjoy psychic fairs.

4. Kurtis and Scott went to Rio de Janeiro last year, and Sandy went to the south of Spain.

5. Impressed beyond words, Gordon met his idol, an actress from his favourite situation comedy, "Gilligan's Island."

6. If there were any truth in advertising, my teeth would be as white as pearls.

7. Judging from what Aline buys, the people at Amazon must figure that she is an intellectual snob with a great deal of money, a taste for trendy fiction, no social life, and lots of time on her hands.

8. Ewan celebrated his fiftieth birthday by buying a kilt and leaving his wife for someone twenty years his junior.

9. Rhonda displayed her new tableware, polished and shining as if they were her very own front teeth.

10. While elegant dishes may look splendid at picnics, I prefer paper plates that can be thrown away and don't need to be washed.

CHAPTER 16 PUNCTUATION EXERCISE B

1. As the thunderstorm raged outside, Faisal and Beenish ate their picnic in the backseat of the van.

2. When our guests left, we gathered up the leftovers and realized we would be eating finger food for the next week, yet there wasn't a drop of gin left in the house.

3. Knowing that she probably would never see the money again, reluctantly Maya agreed to grant Walter the loan.

4. The escaped Labrador retriever had a mission; you see, he was very attracted to an Akita hound that he met in the park yesterday.

5. Axel drove her to the interview at 160 km an hour, an action which resulted in his licence being suspended for a few days.

6. As age creeps up on you, you can always resort to Botox, plastic surgery, or, at the very least, to clothes that conceal your stringy neck, your flabby upper arms, and your love handles.

7. After the parrot fell off its perch, Kathie, who was sitting her friends' pets, went into the house to count the cats to see if they were all still there.

8. Despite her best efforts to comfort her neighbours, they did not seem to appreciate her references to a Monty Python sketch about a dead parrot.

9. It's my lucky day: today I was accepted into university.

10. The resort had been advertised as having twenty-four-hour room service, but, in reality, the guests had to rely on expensive snacks and drinks from an overpriced mini-bar.

CHAPTER 16 POSSESSION EXERCISE A

1. According to the stockbroker's prediction, the financial mistakes you made in the past few years will not affect next year's earnings.

2. Rebecca's son now shops in the men's clothing department, but he still reads children's books.

3. Ross's vacation plans were cut short last year, but next year's trip to Haifa should be glorious.

4. Yesterday's chaperone is today's cruise director.

5. To get a good night's sleep, you need to keep the cats from getting into the bedroom, for Pete's sake.

6. My friend's sister Carmen said that Santa's elves had made her a present.

7. The actor's talents were considerable, but his performance just was not enough to ensure the play's success when all the critics' reviews were so vicious.

8. Dickens's novels and Shakespeare's plays normally make up a secondary school's curriculum in Canada.

9. Men's and women's washrooms are conveniently located near the mall's entrance.

10. I would make a citizen's arrest if I thought the community's by-laws had been violated.

CHAPTER 16 POSSESSION EXERCISE B

1. The bedroom's appearance was similar to that of an eldercare facility, in the housekeeper's opinion.

2. Pearl Josephine's mother thought her daughter's name was appropriate, but her classmates' teasing prompted Pearl to change it to P.J.

3. John's idea of a birthday favour included asking if the lovers' quarrel could be settled peacefully.

4. Abel watched the bank manager's face when he tried to cash his travellers' cheques.

5. Canada's history is full of unacknowledged heroes like Lionel Conacher, who won hockey's most prestigious award, the Stanley Cup, and also won football's most

coveted prize, the Grey Cup, while being one of this country's most accomplished track runners and a boxer who fought Jack Dempsey.

6. Tim Horton's success as a hockey player prompted him to start a business which has become a landmark among Canadian businesses; coffee's pre-eminence as Canada's favourite drink is beyond question.

7. Man's best friend may be his dog, but in Rudyard Kipling's view, a woman's best friend may well be a cat.

8. She enjoyed reading Horace's poetry for its depth, Henry James's novels for their sophistication, and Sears's catalogue for its sales.

9. Everything Ruth cooks looks like a dog's breakfast, but her family's appetite is powerful after a long day's work.

10. Her purse's contents included yesterday's credit card receipts, tomorrow's theatre tickets, and today's unfinished lunch.

CHAPTER 17 SENTENCE VARIATION EXERCISE

Suggested answers

1. a. Wanting to buy a notebook computer, Vidia checked the advertisements on eBay every day, but a reliable notebook seemed too expensive.
   b. Trying to keep the morale of employees high, Bruce provided incentives and collegial activities for employees, instituting a yoga class and inviting people to company picnics.
   c. Attending few classes, the indolent student refuses to complete homework assignments and avoids eye contact with the instructor when he does go to class.

2. a. Toes pointed, Karen executed the pirouette.
   b. A wealth of information, the training session was attended by those who wanted practice in designing Web pages.
   c. Their honeymoon over, Hiram and Edwina decided to start a family.

3. Not a nobleman, John Keats was a member of the lower classes who managed to become a surgeon with some financial assistance from his family. In those days, a surgeon was a tradesman rather like a barber. Although it was an honourable trade, Keats nevertheless wanted to be a poet. Despite the fact that he wrote only a small number of poems, his poetic development is amazing. While it is true that Keats never became famous in his lifetime, he did, however, leave a small, brilliant body of work that is still read today. In 1821, at the age of 25, Keats died, succumbing to tuberculosis. Considered one of the greatest English poets, Keats produced work that is now much admired.

4. a. In the basket on the shelf at the top of the wall unit lay the cat.
   b. Frances enjoys eating fried fish although it has too much fat.
   c. Young people in North America are eating more junk food these days.

CHAPTER 17 PARALLELISM EXERCISE A

1. The dentist advised me to give up soft drinks and remember to floss.
2. Quickly and gracefully, the dancer accepted the bouquet from the conductor.
3. Either I am overtired or I am ill.
4. The piano is elegant, enormous, and out of tune.
5. My best friend has a new house in the country, an in-ground pool, and a huge mortgage.
6. The dog is either scared or upset; he normally does not growl at visitors.
7. The weak Canadian dollar affects the market and severely reduces tourists' buying power in other countries.
8. The money you spend on video rentals and snack food could be spent on tuition and invested in your future.
9. My general practitioner is dedicated, hardworking, and knowledgeable about medicine.
10. You can end your speech with a snappy anecdote, with an intriguing rhetorical question, or with a basic summary of your points.

CHAPTER 17 PARALLELISM EXERCISE B

1. Rover is flea-bitten, smelly, and disobedient, but he is ours.
2. Gord found shopping on eBay as addictive as smoking cigarettes.
3. This movie is a box-office blockbuster: it is full of action, steamy sex, and gratuitous violence.
4. Vacations in exotic lands are relaxing, recreational, and expensive.
5. Canadians are polite, they are deferential, and they distrust Americans.
6. Animation films are becoming popular because they entertain every member of the family, they are artistic, and they demonstrate surprising technological advances.
7. When I go to a wedding, I look forward to the banquet, the dance, and the company of the other guests.
8. A good teacher is funny, enthusiastic about work, and strict.
9. Cars should be big enough to hold more than two people, impressive enough to show off to your relatives, and able to work even under difficult weather conditions on Canadian roads.
10. My grade in this course is better than Homer's.

CHAPTER 17 ACTIVE AND PASSIVE EXERCISE A

1. ACTIVE
2. PASSIVE
3. PASSIVE; PASSIVE
4. PASSIVE

5. PASSIVE
6. PASSIVE
7. ACTIVE
8. ACTIVE
9. PASSIVE
10. PASSIVE

CHAPTER 17 ACTIVE AND PASSIVE EXERCISE B

1. ACTIVE
2. PASSIVE
3. PASSIVE
4. ACTIVE
5. PASSIVE
6. PASSIVE
7. ACTIVE
8. ACTIVE
9. ACTIVE
10. PASSIVE

CHAPTER 18 WORDINESS EXERCISE

Suggested answers

1. Amelia has no experience as a composition teacher, so it was difficult to recommend her for that position.
2. If there is a thunderstorm, turn off your computer; we cannot replace the equipment, so we have decided to be cautious.
3. Students who work hard receive excellent grades, according to my experience.
4. He thinks Gio and Carmen should not collaborate on the project; whenever they are near each other, they do not accomplish much because they both have bad tempers.
5. I assume I will need a new job, because I received a pink slip.
6. Martin studied the fundamentals of kung fu fighting, but his plans for an action movie career were eliminated by his failure to work out regularly.
7. In the court's view, we owe $2000 for refusing to pay the fine on time; we concluded that tickets are to be taken seriously.
8. Rude behaviour will not be tolerated by anyone in contemporary society.
9. Taxes have been raised because the government needs revenue to support the new programs before its term in office ends.
10. Drivers who talk on cell phones should remember that those who are attentive to one task are less likely to have to call their insurance companies.

Index